# THE STORY KEY TO
# GEOGRAPHIC NAMES

**KENNIKAT PRESS SCHOLARLY REPRINTS**

Dr. Ralph Adams Brown, Senior Editor

Series on

**MAN AND HIS ENVIRONMENT**

Under the General Editorial Supervision of

Dr. Roger C. Heppell

*Professor of Geography, State University of New York*

# THE STORY KEY TO GEOGRAPHIC NAMES

BY

O. D. von ENGELN, Ph.D.

PROFESSOR OF PHYSICAL GEOGRAPHY IN CORNELL UNIVERSITY

AND

JANE McKELWAY URQUHART, A.B.

FORMERLY TEACHER OF ENGLISH AND FRENCH IN CASCADILLA SCHOOL

KENNIKAT PRESS
Port Washington, N. Y./London

THE STORY KEY TO GEOGRAPHIC NAMES

First published in 1924
Reissued in 1970 by Kennikat Press
Library of Congress Catalog Card No: 72-113299
ISBN 0-8046-1330-3

Manufactured by Taylor Publishing Company     Dallas, Texas

KENNIKAT SERIES ON MAN AND HIS ENVIRONMENT

# PREFACE

This is a quite unusual kind of book. Hence it may not be inappropriate that the Preface also departs from the conventional form.

One expects a preface to present an outline of the conscious purpose of the book it introduces and an indication of its content. Not infrequently there is also some apology for its defects and limitations. The first part of this Preface endeavors to meet those requirements.

But thereto is appended a second part. This second part is devoted to an exposition of a purpose the book serves and an end it achieves which were not wholly realized by the authors until after the manuscript took form in type.

Because the book was originally conceived and designed to serve a certain purpose in promoting effective teaching of elementary geography, the first part of this Preface is addressed specifically to teachers in the grade schools.

Learning geographic names and fitting them mentally to their correct positions on the map is a basic requirement for attainment of geographic competence. This essential is too slightly recognized by the modern texts.

In the reaction from an earlier type of geographic instruction, in which *lists* of rivers, capes, countries, and cities were learned by *rote,* there has developed a like undue and exclusive emphasis on mastering cause and effect relationships. Nowadays the child is taught "human geography" and "natural regions," and during elementary school years fails altogether to acquire an accurate and comprehensive knowledge of geographic names and locations.

However much emphasis the textbook writers may put on

human and regional relationships, teachers still consider it
essential that pupils in the grades *learn exactly* the facts of
place names and locations. That examination questions are
still prevailingly of the type: "What and where is New
Orleans?" "Name and locate the chief rivers of the United
States," "What are the countries of South America?" indicates this. The child that fails of ability to answer such
questions also fails geography examinations.

In other words, teachers, though convinced of the interest
and desirability of teaching "relationship geography," recognize also that children of grammar-school age cannot be
expected to reproduce the arguments and explanations ad-
vanced in the texts as responses to examination questions.
The children may grasp the situation at the time of the
lesson, but they do not retain the facts of cause and effect
exactly enough to be able to restate them logically and con-
cisely at the time of a test.

And it is unreasonable that they should be expected so to
perform. The texts are formulated by professional geographers after mature study. These authors take considerable
pride in the results of their efforts as set forth in the books.
But that grade-school children should attain to the accom-
plishments of these mature professionals simply by using the
texts they provide, is not to be looked for.

Geographic places and features and their positions in the
world are marked by names on the map. The number of
these names that must be mastered in acquiring even an
elementary knowledge of geography is, in proportion to the
sum of items needed to form a special vocabulary in other
subjects, very great. But it does not follow that the task
of memorizing these names must be altogether dreary, like
calling the roll of the names of the counties of the state
as of old. In maturity, association of ideas is found to be
the greatest aid to memory, and there is no good reason why
association should not be employed also to lighten the task

of the child in memorizing geographic names. Hence *The Story Key to Geographic Names.*

Practically all the geographic terms and names appearing in the "First Book" and "Second Book" texts are explained in the *Story Key.* When an item of importance is omitted, its absence is due to the fact that no explanation of the name is available. In order that teachers may meet the demand, almost sure to develop where the book is used, for explanations of less important terms, a list of the available compendiums on geographic names is provided; these, with consultation of local archives for district names, should afford the required information. The two indexes will facilitate the ready use of this book for reference purposes.

It should be stated emphatically that *The Story Key to Geographic Names* makes no pretense of being an etymological or philological treatise. While effort has been made to exclude conjectures that have no basis in fact, and while derivations known to be unsound are omitted, interest has been considered paramount in decisions as to what should be presented. Explanations, even though not of unquestioned authenticity, have been included where it was deemed that these would serve the purposes for which the book is intended. In these instances, however, the doubt is indicated by a restrictive word or phrase.

*The Story Key to Geographic Names* may be used in the following specific ways to serve its purpose as an aid to the learning of names and places:

1. Systematically in the classroom as a guide to map study.
2. As a book to recommend to parents who wish to help their children with the geography lessons.
3. As a source book for stories by which the teacher may enliven lessons on places and locations.
4. By the child as an aid in mastering pronunciations.

5. As a project source, *e.g.,* picture-name maps.
6. As a clue to historic and other correlations with geography.
7. As a reference book in which the names of places may be looked up as they are met with in lessons and in the daily news.

1. In the classroom the book may be read either aloud by the teacher or silently by the students themselves, the while the maps in the regular texts are conned and each feature and place located as mentioned. *The Story Key to Geographic Names* furnishes the incentive and stimulus to a systematic study of maps to a degree not readily supplied by any other device.

2. Teachers may confidently recommend *The Story Key to Geographic Names* to parents who desire to help their children in the study of geography but who are at a loss as to how to proceed for effective results. The parent reads aloud, the child has the geography text open at the appropriate map. The chapter or pages chosen for reading are each time those which correlate with the day's assignment in the regular text. As each name is encountered and explained, the child finds the place on the map and associates both its name and the location with the story. The content of *The Story Key to Geographic Names* will be found sufficiently interesting to hold the attention of the parent. Hence the enthusiasm will keep up from lesson to lesson.

3. If time is not available in the classroom or if parents are not induced to coöperate for systematic use of the book, the teacher may nevertheless employ it to advantage as a source for the explanations and stories of the names in each day's lesson. These explanations and stories may be introduced informally, as opportunity presents, in the course of successive recitations. Ample material is provided for a story or two each day.

4. It would be worth while to have this book in the hands of every child engaged in the study of geography, if only for the benefit to be derived from the simple and systematic teaching of *pronunciations* it furnishes. It is unreasonable to expect that a pupil in the grades will consult the index and solve the complicated pronunciation keys given in the regular texts. The device used in *The Story Key to Geographic Names* makes learning correct pronunciations an easy and natural performance.

The path leading to a correct and "standard" pronunciation of each name is beset with obstacles which the reader would do well to consider before objecting to any pronunciation as given. For the great majority of names Webster has been our guide. There are some names, however, which Webster does not give at all, a few where he indicates a choice, and several more where local usage or other authoritative sources are definitely opposed to him. To the first class belong a considerable number of foreign names, those of places in Asiatic countries particularly. In most instances we have consulted students from these countries in addition to whatever written evidence we could find. To the second or the third class belong words which apparently have more than one "correct" pronunciation, as, for example, Spanish and French place names that have been transplanted to new countries and are actually pronounced in two ways in their new locality. There are, too, some ancient and honorable names undergoing a temporary (let us hope) transformation, mainly through a general debasement of foreign pronunciations during the World War. In brief, we have endeavored to keep Spanish names Castilian, French words Parisian, etc., but there are cases where the local or "colloquial" has established a change too strongly to be overlooked.

We shall welcome any constructive suggestions based on conclusive authority from those who differ from us on the accuracy of the pronunciations herein offered.

5. A variety of projects are indicated in different chapters of the book. These, if carried out either in the school or in the home, will conduce to a more intensive study of names and locations. Chief of these are the picture-name maps, for the making of which detailed suggestions are given. A similar project is that of a translation map of China. Various suggestions are made for projects in the classification of different types of place names. The reference list of compendiums can be used as a source for the study and compilation of the origins and explanations of local place names.

6. The book abounds in allusions which should be a stimulus to the study of language, history, literature, and science, and which should induce the use of dictionaries, encyclopedias, and other works of reference. Incidentally, a number of delightful children's books, which are not so well known as they should be, are directly recommended to the attention of young students.

Now we come to the second part of this Preface.

Both the authors and the publishers felt that *The Story Key to Geographic Names* was somehow worth while quite aside from the direct and specific purposes for which it was designed, and which are set forth above. They thought of its content in general as comprising a "supplementary reader" which would be a valuable aid in geographic study. The nature of the material was obviously interesting. But why the reader's curiosity kept up from chapter to chapter, in view of the fact that each successive one of these chapters introduced only words and yet more words, was not at all appreciated.

Only after the matter was in type did it suddenly become clear that in linking up the explanations and stories of the names into a connected account *a very great content of other phases of geography had been quite unconsciously introduced.*

And this had been done very effectively chiefly because it was so unstudied. The conscious endeavor was only to introduce material that would link up the names successively considered and to make this connecting matter as concise as possible. The result is that the various regions and countries have their outstanding geographic features sketched in the briefest possible way, or perhaps only suggested, but yet so clearly indicated that one comprehends them broadly and to a degree that would not be possible if they were encumbered by the details and qualifications which would ordinarily be included as a part of such description.

Consider in this connection the parts of the book that deal with Siberia and names and places in Siberia. A real insight of the country is got from these paragraphs—the topography, the nature and significance of the rivers, the characteristics and occupations of the people, and the history of the area. What is not actually said is suggested. Further, the explanations of the words themselves convey much geographic information.

Thus what set out to be a word book exclusively has by indirection acquired a variety of features which make it a geographic reader of sorts. It is informative. Moreover, it links up geography and history, history and language, language and people. It teaches by persuasion and yet without insistence.

The conventional supplementary reader in geography is helpful in the study of geography. But it gives aid by *adding to* the content of the regular text. As most texts are so voluminous that children find difficulty in absorbing all the matter presented, it follows that what is needed is an aid and a guide to a mastery of what the ʽegular texts present rather than additional matter. This is what we feel *The Story Key to Geographic Names* accomplishes—by design with regard to the words, without premeditation with regard to the other features.

O. D. von E.

J. McK. U.

# BIBLIOGRAPHY AND SOURCE MATERIAL

*Century Dictionary and Encyclopedia.*

EGLI, J. J., *Nomina geographica,* in German (Leipzig, Fr. Brandstetter, 1893). This is the most comprehensive of books devoted to geographic names and is encyclopedic in form. In it 42,000 items are considered.

TAYLOR, ISAAC, *Names and Their Histories* (London, Macmillan Co., 1896, second edition, revised, London, Rivingtons, 1898).

PULMAN, G. P. R., *The Names of Places* (London, 1857).

In the first of the two items above the more important geographical names are explained in dictionary form. Much linguistic and historical matter is included. The second is of similar type.

KNOX, A., "Glossary of Geographical and Topographical Terms," in Stanford's *Compendium of Geography and Travel,* supplementary volume (London, 1904).

BLACKIE, C., *A Dictionary of Place Names* (third edition, revised, London, John Murray, 1887).

GANZENMULLER, KONRAD, Definitions of Geographical Names: *Journal of the American Geographical Society,* Vol. 21, Bulletin No. 4 (1889), pp. 516-525; Vol. 22, Bulletin No. 2, pp. 211-217; Bulletin No. 4 (1890), pp. 566-574.

These three references are particularly useful in elucidation of roots, prefixes, and suffixes.

GANNETT, HENRY, *Origin of Certain Place Names in the United States,* U. S. Geological Survey Bulletin No. 258 (Washington, D. C., 1905). As this contains explanations of the names of most of the smaller places in the United States it will constitute a valuable supplement to the volume in hand. The school library will probably be able to obtain a copy free of charge on application to the congressman from the local district.

———, "Origin of Washington Geographic Names" (Seattle, University of Washington Press, 1923).

BAKER, MARCUS, "Geographic Dictionary of Alaska," U. S. Geological Survey Bulletin No. 299 (Washington, D. C., 1906).

*Handbook of North American Indians,* Smithsonian Institution, Bureau of American Ethnology, Bulletin No. 30, Parts I and II (Washington, D. C., 1907 and 1910).

BEAUCHAMP, W. M., "Aboriginal Place Names of New York," New York State Museum Bulletin No. 108 (Albany, 1907).

RUTTENBER, E. M., "Footprints of the Red Men, Indian Geographical Names" (New York State Historical Association, 1906).

These three references will be found interesting in connection with Indian names. The *Handbook* is encyclopedic in form and constitutes a ready reference and index to the sources for Indian names.

McKNIGHT, G. H., *English Words and Their Background* (New York, Appleton, 1923), Ch. xxiv.

WEEKLEY, ERNEST, *Etymological Dictionary of Modern English* (London, 1921).

——, *The Romance of Words* (New York, 1912), Ch. iv.

——, *The Romance of Names* (New York, 1914), Chs. xii, xiii.

KER, E. T., *River and Lake Names in the United States* (New York, 1911).

LAWRENCE, F. W., "The Origin of American State Names," *National Geographic Magazine,* Vol. 38 (1920), pp. 105-143.

EFVERGREN, CARL, *Names of Places in a Transferred Sense in English* (Lund, Sweden, and Cambridge, England, 1909). Use of place names to distinguish other objects, as madras for cotton cloth.

HARRISON, HENRY, *The Origin of Yankee* (London, Moreland Press, 1917).

WHITBECK, R. H., "Regional Peculiarities in Place Names," Bulletin of the American Geographical Society, Vol. 43 (1911), pp. 273-281.

WATERMAN, T. T., "The Geographical Names Used by the Indians of the Pacific Coast," *Geographical Review,* Vol. 12 (1922), pp. 175-194.

This paper is interesting in that it demonstrates convincingly that these primitive peoples (and presumably others) are acquainted with the world only as a very limited area, that they have few or no names for the larger elements of the landscape, a mountain range, for example, is nameless as a whole, but that, on the other hand, every minute natural object has a specific name. In this may be found an explanation of the nature of many primitive place names which have persisted in civilized countries.

KLEINPAUL, RUDOLPH, *Länder und Völkernamen* (second edition, 1919, Vol. 478, Sammlung Göschen).

# CONTENTS

# CONTENTS

# THE STORY KEY TO GEOGRAPHIC NAMES

He thought of the present world no longer as a wonderland of experiences, but as geography and history, as the repeating of names very hard to pronounce, and lists of products and populations, and heights and lengths, and as lists and dates— O! and boredom indescribable.

H. G. WELLS, *The History of Mr. Polly.*

# THE STORY KEY TO GEOGRAPHIC NAMES

## CHAPTER I

### GENERAL GEOGRAPHIC TERMS

"Good enough," you say, as you open the pages of this book; "we shall be glad to know what many of those words and names mean. They are hard to remember, hard to spell, hard to pronounce, and usually they don't seem to have much sense anyway."

That is about the way most children feel when they first begin the study of geography. They can't be blamed so very much for thinking it stupid and tiresome, for they have to learn and remember such a number of things that the task seems endless, and hardly worth while at all. The pictures that the geography book contains are its most interesting feature, for they show different and strange things from all over the world. Anyone can look at these and wonder at the funny people in the South Sea Islands or in Siberia. In this way one learns to understand something of what geography is about. If it were not for the pictures now so freely used in geography books, children would hate to do their geography lesson even more than most of them do, and they would feel more hopeless about ever learning it, because it would be so much more difficult to understand and to enjoy.

Now it is the same with the words and names in geography as it is with the pictures. If one could look at those words and see right away what they are about, as one can with the pictures, this would certainly keep the student interested. Here we have the reason for this book. Its purpose is to make the words and names in geography like the pictures, things one can look at and understand right away. Then, because they are understood, they will be remembered. It may be a new and surprising idea that such a thing is really possible, but it is, as anyone will find who reads on a bit further.

Before we can use a word, we must be able to pronounce it. This may help us to know what it means, too. For that matter, we couldn't ask anybody else what it means if we couldn't pronounce it properly. There are a few simple marks that show in just a glance how letters are sounded. Now when we come to the name of a place or river or something of that sort in this book, we shall first find it divided into syllables and at the same time *phonetically* spelled. This means spelled as it sounds. But since the vowels (*a, e, i, o,* and *u*) each have several different sounds, each sound will be marked, and then it will be put down at the bottom of the page in a word that everyone will surely know.

The word that everyone will naturally want to know about first is geography. This is phonetically spelled jē-ŏg′rǎ-fĭ. The key at the bottom of the pages shows how those vowels go according to the marks. After a little practice it will be easy to remember what the marks

āle; câre; ăm; ärm; ēve; ĕnd; makēr; īce; ĭll

mean, and then it will not be necessary to use the key often. Everyone has at some time or other pronounced this word something like "jog-raf-fy." Well, such a pronunciation as that is treating a good old word rather unkindly. The fault is really a greater one. For the word **geography** is put together by using a Latin word, *geo,* which was what the Romans said when they meant 'the earth,' and a Greek word *graph,* which meant 'a writing.' So geography means 'a writing about the earth.' "Jograffy" puts such a false face on the word that some people would not recognize it. All our good words have surely a right to be treated more fairly than that.

To tell the whole truth about the word geography, we must add that the Romans took *geo* from a similar Greek term, and it may be true that the Greeks in turn took it from a language even older. There are a good many English words which come from both Greek and Latin, or rather from Greek plus Latin. Sometimes the spelling has been changed so much that we have to look hard to find out what language did start a word out upon its journey down the years. There is usually, however, one part of it which we see has never disappeared entirely, no matter how far the word has traveled. This part is called the *root.* Words, like plants, are made of roots and stems. The stem may get broken or die down, but the root is very hard to kill. It may produce more than one stem, too. Some plant roots can be separated and make many plants if they are properly cared for. In the same way word roots can be taken from one language into another and make words of almost the same meaning in each language. Then, too, one root can furnish many

ōld; ôrb; ŏdd; ūse; ûrn; ŭp; fo͞od; fo͝ot; out; oil

different words in the same language. The stem may be a little different, and the leaves not at all alike, as in the many varieties of geraniums, for instance. Its endings are what we may call the leaves of a word.

Everyone ought to know where most English words come from. If we turn to a map of the world, and find on this map, first, the Mediterranean Sea, then the Italian and Balkan peninsulas which extend into it, then Scandinavia, the big peninsula in the northern part of Europe, then the peninsulas of India and Arabia in Asia, then the island of Great Britain, and, finally, North America, we shall have the beginning of a fascinating geography lesson. Perhaps we may draw light pencil lines extending from Italy, the Balkan peninsula, Scandinavia, India, and Arabia to Great Britain, and a little heavier pencil line from Great Britain to North America. This will show where the language we speak came from.

The map of the whole world in all geography books except the large atlases has to be crowded even to make only the greater lands and the oceans appear on it. So it is not possible to show the smaller divisions of the continents and seas. But if we turn to the map of Europe alone, we can locate and find named, Rome, the city on the Italian peninsula; Greece, the country on the Balkan peninsula; Denmark, the little country on a peninsula just south of the Scandinavian peninsula. Then on the map of Asia we can find the Ganges River, in the north of India, and the land of Arabia.

Our Greek expressions come from the language of the peoples who lived in ancient times in the general area that is now the country of Greece. Words of Latin origin

āle; câre; ăm; ärm; ēve; ĕnd; makĕr; īce; ĭll

came from the Romans who spread out from the same
site that the city of Rome occupies to-day. Anglo-Saxon
refers to the language of the Angles and Saxons, the
people who lived originally on the Danish peninsula and
moved later in large numbers to Great Britain, where they
were joined by other people of similar type from Scandinavia. Sanskrit was the language once used by the
population of the plain of the Ganges River in the north
of India. Thus it is evident that English is made up
of words that come from a great variety of sources. Now
we can see that the lines from Greece and Rome may
be made one line, extending from Greece to Rome, and
from Rome through France to Great Britain, for the
Greek words were used in Rome; and the Latin language
of the Romans, mixed with Greek, was brought into
England largely through France and the French language.
Here, then, is a very interesting lesson in geography as
related to language.

Although the sources of the English language, as a
whole, are so geographically varied, nevertheless three-
fourths of the most common English words are of Anglo-
Saxon origin. That is, they were handed down to us
from the languages of the peoples who formerly lived
on the Danish and Scandinavian peninsulas and later, in
part of their number, settled in England. Sometimes
an ancient Anglo-Saxon word was spelled exactly as we
spell the same word in English, but it may not have
meant quite the same thing when first used. Thus **world**
was *world* in Anglo-Saxon, but it meant 'the human
family,' 'all of mankind.' **Earth,** on the other hand, was
*eorthe* in Anglo-Saxon, but it meant *earth* as it does now.

ōld; ôrb; ŏdd; ūse; ûrn; ŭp; fōōd; fŏŏt; out; oil

Perhaps *eorthe* got its start (if one may speak that way about a word) from a root word *ar,* meaning 'to plow,' the root from which we get the word *arable.* **Land** and **sea** are also Anglo-Saxon words that had the same meaning in early times as they have now, but sea was spelled *sae,* and was like the Latin word *saevus,* which meant 'wild,' 'cruel.' It is not thought, however, that the old Angles, when they said *sae,* intended to give the idea that the sea was always raging. All they had in mind was that *sae,* 'great waters,' were different from the wide lands. Still it is interesting that the Anglo-Saxon word and the Latin word are so much alike, and can be so easily linked together.

**Weather** is from the Anglo-Saxon *weder* = 'weather' or 'wind'; so also is **spring,** from *spring* = 'a leap.' **Winter** was always *winter*; but **summer** was formerly *sumer.* **Autumn** we get from the Latin *autumnus,* perhaps related to the Latin verb *avere* = 'be well.' There is also a Sanskrit root *av,* which means 'satisfy one's self.' We think of the bountiful crops of the fall season, and autumn, therefore, appeals to us as a very pleasant and appropriate term to use for that time of year. **Season,** too, we have from the Latin *satio* = 'a sowing' or 'sowing time'; from denoting the particular season, spring, the meaning was extended to any season.

**North** was *north* in Anglo-Saxon, as now; **south** was *suth,* but had the same meaning as it does now. But though **west** was also *west* in Anglo-Saxon, it was connected in origin with the Latin word *vesper* = 'evening,' and the Sanskrit *vastu* = 'a house' or 'the place where the sun stays at night.' **East,** however, came directly from

āle; câre; ăm; ärm; ēve; ĕnd; makēr; īce; ĭll

the Sanskrit *ushas* = 'the dawn,' and of this the *ush* part meant 'to burn.'

North, south, east, and west are spoken of as the **cardinal** (cär'dĭn-ăl) **directions.** Cardinal, however, has no relation to a compass card, on which these directions are printed, but comes from the Latin *cardinalis* = 'pertaining to a hinge,' and that from the noun *cardo* = 'that on which something turns or depends'; hence, important or chief thing, thus, the chief directions. East and west were much more important to the peoples of the early civilizations, partly because they thought that the north was too cold for people to live in and the south too hot, and also because the ancient peoples attached a vast importance to the sun in their religious observances. Accordingly, we have in English the word **oriental** (ō-rĭ-ĕnt'ăl), meaning things from or pertaining to eastern lands, from the Latin *oriens* = 'rising' or 'quarter where the sun rises.' Like *oriental* in origin is the verb **orientate** (ō'rĭ-ĕn-tāt'), to locate one's self or a thing with reference to the chief directions. But orientate once meant only to place a church so that its altar would be toward the east. The idea that this was the proper way was due to the practice of sun worship by ancient peoples. It was in early times the custom also to bury the dead with the feet toward the east. In the same way, **occidental** (ŏk-sĭ-dĕnt'ăl), 'western,' is from the Latin *occidens* = 'quarter of the falling sun,' and the Romans made up *occidens* out of two other words they had, *ob* = 'before' and *cadere* = 'to fall,' thus, 'before the sun fall.'

Two words used in geography and astronomy for the up and down directions are taken from the Arabic tongues.

ōld; ôrb; ŏdd; ūse; ûrn; ŭp; fōōd; fŏŏt; out; oil

**Zenith** (zē'nĭth), the point directly above a person's head, was *samt ur-ras* = 'the path of the head'; whereas **nadir** (nā'dēr), the point in the heavens vertically below any given place on the earth, came from the words *nazir assamt* = 'corresponding to the zenith,' which was their way of saying, a place like the zenith but on the other side. If we want to speak of a place, not in the heavens, but on the other side of the earth, in a line going through the earth directly below us, we say it is **antipodal** (ăn-tĭp'ō-dăl). Antipodal is made up of two Greek words meaning 'against' and 'foot,' hence, 'people with their feet against each other,' and no doubt everyone will agree that that was a happy way to express the idea. Most commonly you will find in geography, "the **Antipodes**" (ăn-tĭp'ō-dēs), and when so capitalized, New Zealand, Australia, and their surrounding regions are usually meant, because those are the lands antipodal to England. But of course North America has a different antipodes from western Europe, and even though the Europeans have been rather saucy in taking the capitalized form for themselves only, we have our very own antipodes nevertheless.

Anyone can go to a globe map and find out where the antipodes of his home is by putting a finger of one hand on the globe at his location and the corresponding finger of the other hand on the point just opposite. One must be sure, though, that the line connecting the two fingers goes through the center of the earth.

The moon, we read, is the earth's **satellite** (să'tĕl-līt), and in Latin *satelles* was 'an attendant' or 'guard.' So we may think of the moon attending and guarding the

āle; câre; ăm; ärm; ēve; ĕnd; makēr; īce; ĭll

earth. The course which the moon follows in going around the earth is called its **orbit** (ôr'bĭt) from the Latin *orbita* = 'the track of a wheel,' and *orbita* was derived from *orbis* = 'a circle.' As the full moon appears as a circle, and as its course about the earth is also a circle, the word *orbit* seems entirely fitting.

Another astronomical term is **zodiac** (zō'dĭ-ăk) which meant, in the Greek, 'of animals' or 'the circle of animals.' Twelve different groups of stars appear in the course of a year in a belt around the heavens, a sort of panorama of stars in monthly installments. These groups were singled out by the ancients in Babylon as early as 2200 B.C., and the name of a different animal given to each of them. It surprises us how much the ancients knew of the stars, while most of us in this day and age know so little, but when we apply our knowledge of geography we find several reasons why this should be true. Egypt, Babylon, Greece, and Italy all are countries with prevailingly clear skies so that the stars at night show brightly and distinctly. Moreover, the people in those lands commonly spent the cool of the evening (for the days are hot) on the flat roofs of their homes, so they had time to observe and talk about the stars and to see how they change. In ancient days, moreover, there were no clocks or watches, and people observed the stars to see how far the night had passed; just as we, even now, note the position of the sun during the day to get some idea of the time, when there is no clock at hand.

**Revolution** (rĕ-vō-loo'shŭn) comes from the Latin, *re* = 'back' and *volvere* = 'turn,' hence, 'turn back' or 'turn round.' **Rotation** (rō-tā'shŭn) is from the Latin

ōld; ôrb; ŏdd; ūse; ûrn; ŭp; fōod; fŏŏt; out; oil

*rota* = 'wheel' or 'vehicle.' There is a nice distinction in the use of these words, as referred to the earth, which will be quite clear when one thinks of a wheel turning or rotating on its axle or **axis** (ăx′ĭs) as does also the earth, especially as, in Latin, axle and axis are quite the same thing. **Pole** (pōl) is from the Greek word *polas* = 'pivot' or 'hinge,' and this had its origin in an earlier word that meant 'urge on.' Hence, we can think of getting hold of the North Pole of the earth and giving it a spin, as one does with one kind of small top. But it would not be very practical to attempt that, even if we could put ourselves outside the earth and were big and strong enough, for the earth exists in space much as a soap bubble floats in air. If a soap bubble were caught in a whirling current of air, it would start to spin, and would then be rotating on an axis, which would, of course, have two poles. But although we would know that the soap bubble had the axis and the poles, we could no more see or touch them than we can touch or see the earth's axis and poles.

On the rotating soap bubble there would be a middle belt or girdle, exactly half-way between the two poles, its equator. **Equator** (ē-kwā′tôr) is from the Latin *aequare* = 'to make equal.' Thus the top part and the bottom part, as separated by the equator, are each exactly half a ball, or a **hemisphere** (hĕm′ĭ-sfēr), from *hemi* = 'half,' and *sphaerium* = 'a sphere or globe.'

We learned in an earlier paragraph that the ancients were much more concerned about east and west than they were about north and south, because they considered only that part of the world which was (to their minds) habita-

āle; câre; ăm; ärm; ēve; ĕnd; makĕr; īce; ĭll

ble by man to be a fit subject for geography. A North-Pole expedition they would have thought to be the height of foolishness. For this reason the world seemed longer to them in the east-west direction than in the north-south direction. Hence, they thought of the north-south direction as the width of the world and called the measurement of this width **latitude** (lat'i-tūd), from the Latin word *latus* = 'broad.' The idea that the "home of man" was longer in an east to west line than on a north to south line was due, as has been said, to the fact that the ancients thought the north too cold and the south too hot for men to inhabit, and also because, although the Atlantic Ocean bounded their known world on the west, on the east they considered the habitable world to extend indefinitely, for they encountered more lands and new peoples no matter how far east they traveled. Thus **longitude** (lŏn'ji-tūd) from the Latin *longus* = 'long,' was the proper word for measurements east and west. Latitude and longitude measurements are in **degrees**, from the Latin *de* = 'down' and *gradus* = 'a step,' thus 'a step down'; but when they put the two together to form the word degree this meant 'a step up' or 'a step sideways' just as well.

As the lines which on a map mark off one degree of latitude from the next are the same distance apart at all points on the earth they are called **parallels** (pär'ăl-lĕlz) from the Greek word meaning 'beside one another.' Although the ancients thought that the sun revolved about the earth and not the earth about the sun, as is actually the case, that error did not prevent them from reasoning out that every place that had noon, midday, at the same instant must have the same longitude; hence it

ōld; ôrb; ŏdd; ūse; ûrn; ŭp; fōod; fŏot; out; oil

must be at the same distance east and west. For if the sun followed a path from east to west across the earth, all the places on a single north to south line must necessarily be crossed at the same instant. Hence the ancients spoke of the line that joined up all places having noon at the same time, in the Latin, as *meridianus* = 'of or pertaining to the midday or to the south,' and we say **meridian** (mē-rǐ'dǐ-ăn).

After the middle of winter the sun mounts higher in the heavens each day, and the days become longer until finally they are as long as the nights. Then it is the time of the spring **equinox** (ē'kwǐ-nŏks), from the Latin *aequus* = 'equal' and *nox* = 'night.' But after the spring equinox the sun does not stop climbing higher in the sky; it goes on up until the beginning of summer, when we have the longest day of the year and the sun stands still, that is, does not go higher in the heavens the next day. This we call the summer **solstice** (sŏl'stǐs), from the Latin *sol* = 'sun' and *status,* past participle of *sistere* = 'to make to stand still.' After the summer solstice the sun sinks lower and lower until we have days and nights once more of equal length, the autumn equinox; and still farther down until it reaches its lowest point and the time of the shortest day, which is the beginning of winter and the time of the winter solstice.

Where you live, probably, the sun, even at the summer solstice, never reaches a point directly overhead in the zenith at noon. But if you were to travel south along your meridian you would come to a place where the sun was directly overhead just at the time of the summer solstice. That place would be in the latitude of the **Tropic**

āle; câre; ăm; ärm; ēve; ĕnd; makẽr; īce; ĭll

of Cancer (trŏp'ĭk ŏv kăn'sēr). Tropic is from a Greek word signifying 'a turn' or 'change,' that is, the sun turns or changes at that latitude, and on succeeding days one would need to go farther and farther south in order to have the sun overhead at noon. Cancer is from the Latin *cancer* = 'a crab,' and that was one of the animal groups of stars in the zodiac; the one that marked the limit of the sun's course northward among the stars. The sun is directly overhead at noon on the equator at the time of the autumn equinox and when it is farthest south, at the time of the winter solstice, it is over the south latitude of the **Tropic of Capricorn** (kăp'rĭ-kôrn). Capricorn is from the Latin *caper* = 'a goat' and *cornu* = 'a horn,' in other words, the 'goat-horned group of stars.'

Now when we turn to a map of the world and locate the Tropic of Cancer and the Tropic of Capricorn we have a very real idea as to why they are located where they are, and why they should have special names. But we are not done with them yet. Between them are located all the parts of the earth where the sun at any time of the year is directly overhead at noon. That is, they mark out a **zone** (zōn), a term from the Greek which means 'a girdle' or 'belt.'

It is easy to understand that the zc ⌐ between the two tropics must also be the hottest one the earth, for it contains all the places where the sun's rays at some time in the year fall vertically; and everyone knows how much hotter it is when the sun is high at noon than when it is low in the morning or in the evening. We speak of this zone, therefore, not only by calling it the **Tropical Zone** from its position between the two tropics, but also as the

ōld; ôrb; ŏdd; ūse; ûrn; ŭp; fōōd; fŏŏt; out; oil

**Torrid** (tŏr'rĭd) **Zone,** from the Latin *torridus* = 'dry with heat.' This, however, is not a very descriptive word, for much of the Tropical Zone is really very wet. It would have been better to use some Latin word, if there were such a one, that meant 'hot from the sun,' for that would be much more true to the facts. Indeed, there seems to have been a little misunderstanding, also, in calling the zones next north and south of the Tropical Zone, the **Temperate** (tĕm'pẽr-āt) **Zones.** Temperate comes from the Latin *temperare* = 'to divide' or 'apportion duly,' the notion being that the Temperate Zones are neither very hot nor very cold. To some extent that is true, in that summer follows winter, according to how high the sun is; but actually the Temperate Zones have greater extremes of heat and cold, both, than does the Tropical Zone. **Frigid** (frij'ĭd) **Zone,** though, is rightly enough named from the Latin word *frigidus,* meaning 'cold.'

The Frigid Zones, for there are two of them, are called, also, the **Arctic** (ärk'tĭk) and the **Antarctic Zones,** respectively, the one around the North Pole and the other about the South Pole. Arctic is from the Greek *arktikos* = 'northern,' because a group of stars (like the groups in the zodiac) which was called the Great Bear (*arktos*) was to be seen in the north. The group of stars that we call the Big Dipper is a part of the Great Bear. Anyone who does not know the Big Dipper should ask someone who does to point it out on the first clear night and also to explain how to locate the North Star, called Polaris, which is directly over the North Pole, by means of it. As the Latin *anti* means 'against' or 'opposite,' it is easy

āle; câre; ăm; ärm; ēve; ĕnd; makẽr; īce; ĭll

to see why the zone around the South Pole should be called the Antarctic Zone.

Each tropic forms one boundary of a Temperate Zone; the other boundary is formed by the **Arctic** or **Antarctic Circle,** the parallel of latitude in the northern or southern hemispheres where the sun is seen just on the horizon at midday at the time of the winter solstice for each hemisphere. Thus the Temperate Zones are also those zones that have a division between day and night every twenty-four hours, on every day of the year, though December 21st is a very short day, to be sure, at the Arctic Circle. What, then, must be the conditions of day and night through the year at the North Pole? That is a very interesting question we will leave to the reader to work out for himself.

The ancients knew that the earth was a globe. Later that knowledge was lost and at Columbus's time discovered again. But there was a time before the ancients first knew the earth to be a ball, yet knew that at the same time of year the sun's rays had a different slope at different places, and that this difference in the directness of the sun's rays brought about the differences in the degree of heat felt in the several zones. To account for this condition they supposed that the flat earth was set on a slant from equator to pole, and that this slant made the different zones. Hence, we have the word **climate** (klī'māt) from the Greek for 'a slope.'

A Dutchman to whom a Californian had been boasting of rose bushes as big as trees and of watermelons the size of a tub, as they grew in the home state of the Californian, after asking each time he was told of one of these wonders,

ōld; ôrb; ŏdd; ūse; ûrn; ŭp; fōōd; fŏŏt; out; oil

why it was, and being told that it was due to the climate, finally retorted by telling the Californian of a building in Holland. The Dutchman said this building was ten stories high and had doors and windows on each floor but no stairs or elevators. "But how can you go to the upper stories?" asked the Californian. "Climb ut," replied the Dutchman. And while the Dutchman probably did not mean his joke that way, we, who know what the word *climate* first signified, see how apt his pun really was.

# CHAPTER II

PERHAPS it is a relief to have passed all those words that have to do with imaginary lines and the things that they mark out. It is bad enough to be asked to remember exactly how everything is located, say, down at the park, or down by the creek, when one is away from those places, but it's worse when one is expected to imagine a whole state or country, and it's still worse when one must think at once of all the earth and the sun and the heavens besides; and that is what is necessary when the solstices are to be understood. But we are past those now, and are to consider next words that stand for real things on the earth, things that one could go and see if it were convenient.

The biggest thing on the earth is the continuous water of the **oceans** (ō'shănz). In Latin ocean was *oceanus,* and this tèrm the Romans obtained from a word used by the Greek poet, Homer, which meant the 'great stream that encircled the earth,' for in those times they thought of the ocean as a great river that flowed around the lands of the earth, as if those lands were islands in the midst of vast waters. When it was realized instead that the sea south of Italy and Greece was everywhere enclosed by lands, the name **Mediterranean** (mĕd-ĭ-tẽr-ā'nē-ăn),

ōld; ôrb; ŏdd; ūse; ûrn; ŭp; fōōd; fŏŏt; out; oil

from the Latin *medius* = 'middle' and *terra* = 'land,' was
given to that part of the ocean, and the great sea to the
west was called the **Atlantic** (ăt-lăn'tĭk) after the **Atlas**
(ăt'lăs) **Mountains** in the northwestern part of Africa,
*atlantes* being the plural of *atlas*. According to Greek
mythology, it was on these mountains that Atlas stood
and supported the sky on his shoulders. Hence Atlas, as
a word, had its origin in Greek terms signifying 'to
endure,' 'to bear,' and though it is twisting the original
sense somewhat, still it would not be very wrong to
think of the Atlantic, therefore, as 'bearing' many ships,
in view of the vast commerce that moves over its waters.
The other great ocean, the **Pacific** (pă-sĭf'ĭk), was so
named by the explorer Magellan, who, in his voyage over
it in 1520-21, encountered no storm. Pacific is made
up of two Latin words, *pax* = 'peace' and *facere* = 'to
make.' When Balboa discovered the Pacific in 1513, he
looked to the south, hence called it *Mar del Sur*, or, 'Sea of
the South,' and we often now use the name the **South
Seas** for the portion of the Pacific about Australia and
to the north and east of that continent.

Where the sea touches the land it does not always
make a straight or even coast line. In many places the
coast waters are broken up into smaller expanses to which
separate names are given, according for the most part
to the extent and the way in which these bodies of water
are enclosed by the lands. Thus we have a **sound**, a
shallow expanse of water open at both ends, the word
being from the Anglo-Saxon *sund,* which had the same
meaning. Hence *sound,* the expanse of water, is different
from the word *sound,* meaning noise, which comes from

āle; câre; ăm; ärm; ēve; ĕnd; makẽr; īce; ĭll

Latin *sonus*. This suggests one reason, then, why often words in English spelled the same way and pronounced the same way have, nevertheless, different meanings.

A **strait** is a narrower, and commonly a deeper, passage of the same kind as a sound, and the term came originally from the Latin *strictus* = 'narrow,' through the old French *estrait* = 'a narrow passage of water.' *Straight*, as a line is straight, spelled differently but pronounced the same, on the other hand, comes from the Anglo-Saxon verb *streccan*, past participle *streht* = 'to stretch,' and is an example of another way in which English words develop.

An **estuary** (ĕs′tū-ā-rĭ) is, like a strait, also a narrow arm of the sea, but one that extends inland, and it occurs usually at the mouth of a river into which the tides run; from this condition the name is derived, for *aestuarium* in the Latin meant 'mouth of the tidal river.' A **bay** is a much wider inward bend of the coast line than an estuary, and the term has an interesting history. It evidently dates back to a Roman seashore resort which was called *Baiae*. Accordingly, when we say Chesapeake Bay, it would sound to a Roman as if we said 'Chesapeake Atlantic City!' It was once thought that bay was from the Latin verb *badare* = 'to gape open,' but whereas that verb is responsible when we say that dogs bay, it has nothing to do with a bay of the ocean, though it would be quite appropriate there too. **Gulf**, an opening wider and bigger than a bay, comes from the Greek and Latin signifying 'lap' or 'bosom,' giving us then the feeling that a gulf is a place where the little ships that sail the great seas should rest comfortably. That, however, is not always true of

ōld; ôrb; ŏdd; ūse; ûrn; ŭp; fōōd; fŏŏt; out; oil

gulfs, and so we have **harbor** (här′bôr), meaning in
Middle English, not only a place where ships could be
safe, but also 'a place of shelter.' Sometimes, even now,
we use the word harbor in that sense when we are writing
poetry.

It is perhaps not strange that **archipelago** (är-kĭ-
pĕl′ă-gō), the word for a large group of islands in the sea,
should really be a word that originally meant the sea
itself, for an archipelago is so much in the midst of the
sea that it seems part of the sea. *Archi* in the Greek
meant 'chief' or 'principal,' and *pelago* = 'the sea.' At
first the word was applied to the part of the sea that we
now call the Aegean. Instead of saying "the Aegean" the
ancient Greeks simply said "the Archipelago," and they
would have expected you to know that they meant what
was to them the one chief sea, which was studded with
islands. Now we know of several other seas studded with
islands, and we call each of them an archipelago and add
another name to distinguish it from the rest. **Island**
(ī′lănd) was from the Anglo-Saxon *igland,* which had the
same meaning; **isle** was patterned on the Latin *in* = 'in'
and *salum* = 'the main sea,' and back in the 1500's, when
some people thought they knew a great deal about words,
they put an *s* instead of a *g* in *igland* to make it more correct, as they thought.

**Isthmus** (ĭs′mŭs) was the same in Latin as now, but,
like archipelago, only a certain isthmus, that of Corinth,
was meant. **Peninsula** (pĕn-ĭn′sū-lă) is from the
Latin *paene* = 'almost' and *insula* = 'isle.' **Promontory**
(prŏm′ŭn-tō-rĭ) is from the Latin *pro* = 'forth' and
either from *mons* = 'mountain' or from the verb *promi-*

 āle; câre; ăm; ärm; ēve; ĕnd; makẽr; īce; ĭll

*nere* = 'to jut out.' **Cape** comes from the Latin *caput* = 'a head.'

**Continent** (kŏn'tĭ-nĕnt) is derived from the Latin verb *continere* = 'to hold together,' 'to be continuous, uninterrupted,' and is, therefore, an altogether fitting term for the great, unbroken stretches of land that are the sites of the great nations. **Land,** itself, is Anglo-Saxon and always had the same form as it has now, and also the same meaning, that is, it signifies the solid part of the earth on which we live.

On the continents we find mountains, valleys, and plains, that is, hills, hollows, and flat places. All three of these words are from the Latin. *Mons* was the Latin word for **mountain,** *vallis* for **valley,** and *planum* for **plain.** As we shall see later, the word for mountain, taken from many different languages, is used either as a whole, or in part, or in some distorted form, for very many names of places where people live in numbers, that is, cities and towns. It is easy to understand why this should be true. A mountain sticks up; it can be seen from far away; it is an obstacle to travel and to the movement of materials by man; it is also a hard place for an enemy to attack, and hence forts were commonly built in or on the sides of mountains. Therefore it was only natural that since mountains impressed themselves in so many ways on the senses of the people living near them that a name connected in some way with a mountain should have become part of the names of many places.

**Plateau** (plă-tō') comes from the French, meaning 'a little flat place.' We usually mean, however, a flat place which is elevated some distance above the sea level.

ōld; ôrb; ŏdd; ūse; ûrn; ŭp; fōōd; fŏŏt; out; oil

Although continents are wide stretches of uninterrupted land, as compared with islands, peninsulas, isthmuses, and so on, still they do have bodies of water on them, and flowing across them. If the body of water is of wide extent, it is a **lake,** from the Latin *lacus* = 'a large body of water.' Variations of *lacus* occur in many languages to signify lake: thus the Scottish *loch* and *lough,* for instance, Loch Katrine, of which you have heard; in French we have *lac,* in Spanish, Portuguese, and Italian, *lago,* as Lago di Garda. A small lake is a **pond,** a term that comes from a Middle-English word *pound* = 'an enclosure,' in which sense we still use it when we say a dog has been put in pound; *pound,* perhaps, came from an Anglo-Saxon word *pund* = 'to dam up.' From either origin *pond* is a fitting word, since a mill pond, for example, is both enclosed and dammed up. **Pool,** an even smaller body of water than a pond, is from the Anglo-Saxon *pol* = 'a hole' or 'a pit.' This Anglo-Saxon *pol* also means mire and mud, as does an ancient Greek term similar to pool. The old swimming pool had a pretty muddy bottom as many of us remember from our boyhood days.

If the water on the land has a distinct flow, it is either a stream, or a river, or a creek, or a rivulet, or a brook. Of these words, **stream** is the class name, that is, it is used for all kinds of flowing water: a river is a stream, so is a brook. Stream is also, perhaps, the most ancient term of all these. Stream was *stream* in Anglo-Saxon but seems to have come originally from a Sanskrit root word *sru* = 'flow,' and as you pronounce *sru,* you get the idea of the sound of flowing water. **River** is from the

āle; câre; ăm; ärm; ēve; ĕnd; makēr; īce; ĭll

French *rivière* = 'a river,' but that term itself came from
the Latin *ripa* = 'the bank of a stream' or 'the coast of
the sea.' In the latter sense it is still used by the Italians,
as we see in the place name Italian Riviera, of which you
have heard as a winter resort. **Rivulet** (rĭv'ū-lĕt), however, does not come from river, as one might think, but
from the true Latin word for river, *rivus*. A little river
in Latin was *rivulus*, and we have simply used *et* instead
of their *us* as an ending to signify that it is a small river.
Like stream, river also goes back to a Sanskrit root word
*ri*, meaning 'to flow' or 'run.' Accordingly, when we
write that a word is de*ri*ved from some other word, we
mean that it 'flows' from that word. Again, when
you say that someone is your *ri*val, you mean that he or
she 'runs' the same way that you do, not literally always,
but in the broader sense of having the same object at the
end, as most rivers run down to the sea finally.

**Brook** is an Anglo-Saxon word *broc* = 'a stream,' and
may have some connection with the Anglo-Saxon
*brecan* = 'to burst forth,' which certainly would fit a
mountain brook. **Creek** comes from the Icelandic *kriki*
= 'a nook' or 'bend,' and perhaps is also related to the
Anglo-Saxon *crecca* = 'a creek.' At any rate, there are
place names in England, like Creccanford, that is, the ford
of the creek. They do not use the word *creek* much in
England nowadays, but we have it for winding, shallow
streams, larger than a brook but smaller than a river,
and that use is in keeping with the original Icelandic sense.

The continents are divided up into countries inhabited
by different nations. The word **country** is a curious one
in its derivation. One would not guess easily how it came

old; ôrb; ŏdd; ūse; ûrn; ŭp; fōōd; fŏŏt; out; oil

to be used. It comes from the Latin preposition *contra* = 'over against' or 'in front of,' the idea being that a country is a land that is laid out over against, or in front of, a person, to be examined or thought about. So when one looks at a country on a map, or imagines it from reading about it, one is acting quite properly. **Nation** is from the Latin word *natio* = 'birth' or the verb form *nasci* = 'to be born,' hence the idea of a race or people. From that one would get the idea that all the people of a nation ought to have the same country of origin. When nations were very small, that is, when they were really tribes, that was true, but it is so no longer. If, however, a people live in one region for any considerable length of time, they tend to become a nation in the original sense, for there are very few marriages outside the country, and thus the whole people, after not many generations, tend to become connected by ties of blood.

**People** is a comfortable word to use, for its connections are simple and satisfying. It comes from the Latin *populus* = 'the people.' **Race**, like nation, has been confused. Race is from the Old High German *reiz* = 'a line' or 'a scratch.' We get our English word *write* from the same term. As in the case of nation, we think of a race as a people having had the same ancestry, but on the basis of the origin of the word all one could say would be that a race was made up of people who scratched or wrote the same way. What perhaps was in mind was that a race has a certain line of descent. **Tribe**, too, is only indirectly connected in origin with its present meaning. Tribe is from the Latin *tribus* = 'a division of the people,' thus very general in its sense and not originally significant

āle; câre; ăm; ärm; ēve; ĕnd; makēr; īce; ĭll

of a common father or blood relationship. However, the Romans perhaps originally meant by *tribe* a third part of the people, for in early days the Romans were divided into three great families.

Within a nation the people live in single families on farms, with houses often far apart, or in groups of houses making up villages, towns, and cities. The word **village** is directly from the Latin word *villa* = 'a country house,' and this in turn probably came from *vicus* = 'a village.' Farmers and villagers usually regard city people as villains; 'the wicked city,' is a common phrase, but, curiously enough, the word *villain* is from the same Latin words as village, and villain meant originally a farm servant or peasant. If one lives in a city or town, he may have reasons, because of the cost of food, to regard farmers as villains, even to-day; so perhaps the score is even.

Anyhow, people living in towns have no special reason for turning up their noses at country people, or villagers, on the basis of the origin of the word **town,** for this word was the homely Anglo-Saxon *tun,* which meant 'a hedge' or 'an enclosure,' or a simple farmhouse. **City,** however, is more lordly; it is derived from the French *cité,* and this grew out of the Latin *civitas,* which meant first 'a state' and later only the city in the state. Possibly, also, city goes back to an old Sanskrit root word *ci* = 'to lie down.' And a chief city, or **metropolis** (mĕ-trŏp′ō-lĭs), is even more dignified, for it gets its title from Greek words meaning 'mother' and 'city.' Hence a metropolis was originally a mother city, that is, a city which guided and ruled smaller cities. But the dwellers in a metropolis need to remember that they have to have a number of

ōld; ôrb; ŏdd; ūse; ûrn; ŭp; fōōd; fŏŏt; out; oil

*police* to keep them in order, and you can see that the name of the officer is pretty closely related to the region in which he is most needed. The word **region** (rē'jŭn) was purposely used in the sentence above, because it is derived from the Latin *regio* = 'a territory' and, to go farther back, from the Latin *regere* = 'to rule.'

Now we have straightened out a lot of the common words in geography, but we constantly find new ones appearing. Thus, just above, is **territory** (tĕr'rĭ-tō-rĭ). It will be easy to guess its derivation from another word that has already been described. But that is not saying that one could solve so easily all the new words that may be found. Therefore, we are going to suggest here a sort of game that ought to be very interesting, and helpful too, and one in which a number of persons can take part at the same time. It is this. Go over all the pages of this book up to this point, and pick out the words (they do not all need to be geography words) that seem to have some sort of a story connected with them, that is, which appear to have had a history. Write these down in a list in their alphabetical order. Then compare lists and see what ones ought to be added to other lists from your list, and what ones you skipped that others found. Next let everyone have guesses at what each of these words originally meant, from what language it was derived, and whether it is just one word or was made up of two earlier words. Then let each person take two or three of the words and look them up in a big dictionary and find out what their true history has been. For this purpose the *Century Dictionary and Encyclopedia* is especially good, and a copy of that work is generally at hand

āle; câre; ăm; ärm; ēve; ĕnd; makĕr; īce; ĭll

in every library. If one does not know, it is easy to learn how to look up the different words and to work out their derivations. Then it will be interesting to see how different the true derivations are from those which were guessed.

ōld; ôrb; ŏdd; ūse; ûrn; ŭp; fōōd; fŏŏt; out; oil

# CHAPTER III

IN a geography class one day the teacher said, "Now remember:

> In fourteen hundred ninety-two
> Columbus sailed the ocean blue."

The next day she called on Henry: "Henry, tell me about Columbus," and Henry recited:

> In fourteen hundred ninety-three
> Columbus crossed the deep, blue sea.

So he did, yet it must be admitted that Henry was muddling things a bit in his version. But we can take a hint from Henry and have a very interesting game if we look up the facts of the life of Columbus and then try to make other good verses of the same form, thus:

> In fourteen hundred fifty-three
> Columbus was a boy—care-free.

If a large group tries, some quite interesting rhymes ought to result. This might be fun at a party.

However, the point to quoting Henry is that it seems to have been the fate of Columbus to be muddled, both by himself and by others. As he was the discoverer of the New World, it would appear only fitting that he should have named North America, or in any

āle; câre; ăm; ärm; ēve; ĕnd; makēr; īce; ĭll

28

event had the continent named after him "North Columbia" instead of North America. But Columbus died without even knowing that he had discovered a new world, and because of his ignorance of this fact his mistaken ideas are perpetuated in many geographical names, and another man's given name is used to designate the two great continents of the New World.

When Columbus arrived at the island of Haiti, he thought that he had reached Japan. Cuba he identified as China, and Costa Rica was to him Malakka. As these were all places at the west of the East Indies archipelago, Columbus naturally enough called them, as a group, *las Indias Occidentales,* which is Spanish for the **West Indies.** Accordingly, the natives of the new lands became known as **Indians,** which they were not at all, and there has been confusion on that account ever since. If the American Indian is an Indian, what shall we call an Indian Indian? Surely, the Indian Indians have the first right to the name.

It seems curious, too, that Columbus should have been made so confident about having arrived at the true Indies, by the fact that the natives he encountered had a reddish skin color, which resembles the skin color of the true Indian peoples. We shall be less surprised that he was so badly mixed up, however, when we remember how the occurrence of the archipelago of islands, the tropical conditions, and the nature of the inhabitants all fitted in very nicely with his notion of sailing to the East Indies by a route to the west. If the natives had had bright green skins, Columbus would have known at once that something was wrong.

ōld; ôrb; ŏdd; ūse; ûrn; ŭp; fōōd; fŏŏt; out; oil

It remained for another man, Americus Vespucius, like Columbus, an Italian, first to conceive that a new world had been found. Vespucius made a voyage to the scene of the discoveries of Columbus, and perhaps sailed to the south and east along the coast of Brazil. There are those who doubt that Vespucius arrived at the coast of South America first, as he let it be understood. In any event, he sent letters saying that he had discovered a New World, a new Fourth Part of the Globe (Europe, Asia, and Africa being the three known parts), and described the new lands.

A professor in Lorraine, then a German frontier province, wrote a book based on these letters in which he suggested that as Americus Vespucius had discovered the New World, "we may call it Amerigé, or **America**." This book was widely read, and the idea of so naming the New World seemed to please people. By that time it was known that South America could not be part of India, for South America was found to extend south of the equator, and India did not. At first America was meant to apply only to the land east and south of the Caribbean Sea, but when the new land was found to be continuous for the whole length of North and South America, the term was used for both continents. And it is a name that does fit very well, first because it has the same form as Asia, Africa, and Australia, and second because by simply adding *s* we get the English plural form **Americas** to use when we want to speak of both continents as a unit.

The name of the **Caribbean** (kăr-ĭ-bē′ăn) **Sea** in which the West Indies are situated recalls another of the

āle; câre; ăm; ärm; ēve; ĕnd; makēr; īce; ĭll

mistakes of Columbus. The more peaceful of the natives
of the West Indies called some fierce invaders, who had
come in from South America and conquered certain
islands, *Cariba,* a word meaning 'fighters,' and from this
the sea derives its name. Columbus misunderstood them
to say "Caniba" and, always thinking that he was near
to China, he set down in his record on December 11,
1492: "Caniba must mean subjects of the Chan who
must reside in the neighborhood." The Great Khan or
Chan was the name at that time applied to the emperor
of China. Later, when man-eating savages were discovered in South America, the term cannibal, a corruption, thus, of the word *Cariba,* was used to designate
them; but the true source of the word was overlooked,
and people thought it was derived from the Latin *canis* =
'a dog.' One may see from this how easily words get
twisted about.

The West Indies are divided into two groups, the
**Greater** and the **Lesser Antilles** (ăn-tĭl'ēz). This name
is the record of still another error. Columbus had along
with him a map made in 1474 on which the maker, one
Toscanelli, had put a large island, Antilia, as located in
the middle of the Atlantic Ocean. Toscanelli had little
better excuse for putting Antilia there than pure imagination and the further idea that the presence of the island
ought to make easier the westward voyage from Europe
to Asia. In the Spanish form, *Antilias,* the word translates as the 'island in front,' that is, of Asia.

The Lesser Antilles are divided again into the **Windward** and the **Leeward Islands,** because those to the
east, the Windward Islands, receive the Trade Winds

ōld; ôrb; ŏdd; ūse; ûrn; ŭp; fōōd; fŏŏt; out; oil

before those winds reach the Leeward Islands, which are located farther to the west. But as the Trade Winds blow as much from the north as they do from the east, this division and naming are misleading, and hence as out of place as the errors of Columbus. Study a map of the West Indies and of the Trade Winds to understand the situation.

Columbus, however, was not the only person who slipped in giving names, as we shall see. In fact, the name of the peninsula of **Yucatan** (yū-kă-tăn'), quite near the West Indies, is again the record of an error. Cordoba, who discovered the peninsula, asked the natives on landing, "What is the name of this place?" Not knowing Spanish, their spokesman naturally answered, *"Tectelan"* = "I do not understand." Cordoba not only thought he had the name of the country, but he also failed to hear correctly, so he put down Yucatan, and thus it remains to this day.

The islands north of the West Indies, the **Bahamas** (bă-hā'măz), were originally called, in the Spanish, *Bimani,* and this word later was corrupted to the pronunciation Bahamas, as it is now spelled. Possibly it was so easily changed because whoever called them *Bimani,* in the first instance, was not very sure of himself and was, moreover, trying to locate in the Bahamas a place that existed only in the imagination of certain people of that time. What he wanted to do was to call these islands *Palombe,* for that was the name given to a supposed place in Asia where the Fountain of Youth was thought to flow. In those days even grown men when they wanted something nice "just supposed" it.

āle; câre; ăm; ärm; ēve; ĕnd; makēr; īce; ĭll

Boys and girls nowadays like to play "just suppose" and find it lots of fun, but they know it is very, very difficult to make "just suppose" come true.

Out to the east of the Bahamas is a place in the ocean called the **Sargasso** (sär-găs'sō) **Sea,** after a kind of seaweed that collects there. This is said to be the longest plant that is known. You will be interested to find, on a map, just where the Sargasso Sea is located, and then look up "sargasso" in the encyclopedia to find out how long single plants of the weed are and why so much of it is found at that one place in the Atlantic. If it is possible to get a copy, it will be worth while to read a book by Thomas A. Janvier entitled *In the Sargasso Sea.* It is a "just suppose" story about the Sargasso Sea which is very interesting, and one which boys will like immensely because it tells about mystery and treasure. The sargasso weed being so long makes me think of a tree in the West Indies which is like our pine trees but grows very tall. Hence the negroes call it the "mile tree."

North and east of the Bahamas are the **Bermuda** (bĕr-mū'dă) **Islands,** so called after Juan Bermudez who discovered them by being wrecked there, probably in 1522. Shakespeare's play *The Tempest,* which appeared in 1610, was suggested by this shipwreck, and in it Shakespeare mentions the "Bermoothes."

Before Columbus came upon the West Indies, Eric the Red, sailing from Iceland in 983, landed on a very large island far to the north, which he called **Greenland.** That name was no more appropriate to the vast extent of glacial ice that covers Greenland, for the most part, than the names that Columbus fixed on the lands to the south.

ōld; ôrb; ŏdd; ūse; ûrn; ŭp; fōōd; fŏŏt; out; oil

But Eric was not laboring under any delusions when he called his discovery Greenland. The sly fellow had in mind inducing many people to come to his discovery as colonists, for he wrote, "Much people will go thither if the land has a pleasant name." His trick is an old one; it was practiced by ancient peoples, as, indeed, it is now, when men who wish to sell building lots on new lands at the outskirts of cities call their plots "Glendale" and "Garden City." It must be said for Eric that the grassy spot he chose for his colony was perhaps the pleasantest place in all Greenland, but that is not saying much. Just because a place has one oak tree on it is not a good excuse for calling it "Oakmont."

In Greenland, natives unlike the Indians were found, the **Eskimo** (ĕs′kĭ-mō). That name is a Danish way of writing the Indian word for the Eskimo, which was *Askimeq* and meant 'eaters of raw flesh.' To the Indians it must have seemed that the Eskimo did eat much raw flesh, as these dwellers along the Arctic shores had no wood to use for fuel. Do you know how the Eskimo manage to cook their food? The Eskimo, however, will not listen to the term "Eskimo"; they call themselves **Innuit** (ĭn′nōō-ĭt) which means 'men, people.' The most notable settlement in Greenland now is **Godthaab** (gŏt′tăb), which is Danish for 'good hope'; the name was given by a missionary, Hans Egede, to express his longing to civilize the Eskimo and convert them to Christianity.

**Newfoundland** (nū′fŭnd-lănd) has a fitting name, for it was an early discovery of the English, and became their first colony. Henry VII, the English king of that time,

āle; câre; ăm; ärm; ēve; ĕnd; makēr; īce; ĭll

in 1498 wrote in his private notebook, "10 pounds [about $40] to him who found the new isle." John Cabot got the ten pounds. That was not a very high sum either for finding so large an island.

**Labrador** (lăb′ră-dôr′), the great peninsula near Newfoundland, owes its name, according to the usual explanation, to the fact that Portuguese navigators captured a number of natives of that region and took them back to Lisbon as laborers or slaves; *llavrador* in the Portuguese means 'a farmer,' hence 'a laborer' or 'slave.' Probably, however, the land received its name from one Fernandez, who accompanied Cabot on his voyage and who afterwards revisited this coast. Fernandez was *llavrador da Ilha Ferceira,* that is, 'a farmer from the island of Ferceira'; hence the name.

Labrador is a bleak region, and to it might well have been applied the term **Canada** (kăn′ă-dă) if we accept one explanation of what Canada means. The Portuguese, sailing up the St. Lawrence River and hoping thus to get to the Indian Ocean, when they found this impossible are said to have expressed their disappointment by saying "*Canada,*" that is, in Portuguese, "nothing here." However, the true explanation is that the word comes from the Iroquois Indian word *kanada* = 'a collection of huts' or 'a town,' which the French explorers understood to mean the name of the whole country instead of simply the village where they landed.

We all know the origin of the name of our own country, the **United States of America**, but do we know how we came to have **Uncle Sam** and to be called *Yankees?* During the Revolutionary War bags of flour for our

ōld; ôrb; ŏdd; ūse; ûrn; ŭp; fōōd; fŏŏt; out; oil

armies were marked "U. S." to show that they were property of the United States, just as government materials still are marked. But a clerk, who did not understand this, thought the shipper had put "U. S." on the bags because he meant that Samuel Wilson, a government commissioner, who was known popularly as Uncle Sam, was to take charge of them. They joked the clerk so much about his mistake that by and by everyone knew of it, and "Uncle Sam" stuck. Europeans sometimes say **Brother Jonathan** instead of Uncle Sam, and that is because George Washington relied greatly on the judgment of Jonathan Trumbull, in those days governor of Connecticut. When a particularly difficult matter came up, Washington would say, "Well, we must consult Brother [thus] Jonathan." Of course, very quickly all the wits began to repeat this in reference to their silly problems, and so Brother Jonathan became the rival of Uncle Sam as a personification of our national existence. **Yankee,** on the other hand, was started either by the Dutch or by the Indians. The Indians, it is said, heard the French in Canada speak of the English settlers in New England as *Anglais,* the French for 'English.' But the poor Indians could not manage the French pronunciation, so they made it *Yengeese,* and let it go at that. The Dutch settlers in the Hudson valley were jealous of the New Englander and called him, contemptuously, a "Johnny," that is, in Dutch, *Janke,* pronounced Yanky. Later on, the people of Virginia wanted the people of New England to help them in fighting the Cherokee Indians. When the New Englanders would not do this, the Virginians called them *Yankees,* meaning cowards;

āle; câre; ăm; ärm; ēve; ĕnd; makēr; īce; ĭll

that is, they called them an "Indian name," pronouncing
it a little differently from the way the Indians did. After
the people of New England had fought the battle of
Bunker Hill and proved that they were brave, they no
longer objected to the name. Accordingly, they are Yankees to this day.

Immediately south of our country is **Mexico**
(mĕk′sĭ-kō). Mexico is an Aztec word which meant 'at
the temple of the war god,' whose name was *Mexitli*.
In the Aztec language *co* was the preposition 'at'; hence
by omitting the *tli* and adding the *co* we have the name
Mexico.

South of Mexico we see on the map six little states,
republics, which plan to become an important federated
nation like our own, and a British colony which has the
same name as one of the republics. The republic next
to Mexico is **Guatemala** (gwä-tä-mä′lä), a word that has
been made easier to pronounce from the native *Quauhte-
mallan* = 'the rotten tree,' not exactly a pleasant name.
**Honduras** (hŏn-dōō′räs), the name of the republic (and
also of the British colony) adjacent to Guatemala, has,
however, a more profound name, if you will allow us
to make a pun. Honduras is the Spanish word for 'the
depths.' It is said that when the Spanish explorers came
to this land, they approached very close to the shore
with their ships, but even so could not reach bottom with
long ropes on their anchors. Hence they "thanked God
that they had been saved from the frightful depths" that
they supposed the ocean over which they had sailed must
have. It is rather difficult to understand why it would
be any worse to have a ship sunk in two thousand feet

ōld; ôrb; ŏdd; ūse; ûrn; ŭp; fōōd; fŏŏt; out; oil

of water than in a hundred—one would drown just the same in the lesser depth. But that is how some people feel about such things.

**Salvador** (săl'vă-dôr) is the Spanish for 'the holy Saviour,' and the founders of the capital in that state put their colony under His protection. **Nicaragua** (nĭk-ă-rä'gwă) perpetuates the name of an Indian chief who lived in that vicinity when the white men first came. **Costa Rica** (kŏs'tă rē'kă) is the Spanish for 'rich coast'; Columbus indeed called this the *Costa del Oro* or 'gold coast,' probably because he got some gold from the natives living there. **Panama** (păn-ă-mä') is a prettier name, if it is, as some say, the native word for 'butterfly'; and even if it only means 'abounding in fish,' as others translate *panama*, it is not an unpleasing idea.

To make our round of the chief features and political divisions of North America complete, we have, finally, to consider the great northwestern territory of the United States, that is, **Alaska** (ă-lăs'kă). Alaska, too, is a native term and one that the natives themselves meant to apply to the country. It has several forms, the Indian being *Illapieasco,* in which the *illapie* meant 'earth' or 'land' and *asco,* 'great,' hence, the 'Great Country.' The Eskimo had it *alakshak,* that is, 'the peninsula' or 'the mainland.' Although we are not quite sure of the exactness of either the Indian or the Eskimo translation, together they express satisfactorily both the size and the form of the territory. It seems strange that across Alaska, from north to south, is as far as from Canada to Mexico; and that from Alaska's most easterly boundary to the outermost of its western islands is as great a distance as from the Atlantic to the Pacific in the United States. But a little measuring on maps will convince anyone who doubts it that Alaska is truly a "Great Country."

# CHAPTER IV

## THE LARGER NATURAL FEATURES OF NORTH AMERICA

PERSONAL place names are usually not interesting. Too often they are bestowed with the idea that by this means the memory of some individual, who would otherwise be soon forgotten, can be kept green. But that is not true of **Hudson Bay,** named after Henry Hudson, who, after discovering the **Hudson River** in 1609, sailed to the north in 1610 in his search for a northwest passage to Asia. It was then hoped that a route into the Pacific, suitable for ships of commerce, would be found to the north of North America. That trip can be made. It is a feat which has been accomplished in recent years, but the attempt cost Hudson his life. His crew rebelled at the hardships, and thrust him, his son, and seven sailors who were ill into a small boat, set them adrift in the middle of the great bay which now bears his name, and abandoned them to their fate. Nothing was ever heard again of the people so cruelly deserted.

Hudson Bay may be important commercially in the future as Canada develops, but the **Bay of Fundy** (fŭn′dĭ), another large indentation of the coast to the south, has long been used by many ships. It was probably named originally *Baya Fonda,* which is Portuguese for 'deep bay,' *fonda* being like the Spanish *hondo,* which we met in the name Honduras.

Chesapeake (chĕs'ă-pēk) **Bay** is an Indian name, which, as originally used by the Delawares, was *Kitshishwapeak,* and meant 'great salty bay.' Elsewhere it is asserted that the original Indian word for Chesapeake was *K'chesepiack,* and that it meant 'country on a great river.' If one tries to pronounce the Indian words, it is easy to understand why we have shortened and simplified the name. **Pamlico** (păm'lĭ-kō) **Sound** was so called after an Indian tribe of the same name that formerly lived on its shores. Another sound, **Puget** (pū'jĕt) **Sound** on the Pacific coast, was named after Peter Puget, a member of Vancouver's expedition which surveyed the coast in 1792-94, as was **Bering** (bā'rĭng) **Strait** after Vitus Bering who was sent out by the Russian Emperor Peter the Great in 1728 to find out how far Asia extended to the east and whether Asia and America were connected.

With the exception of some high ranges, not well known, on the east coast of Labrador, there are no important mountains in the eastern Canadian part of America. The northeastern part of the United States, however, is very rugged. In Maine we find **Mt. Ktahdin** (kĕ-täh'dĭn), a high peak with an Indian name which means 'chief mountain.' It really ought to have had the name given to **Mt. Monadnock** (mŏn-ăd'nŏck), a much lower peak to the south, for *m'an* = 'surpassing,' *adn* = 'mountain,' and *ock* = 'a place'; hence this is the 'place of the surpassing or unexcelled mountain.' Perhaps it was so to those Indians who lived nearby and did not know of greater mountains.

In this part of the United States are a number of

ōld; ôrb; ŏdd; ūse; ûrn; ŭp; fōōd; fŏŏt; out; oil

mountainous districts, famous, as Mt. Monadnock was
to the Indians, not because they are so great but because
they are well known by the very many people who live
near them. Thus the **Berkshire** (bûrk′shēr) **Hills** have
a name that comes from the Anglo-Saxon *Barocscir,* that
is, 'bare oak,' a name that once referred to a bare oak
in Windsor Forest, England. The **Green Mountains,**
north of the Berkshire Hills, were so named because
they are covered with evergreen pines and hemlock trees.

In New York State there are three mountain regions
often mentioned. Those farthest north, the **Adirondack**
(ăd-ĭ-rŏn′dăk) **Mountains,** bear the name that was applied to the Indian tribe that dwelt among them by their
Indian neighbors on the adjacent lowlands. *Adirondacks*
or *Hatirontaks* means 'leaf eaters' or 'they eat trees,' and
it was intended to be an insulting name, something like
calling a person a "poor relation." The idea was that the
Adirondacks Indians had nothing better than leaves or
the bark of trees to eat in times of scarcity. The highest
peak of the Adirondacks is **Mt. Marcy,** named after
William L. Marcy, a former governor of New York
State and Secretary of War in the Cabinet of President
Polk. The **Catskill** (kăts′kĭl) **Mountains** were named
by Dutch settlers in their valleys *Katsbergs,* that is the
'cat's mountains,' on account of the many wildcats found
in their forests in early days. Even now hunters find
and shoot a few wildcats each year in the remote parts.
The name **Shawangunk** (shĕn′gŭm) **Mountains,** south
of the Catskills, have an Indian name that is made up of
*shaw* = 'side,' *ong* = 'hill,' and *unk* = 'at'; hence, 'at or
on the hillside.' Shawangunk is perhaps the hardest word

 āle; câre; ăm; ärm; ēve; ĕnd; makēr; īce; ĭll

to pronounce correctly of all the place names in the United States. If you go to the Shawangunks, the people who live there say they are certain that they can tell whether you are a stranger in those parts by the way you pronounce the name.

The much greater ranges of mountains called the **Appalachians** (ăp-ă-lā′chĭ-ăns) are named after the *Apalachee* tribe of Indians, that is, the 'other side people.' It is evident from this that the Indians who made up the name must have felt that these were the people who lived 'beyond reach,' as it were. And it is likely that the Indians had this idea because they found travel through the mountains toilsome, for a name, **Allegheny** (ăl-ē-gā′nĭ), which they gave to a part of the Appalachians, means 'endless mountains.' As the Indians said it, Allegheny was *oolikhanne,* and some students of the Indian tongues say that this meant rather, 'best river.' Where would that translation fit? Southern portions of the Appalachians are called the **Great Smoky Mountains** and the **Blue Ridge.** Both of these terms refer to the blue haze that generally envelops their summits. The highest peak in the Appalachians is called **Mt. Mitchell** because Elisha Mitchell, state surveyor of North Carolina, lost his life in 1857 in making a map of it. At the base of the Appalachians on their east side is found the **Piedmont** (pēd′mŏnt) **Plateau,** a French name, made up of *pied* = 'foot' and *mont* = 'mountain.'

Out in the middle of the continent there is another upland which has a French name, the **Ozark** (ō′zärk) **Plateau.** Most simply explained, this name is from the French term *aux arcs,* that is, 'at the bends,' and was

ōld; ôrb; ŏdd; ūse; ûrn; ŭp; fōōd; fŏŏt; out; oil

given because the rivers in the Ozarks wind about to an astonishing degree. It is said, however, that the full name of the Ozarks was originally *Bois aux arcs,* that is, 'wood for bows,' because here the Indians got Osage orange wood, which is very elastic and stays springy when dry. They also used the juice of this tree to color their faces yellow when they went into battle. Boys who live in regions where the Osage orange grows ought to use it for bows and to color their faces when they play Indians. But it will be well to try a little of the juice on the fingers first so as to be sure that it will wash off easily and to be careful not to get it into the eyes.

The **Black Hills** also were named by the French, *Côte Noire,* that is 'black hill,' on account of the dark pine forests growing on them. The French, in turn, had translated the Indian name which had the same meaning. The surrounding plains were bare of trees and much lighter in color. The **Ouachita** (wŏsh'ē-tô) **Mountains** in Oklahoma have a curious name, about which nothing seems to be known except that an Indian tribe was so called.

In the far west of the United States and extending into Canada are the really great mountain masses of North America. Taken altogether these are known as the **Western Cordilleras** (kôr-dĭl-yā'räz), a Spanish word meaning 'mountain chains.' Of these chains the **Rocky Mountains** are perhaps the best known. Their name requires no explanation. One of their ranges is called the **Tetons** (tē'tŏns), an Indian word which means 'prairie dwellers' —not very appropriate for a great mountain range. One of the highest summits of the Rockies is **Pike's Peak,**

 āle; câre; ăm; ärm; ēve; ĕnd; makẽr; īce; ĭll

named after Lieut. Zebulon M. Pike who discovered and first ascended it in the course of geographical explorations in the newly purchased Louisiana in 1806-7. Pike himself said the peak was so remarkable, and could be seen from so far off, that the Indians for hundreds of miles about knew of it. When white people first began to emigrate across the great western plains, they painted "Pike's Peak or Bust" on their wagons to show how determined they were to succeed in the journey. Francis Parkman's book *The Oregon Trail* tells in detail what it meant to take such a trip in those days.

West of the Rocky Mountains we find the **Sierra Nevada** (sǐ-ěr′rǎ nē-vä′dǎ) range in the United States and the **Sierra Madre** (mǎ′drā) in Mexico. *Sierra* is a Spanish word which means 'saw tooth' and also a 'desolate, barren mountain range,' and these mountains are very much of both, as they have jagged peaks and bare, rocky slopes. *Nevada* means 'snowy' and *madre*, 'mother.' The first is true, the second a fanciful idea of the Spaniards. **Mt. Whitney**, the highest peak of the Sierra Nevada, is named after Josiah D. Whitney, state geologist of California, from 1860 to 1874 and afterwards professor of geology in Harvard University.

At the south end of the Sierra Madre are three great volcanic peaks which have much more fascinating names. The highest is **Iztaccihuatl** (ĕs-täk-sē′wät′l), an Aztec word made up of *iztac* = 'white' and *cihuatl* = 'woman,' that is, 'the white woman.' The bottom of this mountain is invisible at twilight, and the shape of its snowy top looks like a woman in a white robe lying down; hence, at twilight the mountain appears as a shining, ghost-like

ōld; ôrb; ŏdd; ūse; ûrn; ŭp; fōōd; fŏŏt; out; oil

figure floating in the air. **Orizaba** (ō-rē-sä′bä) is the second of these peaks; its present name is not explained, but the Indians call it *Citaltepetl,* from *citalin* = 'a star' and *tepetl* = 'a mountain.' Its summit, like Iztaccihuatl, shines at night like a bright start. **Popocatepetl** (pō-pō′- kä-tä′pĕt'l) has the same ending as the second peak, and *popoca* means, 'he smokes.' Thus we have 'the mountain —he smokes,' and so he does, for the volcanic activity in "old Popo" has not yet died out.

The only volcano that is active in the United States is **Lassen** (läs′en) **Peak,** named after Peter Lassen, an early explorer. Better known is **Mt. Shasta** (shäs′tä), an extinct volcano named after an Indian tribe, the Shastika, who lived on its slopes. Both these peaks are in the **Cascade Range** of California, so named because the Columbia River has great cascades in its course where it passes through these mountains. The **Coast Ranges** are parallel to the Pacific Ocean coast for almost the whole length of the continent. Behind them is the **Selkirk** (sĕl′kẽrk) **Range** in Canada, named after the Earl of Selkirk, a Scotch nobleman who began the colonization of the present Canadian province of Manitoba on lands granted to him in 1812 by the Hudson's Bay Company. But the title of this lord is a Scottish word which was, in its original form, *Seleschirche,* made up of the words *shiels* = 'forest huts' and *chirche* = 'church'; hence, 'church amid the forest huts.' Here we see how a name may in time be used for a place or a scene that is utterly out of keeping with its meaning.

In Alaska we have, on the other hand, the **Fairweather Range,** so named because of the clear skies that prevailed

āle; câre; ăm; ärm; ēve; ĕnd; makẽr; īce; ĭll

when Capt. James Cook explored that coast in 1778. It is quite a fitting name because, for the most part, the coasts thereabouts are foggy and rainy regions. In this section are found the two highest mountains of North America, **Mt. McKinley,** named after a martyred President, the other **Mt. St. Elias,** after the saint, because it was discovered on St. Elias' day in 1741.

Three of the five magnificent bodies of water that constitute our **Great Lakes** have Indian names. **Ontario** (ŏn-tā'rĭ-ō) was originally *Oniatariio,* a combination which meant 'beautiful prospect of hills, water, and sky.' Another translation makes of *Ontario* only 'beautiful, or great, lake.' **Erie** (ē'rĭ) was *Eriga,* which meant either 'wildcat' or 'cherry' lake. Probably the former idea is the correct one, for the Erie Indians were sometimes referred to as the 'Cat' Indians. If so, the original Indian word for Erie was *yenresh* = 'it is long tailed,' meaning by that the panther. **Michigan** (mĭsh'ĭ-găn) was made up of *missi* = 'great' and *sagiegan* = 'sea,' thus, 'great sea.' There is another Indian name for this lake, *Mishawiguma* = 'wide, expansive waste,' used because the lake has no islands, and this also may easily have been changed to Michigan. The other two Great Lakes were named by the French. **Huron** (hū'rŏn) was a nickname the French gave to the Indians who lived on its shores, because these Indians wore lines of bristly hair across their otherwise shaved heads. They must have been rather striking persons, these Indians, so one can hardly blame the French for thinking of an old word of theirs, *hure* = 'hair in disorder.' What the French meant was to call the Indians "shock heads." Hardly a respectable name for a

ōld; ôrb; ŏdd; ūse; ûrn; ŭp; fōōd; fŏŏt; out; oil

lake, though, unless one thinks of the wild waves which sometimes mark the surface of Huron in stormy weather. **Superior** (sū-pē'rĭ-ēr) is the French *supérieur* = 'higher,' and fits very well, as Superior is the highest in level of all five lakes.

The **St. Lawrence** river and gulf were discovered by Jacques Cartier on the day of that saint in 1535, and the **Laurentian** (lô-rĕn'shĭ-ăn) **Highlands,** which border them, repeat the same name in the adjectival form. As a stream which can be navigated by ships, the middle course of the St. Lawrence is blocked by the **Lachine** (lă-shēn') **Rapids.** This name is another of the relics of the ideas of the early explorers that by some water passage through North America they could easily and quickly sail to China. La Salle thought that by going up the St. Lawrence and down the Mississippi he would arrive at the China Sea, which he believed was at the mouth of the latter stream. These rapids in the St. Lawrence blocked his way, and those who had no faith in La Salle's ideas called them *Lachine* rapids, that is, 'the China' rapids, to make fun of La Salle.

**Delaware** (dĕl'ă-wàr) river, bay and state were named after Lord Delaware, or de la Warr, appointed governor and captain-general of the Virginia colony in America in 1609. The **Susquehanna** (sŭs-kwē-hăn'nă) **River** has an Indian name, originally *Suckahanne,* in which *sucka* meant 'crooked' and *hanne,* 'water.' If you will trace the course of this stream on a map you will give the Indians credit for naming it rightly. However, those who know the Indian languages best admit that they are not sure what the *susque* part of the name came from and say they doubt

that it was had from an Indian word for 'crooked.'
**Ohio** (ō-hī′ō) is also an Indian name; in full it was
*Ohionhiio,* that is, 'beautiful river,' and it is that, really.
The French, who love beauty, for a time, indeed, used the
French translation, *la Belle Rivière,* as their name for the
Ohio. The **Missouri** (mĭ-sōō′rĭ) **River** has a name made
up of *missi* = 'great' and *uri* = 'muddy,' in the Indian
tongues. This stream carries so much mud that in times
of flood it is said that one can see a yellow smoke over
its waters, making its course visible from a distance. The
smoke is the fine mud that is cast into the air as spray
by the river's rapid flow.

The **Mississippi** (mĭs-ĭ-sĭp′i) also has the prefix 'great'
and the suffix *sipi* = 'stream.' That is simple enough, and
quite right. But, as an example of how easy it is to slip
in giving names, consider the one by which the lake that
was long thought to be the source of the Mississippi is
known, **Itasca** (ĭ-tăs′kă). A Lieutenant Allen, who was
with Harry R. Schoolcraft in 1832 when this lake was
found, decided that it should have an Indian-sounding
name, and one that would at the same time tell of its
importance, provided one knew how the name was formed.
So he hit upon Itasca, because this was a word made up
of the last and the first syllables of the two Latin words
*ver* (*itas ca*) *put,* which was, as he translated it, 'true
head.' But the proper way to say "true head" in Latin
is *caput verum,* so his name should have been *Putver,* and
not Itasca. Worse than that, it was discovered that another, **Dolly Varden Lake,** was the highest source of
the Mississippi. Unhappily, this name is a very silly one
for the head of the greatest river, for it is the name of a

ōld; ôrb; ŏdd; ūse; ûrn; ŭp; fōōd; fŏŏt; out; oil

particular kind of flowery cloth, very popular for girls' dresses in 1872.

**Rio Grande** (rē'ō grän'dā) is Spanish for 'great river,' and **Colorado** (kŏl-ō-rä'dō) is Spanish for 'ruddy red.' Although the Colorado stream itself is not that color, the rocks along its sides are, for long distances, quite red in tint. The **Columbia** (kō-lŭm'bĭ-ă) **River** was named after the Boston ship, which in 1792, first sailed into its mouth and the ship's name, of course, is derived from Columbus.

In Canada three of the biggest rivers have names that are either directly of Indian origin or have to do with the Indian occupation of the land. The **Saskatchewan** (săs-kăch'ē-wŏn) was to the Indians the *Ki-sis-kah-che-wan,* or 'the river that flows rapidly.' One can see that it does, too, for long lines of bubbles and foam mark its surface. **Assiniboine** (ăs-sĭn'ĭ-boin) is a name that means 'stone boilers.' One wonders why anyone should wish to "boil" stones. The Indians who lived along the Assiniboine did not do that exactly, but as they had no pots to cook in that would stand fire, they were compelled to heat stones and put them into the water in which they wish to boil their meat. Perhaps this was the forerunner of the fireless cooker of to-day. The **Athabaska** (ăth-ä-băs'kä) is named after a numerous Indian people that occupied a large part of northeastern Canada; the name itself means 'swampy meadow.'

There are three big rivers quite far to the northwest in North America. The **Peace River** is so called because this is the translation of the Indian name of the stream. On its banks the enemy tribes of that section formerly met to agree not to fight for a while. The **Mackenzie**

āle; câre; ăm; ärm; ēve; ĕnd; makēr; īce; ĭll

(mă-kĕn′zĭ) **River** was so named after its discoverer, Alexander Mackenzie, who went down it in 1789 and was the first white man to come to the Arctic Ocean by that route. Finally, in Alaska there is the **Yukon** (yū′kŏn) **River,** with an Indian name which, like Mississippi and Rio Grande, means simply, 'great river.' Many Indian and foreign names that seem so strange are very commonplace when translated into English, but they do have the merit of sounding well when pronounced. One must remember that the Indians in Alaska never traveled to the Mississippi or the Rio Grande and knew only one 'great river'; so what was more natural than for them to call it that, since that is what it was to them?

ōld; ôrb; ŏdd; ūse; ûrn; ŭp; fōōd; fŏŏt; out; oil

# CHAPTER V

THE **New England States** are truly named, for they were quite fully occupied at early dates by colonists all of whom came from England. Many of the names of the places where people live, that is of the cities, towns, and villages, in New England are, therefore, of English origin. But, as everywhere else in North America, the Indians were there first, and the large regions and the natural features of the New England country have in many instances Indian names.

**Massachusetts** (măs-să-ch'sĕts), for example, is a word built up from the Indian *massa* = 'great,' *wadschuasch* = 'hills,' and *et* = 'at.' Hence, this is the state 'at the great hills.' Although it is true that the Massachusetts hills are imposing, the name of **Connecticut** (kŏ-nĕt'ĭ-kŭt) shows a more thoughtful and observing Red Man. Connecticut was *Quonoktacut*, which means 'the river whose water is driven in waves by tides and winds.' Some writers think that Connecticut was made up of the Indian phrase *quinni-tukq-ut* = 'at the long tidal river,' which amounts to the same thing, though not so poetically expressed.

**New Hampshire** (nū hămp'shĭr), however, is named after an old English county. The 'hamp' part is the form that the Anglo-Saxon word *heah* == 'high' has finally become, and *shire* is equivalent to 'share.' Hence the 'high share,' not bad, for much of New Hampshire is high, though those who gave it that name probably had no idea of the original meaning. But the name of **Vermont** (vĕr-mŏnt′) combines the French *vert* == 'green' and *mont* == 'mountain,' hence 'green mountain.' **Maine** either preserves the name of a province in France, originally *Cenomania* == 'a place or district,' or else has been the result of the ocean fishermen calling it "Maine" because it was the 'mainland.' This the seafarers did because there are so many islands along the coast.

About the name of **Rhode** (rōd) **Island** there has been much controversy. Some say that it was originally *Roode Eylandt* == 'red island,' and that it was so named by an early Dutch navigator who noticed banks of red clay on its shores. Recent historians, however, do not find the matter quite so simple. In 1644 the General Court of the settlements of Roger Williams' followers at Portsmouth and Newport changed the name of the large island on which they were located from its Indian name of *Aquidneck* to Isle of Rhodes or Rhode Island. It is thought that the settlers had in mind the following passage in Hakluyt's description of Verrazano's visit to the island in 1524: "We discovered an Ilande in forme of a triangle distant from the maine lande three leagues about the bigness of the Ilande of Rhodes." The name of the Greek island *Rhodos* or Rhodes meant 'rose.' Roger Williams found the name quite fitting, for he later declared that "Rhode Island, like the Isle of Rhodes, is an island of roses."

ōld; ôrb; ŏdd; ūse; ûrn; ŭp; fo͞od; fo͝ot; out; oil

The "island" of Rhode Island was situate in **Narragansett** (năr-ă-găn′sĕt) **Bay.** In the Indian language the name of this bay was *Naiaganset* and meant, not the bay, but 'those at the small point' on the bay, *naiag* being the word for 'small point' and *et* an ending meaning 'at.' **Casco** (kăs′kō), the name of a bay in Maine, is the Indian word for 'heron.' On the Massachusetts coast there is **Buzzards Bay,** so called because of small hawks very abundant there. **Martha's Vineyard** is a name that has a more complicated history. Everyone agrees that the first part originally was not Martha at all, but Martin, and was so called after a sailor friend of the discoverer, Bartholomew Gosnold (1602). But there is doubt whether this man's last name was "Wyngaard" or whether there were actually so many wild grapes on the island that it was named 'Martin's Vineyard.' **Cape Cod,** however, is immediately understood. The waters about it were a good place to catch cod fish.

The important rivers and lakes of New England, with one exception, bear Indian names. The exception is the **Fall River** of Massachusetts. As this stream is only two miles long and falls 140 feet in one half-mile of its course, it well deserves its name.

The largest New England streams, other than the Connecticut, are those in Maine. Here we note the **Androscoggin** (ăn-drŏs-kŏg′ĭn), which seems about the best that the white people could do with the word *Amasagunticook,* that is, 'the fish-spearing tribe' which dwelt on its banks. **Kennebec** (kĕn′ĕ-bĕk) meant 'long, lake-like river,' and **Penobscot** (pē-nŏb′skŏt), originally *Penaubsket,* was 'it flows on rocks,' whereas the **Merrimac** (mĕr′ĭ-măk)

āle; câre; ăm; ärm; ēve; ĕnd; makĕr; īce; ĭll

in New Hampshire and Massachusetts was the 'swift water.'

It is not certain that the **Hoosac** (hōo′săk) **Tunnel** was named after the **Housatonic** (hōo′să-tŏn′ĭk) **River**, but if it was, the name fits. This words is made up of *wussi* = 'beyond' and *adene* = 'the mountain.' If you will say these two words quickly, one right after the other, you may be able to understand how, in time, they came to be Housatonic.

**Winnepesaukee** (wĭn-nē-pĕ-sô′kē) **Lake** still has its exact Indian name and a fine one too, for the word means 'beautiful lake of the highlands.' Others say, however, that Winnepesaukee means 'good water outlet' because *sauk* is an Indian word for 'outlet.' This is used in the name **Saco** (sā′kō) applied to a river and city in Maine. **Moosehead Lake** in Maine has that name because its outline resembles a moose's head, and wild moose are still to be found in the forests nearby. The Indian word *moos*, from which we have our word moose, means 'he strips or eats off.' The Indians called the moose that because it eats the bark and twigs of young trees.

We have already considered most of the mountain names in New England, but there are several others that must not be overlooked. The **White Mountains** are so called because their tops are of bare rocks, white granite. Several of the highest peaks in the White Mountains have been named after our early presidents, and these are sometimes called the **Presidential Range.** The highest, **Mt. Washington,** is the second highest peak east of the Rockies. The **Taconic** (tă-kŏn′ĭc) **Mountains** have a name that is the Indian word for 'wilderness,' and that

old; ôrb; ŏdd; ūse; ûrn; ŭp; fōod; fŏot; out; oil

instance is perhaps the only one in which the Indians used 'wilderness' as a place name. At first one thinks this strange, for the Indians certainly had enough wilderness about them. But for that reason a wilderness had to be bad indeed before they called it so. **Mt. Greylock,** the highest point in Massachusetts, has a very hoary aspect in winter because of the snows which cling to its top.

Although the names of the natural features of New England are, as we have found, quite varied, and have entertaining explanations, it is the place names of this part of the United States that have especially marked characteristics. One may expect this because the colonists were all so very English and because they were earnestly religious. Thus, because the Pilgrim Fathers set sail in the *Mayflower* on September 6, 1620, from the mouth of the River Plym in England, they called the place where they landed in Massachusetts **Plymouth** (plǐm′ŭth). By a curious coincidence, a spot on the map very near the site of Plymouth had, five years earlier, been given the same name by Prince Charles, later King Charles I. **Three** colonists to **Boston** (bŏs′tŭn) came from the small English place called Boston and gave the name of their home town to the new settlement. Boston is a short form of what was earlier *Botolph's tun,* or 'Botolph's town or enclosure'; St. Botolph was a famous monk in the early history of England.

Three New England place names are due directly to the religious fervor of the early settlers. **Salem** (sā′lĕm) in Massachusetts (also in Oregon) is derived from the Hebrew *schalam* = 'peace, quiet, rest.' It appears also in Jerusalem with the same general meaning but with an

āle; câre; ăm; ärm; ēve; ĕnd; makēr; īce; ĭll

even earlier origin. The Puritans had been quarreling
about the extent of their lands, and called this new settlement Salem because they wanted to be at peace. **Concord**
was intended to make clear both the Christian concord of
the group that founded it and that they had acquired the
place by friendly purchase from the Indians. Roger
Williams and five companions were expelled from Salem
(one sees that in spite of the name the Salemites had
troubles) and wandered fourteen weeks in the wilderness.
When they had quite given up hope, the outcasts were
kindly received by Indians at the site of what is now
**Providence** (prŏv′ĭ-dĕns), Rhode Island. Williams
named it that "for God's merciful providence to me in
my distress." If you do not remember the story of the
Pilgrims and their associates, you should read it again
soon, for it is very exciting and interesting.

Next we need to consider a long list of towns that,
like Boston, were named after places in England from
which some, at least, of the colonists had set out. When
they gave the name of the home town to the new settlements, these folk probably had no idea what the significance of the names had once been. They used the names
for sentiment's sake, possibly to make themselves feel
more at home. But to us the names will mean more if
we know their true origin.

In Massachusetts we find **Cambridge** (kām′brĭj),
which was earlier *Camboritan* and meant 'crooked ford';
**Gloucester** (glŏs′tēr), which was once *Gleafanceaster*,
that is, 'town on the bright, clear (stream)'; **Haverhill**
(hā′vēr-ĭl) = 'hill above the haven or harbor'; **Lynn**
(lĭn), which meant 'the pool'; **Malden** (môl′dĕn) after

ōld; ôrb; ŏdd; ūse; ûrn; ŭp; fōōd; fŏŏt; out; oil

the English Maldon, from *mael* = 'a sign or cross' and *dun* = 'a hill'; hence, perhaps, the 'marked hill.' **Taunton** (tôn′tŭn) was once, in Anglo-Saxon, *Tantun,* from the River *Tone* and *tun* = 'an enclosure or town on the Tone.' **Waltham** (wŏl′thăm) started as Anglo-Saxon *Wealtham,* which meant a *ham,* 'place,' in the *weald,* 'forest.' Study the present-day pronunciation of **Worcester** (wo͝os′tẽr), and you can appreciate how this name could have started as *Wigornia,* next became *Wigerceaster,* then *Wireceaster,* and now Worcester. How long will it be before we write it "Wooster"? As *Wireceaster* it meant 'town of the marsh.' **Milford** (mĭl′fôrd) was so called because of the mills on Mill River. In using the name the people who gave it had the English Milford in mind. But that word did not mean at all what they thought. The English Milford is a translation of the Welsh name *Rhyd-y-milwr,* that is, 'the ford over the Milwr,' the Milwr being a stream. Hence, neither the "mil" nor the "ford" fits in the case of the Massachusetts locality.

Outside of Massachusetts we find **Bangor** (băn′gôr) in Maine, after the Irish *Beannchor* = 'a group of hills.' **Burlington** (bẽr′lĭng-tŭn) in Vermont is named after the Burlington family of New York, but their name was made up of the Anglo-Saxon *bur* = 'a storehouse' and *tun* = 'a farmyard enclosure.' **Manchester** (măn′chĕs-tẽr) in New Hampshire, and also in England, was originally the Celtic *Mancenion,* in which *man* was 'place' and *cenion,* 'skins,' that is, 'the place where skins were got or traded for.' Later this was changed to *Manceaster,* and then, as *ceaster* also means 'place,' it was 'place-place.' **Rutland** (rŭt′lănd) in Vermont, named after the English county, is perhaps from *Rootland,* that is, a cut-over forest area where the stumps still remain; **Hartford** (härt′fôrd), Connecticut, is the outcome of the Anglo-Saxon *heart* = 'a stag,' thus 'the stag's ford'; **Norwich** (nŏ′rĭch) meant 'northern city.' **Waterbury** (wô′tēr-bĕr-ĭ), a third Connecticut city, is, surprisingly, not from 'water' but probably from *vadre* = 'a ford' and *beorg* = 'a hill.'

**Brookline** (brŏŏk′lĭn) in Massachusetts and **Brooklyn** (brŏŏk′lĭn) in New York are both named after a Dutch village *Breukelen,* a term that meant 'broken up' or rough land. **Montpelier** (mŏnt-pēl′yēr) in Vermont was named after a city in France. Originally, the French city had the Latin name *Mons pestellarius* = 'grinder's mountain,' and this gradually changed to Montpelier.

Although the English colonists had a good supply of "old home" names for their new settlements, they did occasionally adopt Indian names. Thus in Massachusetts **Chicopee** (chĭk′ō-pē) was the Indian word for 'birchbark place,' and **Nantucket** (năn-tŭk′ĕt) meant 'its sterile soil tempts no one.' In Rhode Island, **Woonsocket** (wŏŏn-sŏk′ĕt) is 'at the place of the mist'; and **Pawtucket** (pô-tŭk′ĕt), 'at the little falls'; whereas **Nashua** (năsh′ŏŏ-wä) in New Hampshire was 'the land between.'

Another group consists of names that explain themselves in their English form. Settlers went out from Boston and established new harbors at **New Haven** (nū hā′vĕn), Connecticut, and at **Newport,** Rhode Island. **Westerly,** Rhode Island, is at the extreme western border of that state. **Rockland,** Maine, is so called on account of its granite quarries, whereas **Springfield** in Massachusetts, and other towns with the same name in

ōld; ôrb; ŏdd; ūse; ûrn; ŭp; fōōd; fŏŏt; out; oil

Illinois, Ohio, and Missouri, are places where springs abound. **Bridgeport** in Connecticut has a bridge at the harbor, whereas **Bar Harbor** in Maine has a long, sandy bar that is visible only at low tide, and **Portland** is, of course, the city at a port.

Finally, there are several names given as memorials to various people. In Massachusetts are **Brockton** (brŏk'-tŭn), an old, resident family name; **Dalton** (dôl'tŭn), after Gen. Tristram Dalton, one of the Massachusetts senators in the First Congress of the United States; **Everett** (ĕv'ēr-ĕt), after Edward Everett, the famous orator, scholar, and statesman who died as the Civil War was drawing to an end; **Fitchburg**, after John Fitch, the inventor of a steamboat which ran on the Delaware River twenty years before Fulton's *Clermont;* **Holyoke** (hōl'yōk), after Rev. Edward Holyoke, an early president of Harvard College; **Lawrence** (also in Kansas), after the Lawrence family of Boston who were identified with the development of the New England cotton industry; **Lowell** (lō'ĕl), for Francis C. Lowell, who established in 1813 the first cotton mill equipped with power looms in the United States; **New Bedford**, after the Duke of Bedford, because the duke's family name was Russell, the same as that of the original owner of the land on which New Bedford was built; **Pittsfield**, after William Pitt, the elder, prime minister of England during the French and Indian War; and **Somerville** for Capt. Richard Somers, a naval officer in the war with Tripoli. In Maine are **Augusta** (ô-gŭs'tă), named after that Princess of Wales who was the mother of George III, and **Lewiston**, after the Lewis family, the founders.

āle; câre; ăm; ärm; ēve; ĕnd; makēr; īce; ĭll

**Proctor** and **Barre** (băr'ē), Vermont, are, in turn, named after Redfield Proctor, a United States senator, and Col. Isaac Barré, a soldier in the French and Indian War and a friend of America in the British Parliament. **New Britain** in Connecticut imitates New England, and **Attleboro** (attl'bŭ-rō) in Massachusetts and **Biddeford** (bĭd'dē-fôrd) in Maine duplicate the names of English towns.

Now that we have found out the origins of many names in New England, it will be interesting to use our knowledge to make a new kind of map.   On a large piece of paper make an outline map of the New England States. Then print in the name of each state.   Next draw in a symbol that will tell what each name means, thus a rose for Rhode Island, high hills in Massachusetts, and so on. Then put the names of the mountains, rivers, lakes, and other features in their proper locations and see how well you can picture them according to the meanings of their names.   In some instances this will be easy, in others quite difficult.   Thus one might use a green pencil for Vermont and put in green pine trees for the Green Mountains.

When one has finished the general map of New England and found its making worth while, he may wish to try each state and its cities separately.   Where the places are named after a man, draw a picture of the man as one imagines he may have looked.   When children are doing the maps, fathers and mothers will perhaps be able to give ideas of how to show the other cities.

If maps such as these are done as a project by a class in geography, it will be interesting, after each pupil has

ōld; ôrb; ŏdd; ūse; ûrn; ŭp; fōōd; fŏŏt; out; oil

completed his "picture-name" map on paper, for the
teacher to pick out the best picture symbol for each place
and have the pupil who made it draw that symbol again
on a big, blackboard map in the classroom. In that way
everyone in the class will have a chance to help make
the blackboard map, and all can see whose the best picture
of each place was.

āle; câre; ăm; ärm; ēve; ĕnd; makĕr; īce; ĭll

# CHAPTER VI

### THE STATES OF THE BIG CITIES

As a group, no five states have so many large centers as New York, Pennsylvania, New Jersey, Maryland, and Delaware, although others, too, have big cities. What other five states that touch each other could one choose as most nearly equal to them in this respect? These five, then, may well be thought of as the States of the Big Cities.

**New York** (nū yôrk), the state and the city, and also the city of **York** in Pennsylvania, were named after a county in England. It took a long while and many changes to simmer the word down to the short and snappy form it has now. To begin with it was *Eburacum*, a Celtic term related to *labar*, a word meaning 'muddy bottom.' By and by this changed to *Eboracum*, and then, in the Anglo-Saxon, became *Eoforwic*, which meant 'wild-boar town.' In changing the form the original meaning was forgotten. Then the Danes came along and found *Eoforwic* a bit clumsy, so they cut it down to *Jorvik*. From *Jorvik* to *York* was an easy change, and about as far as one could go in shortening the word. Perhaps, however, three hundred years from now it will be *"Yok,"* as some New Yorkers already like to pronounce it.

**New Jersey** (jēr'zĭ), after an island in the sea channel between England and France, was so named in honor of

ōld; ôrb; ŏdd; ūse; ûrn; ŭp; fōōd; fŏŏt; out; oil

Sir George Carteret, to whom the province was ceded in 1664 in recognition of his sturdy defense of Jersey as governor against the Roundheads. Perhaps the word Jersey is a relic of Cæsarea, a reminder of the time when the Roman Cæsars ruled over Britain and France. In any event that is all we know of it. About **Pennsylvania** (pĕn-sĭl-vān′ĭ-ă), however, we are certain. It is the only state in the Union named after its founder, and it was so called by William Penn in honor of his father. With the family name, Penn combined the Latin word *sylvania* = 'forest land,' for that described the original condition of the country very well. Indeed, much of Pennsylvania is still covered with forests. **Maryland** was so named in honor of the English queen, Henrietta Marie, the consort of Charles I. The **District of Columbia**, the Federal district independent of all the states, is, of course, named after Columbus. Delaware we know about from the name of the river.

In New York State there are several large lakes, some important in history, others in commerce. The other states of our group do not have such great bodies of water. **Lake Champlain** (shăm-plān′) is named after Samuel de Champlain, who discovered it in 1609; the rest all have Indian names. **Chautauqua** (shă-tô′kwă) is the 'place where the fish are taken out'; **Cayuga** (kā-yū′gă) is the 'long lake,' or perhaps was originally *Kweniogwen* = 'place where locusts were taken out'; **Seneca** (sĕn′ĕ-kă), next to Cayuga, is really longer, but is named after the Seneca Indians, 'the people of the standing stone.' Really, the name *Seneca* has a very complicated history. It started as *sinni ika* = 'at the place of the projecting

āle; câre; ăm; ärm; ēve; ĕnd; makẽr; īce; ĭll

rocks,' the term which one tribe of Indians used in their language to tell of the place where another tribe, the Oneidas, lived. The Dutch took this term, added *ens* to it, thus, *Sinnikens,* and used it as a name for the Indians living at the north end of Seneca Lake. **Keuka** (kē-ū′ka), another of the **Finger Lakes** (a look at a map of New York State will show why they are so called), is perhaps got from *Kaniengehaga,* of which the first part, *kanienge,* means 'dwellers in,' and the last part, 'land where flint is found.' The name recalls the uses the Indians made of flint. **Oneida** (ō-nī′dă) **Lake** is derived from *Oneniute* = 'standing-stone people,' as explained above. **Otsego** (ŏt-sē′gō) **Lake** has the pleasing name of 'welcome water.'

The most famous of the rivers in our group of Big City States, is, of course, the **Niagara** (nī-ăg′ă-ră) with its great falls. There are three Indian words from which Niagara may have been derived. One, *jorakahre,* is quite appropriate, for it meant 'thundering waters.' The second, however, is nearer the sound of the word we use, *nee-agg-arah,* which meant 'across the neck.' This fits the river, as the other does the falls, as one will readily see if the course of the Niagara River from Lake Erie to Lake Ontario is traced on a map. The third is *ohniaga* = 'divided bottom land'; if this was the origin, it probably was intended to describe the way the upper Niagara River flows almost on the surface of a very level plain.

The **Genesee** (jĕn-ĕ-sē′) **River** was the 'shining valley' to the Indians. As seen from the high banks (**Geneseo,** originally *Tyonesiyo* = 'there it has fine banks') on either side of the stream, it does make a wonderful, shining ribbon of light, with many bends and turns. Their enemies called the Iroquois tribe 'cannibals' or 'eaters of live meat,' that is, **Mohawk** (mō′hôk), and that is now the name of the river in the valley of which that tribe lived. The **Chemung** (shē-mŭng′) was 'big horn in the water' because the fossil tusk of a mastodon was found in its gravels. The **Black River** is so called because of the dark color of its waters, which are stained with juices from the decaying vegetation of the great forests in which it has its sources.

In Pennsylvania we find the **Monongahela** (mō-nŏn-gă-hē′lă), which is said to be named after the Indian term *menaun-gehilla*, which is thought to have meant 'river with the sliding banks.' The **Lackawanna** (lă-kă-wăn′nă) **River**, in Pennsylvania, and the **Raritan** (răr′ĭ-tăn) in New Jersey, have quite different names. But some students of Indian languages say the names are different only because they are from different Indian languages. They mean the same thing, 'the stream that forks.' For Raritan, however, there is another explanation—that it is the way the Dutch pronounced the Indian word *eraruwitan* = 'the stream overflows so.' The floods of the Raritan compelled the Indians to move inland.

Around about New York City are a number of names and places that are well known on account of their being linked up with the metropolis. The big city is thought by many to be a wicked place and perhaps its start in badness is due to the island on which it is built, **Manhattan** (măn-hăt′ăn) **Island**. This, it is said by some, was had from the Indian term *manahacteneid* = 'the place of drunken-

---

āle; câre; ăm; ärm; ēve; ĕnd; makēr; īce; ĭll

ness.' The story is that Henry Hudson, in 1609, invited the Indian chiefs into the cabin on his ship and made them drunk. Probably, however, some one who thought New York a wicked city found that term and the translation and made up the story. A more agreeable explanation of the name is that it is derived from *monahtanuk*, which means 'place of dangerous currents,' for there are quite strong currents in New York harbor. But the simplest, hence, more likely, the true, explanation is that the original Indian name was *Manah-atin* = 'island hill,' which best fits the place too. **Coney** (cō'nē) **Island,** where people now go to be gay, has an innocent enough name; it is 'rabbit' island, because of the number of rabbits once found there. **Long Island,** quite clearly, was so named because of its form.

Besides the Hudson River, called the **North River** at New York City, another arm of the sea, in which the water flows back and forth with the tides, on the east side of the island is called **East River.** The **Croton** (krō'tŏn) **River,** along which a great series of reservoirs supply part of the water for the city, was named after an Indian chief, *Kenoten* = 'the wind.' It is asserted by others that the chief's name really was *Kloltin,* meaning 'he contends.'

One of the subdivisions of the city, and also a small river in it, are called the **Bronx** (brŏnks), after Jacob Bronck, an old Dutch settler in that section. Such divisions are called "boroughs," an old English name for incorporated towns. Thus we also have **Queensborough** (kwēns'bŭr-ō), which was Queens County before its incorporation in the greater city. There is a place in England that has the same name; it was once *cyningburh* or 'kingsborough,' but Edward III changed the name in honor of his Queen Philippa.

Near New York City are a number of large cities important in themselves, but owing much of their growth, nevertheless, to being connected with the metropolis. **Yonkers** (yŏn'kĕrz) is from the Dutch *jonkheer* = 'young gentleman,' for that was the way people referred to the young Dutch proprietor of the place in early days. **New Rochelle** (rō-shĕl') was so named by the Huguenot refugees who settled it in 1689 in honor of the French city of La Rochelle which had made a gallant defense of their cause. Some say that **Hoboken** (hō'bō-kĕn), New Jersey, repeats the Indian word *hopoghan* = 'the smoked pipe,' because there the colonists smoked the pipe of peace with the Indians. Probably, however, the city was so named after a Hoboken in the Netherlands, though the Dutch may have been led to choose that name because it was so like the Indian word *hopoghan*. **Newark** (nū'ĕrk), New Jersey, is named after an English city from which some of the settlers in Newark came. This English city was the 'new work' or castle which was rebuilt in 1125.

In addition to those already given, five other cities in New York have Indian names. **Cohoes** (kō-hōz') means 'shipwrecked canoe'; **Oswego** (ŏs-wē'gō) is very much shortened from *on-ti-ahan-toque* = 'where the valley widens'; **Poughkeepsie** (pō-kĕp'sē, colloquially pō-kĭp'-sē) was *Apokeepsingh* = 'a safe, pleasant harbor for small boats,' and truly the Hudson is a big river for small canoes; **Schenectady** (skĕ-nĕk'tă-dĭ) meant 'the river valley beyond the pine trees'; whereas **Saratoga** (săr-ă-

āle; câre; ăm; ärm; ēve; ĕnd; makĕr; īce; ĭll

tō'gă) is from *sah-rah-ka,* that is, 'the side of a mountain,' which fits its location.   Possibly, however, the original Indian word was one which meant 'place where ashes float,' but why this should be the source does not seem to be known.

Back in the early days, when New York was first being mapped, a clerk, apparently one Robert Harpur, in the Land Commissioners' Office in New York City, was told, it is said, that he would have to give names to a lot of divisions on the map that previously had only been numbered.   So he took a dictionary of classical names and put one down wherever it was needed.   Partly on account of his trick, and partly on account of the example he set, there are a number of names in the northern part of the state that were in use when history began.   Thus **Syracuse** (sĭr-ă-kūs') is named after a Phœnician city in Sicily, and the term came from the verb *serach =* 'to stink.'   That seems not a nice word to use for a city, but there was a bad-smelling swamp near the ancient town.   Syracuse in New York also has marshes close by, but it is not likely that they ever make the ancient name a fitting one.   **Utica** (ū'tĭ-kă) is a pleasanter name, and quite fitting too, for it means 'to settle on' or 'to colonize.'   **Troy** (troi) and **Ithaca** (ĭth'ă-kă) are names made famous by the Greek poet, Homer.   Some readers of this book will be able to read about Troy and Ithaca in the Greek, but there are good English translations of Homer which serve those who do not know Greek (notably the one by Butcher and Lang).   The name of **Auburn** (ô'bûrn) came from an English poem, "The Deserted Village," by Oliver Goldsmith which most people have read with much pleasure.

ōld; ôrb; ŏdd; ūse; ûrn; ŭp; fōōd; fŏŏt; out; oil

It has the line "Sweet Auburn, loveliest village of the plain."

**West Point** seems simple enough but is, nevertheless, possibly the result of a mix-up. Originally, it was called Gees Point by the Dutch settlers on the other side of the river. Now *geest* in Dutch means 'dry, high, infertile land,' and that fitted very well. But later on, when English people lived there, people who had no idea what *geest* meant, they naturally enough called it West Point, for it was on the west side of the river.

There are a series of names in New York that define themselves in plain English. **Buffalo** got its name in 1801 when buffalo were still found as far east as its site. **Gloversville** tells of the glove factories there. **Kingston** (also in Canada and Jamaica) was named in honor of the English king; **Lockport** on account of the locks, many of them, in the Erie Canal at that place; **Newburgh** means 'new castle' or 'new fort,' an appropriate name when the place was settled in 1709; **Watertown** is thus named because there is so much water-power there for mills. You might guess all of those, but suppose you try to solve **Penn Yan** without looking at what follows. Settlers came there from two regions, Pennsylvania and New England, and as each group was unwilling to have the other name the place, they called it Penn Yan.

At best, names of places from names of persons are tame, because after a generation or two there is no longer anyone really interested in the derivations. If ever one has a chance to name a place, one should not do it in that way. **Albany** (ôl′bă-nĭ) was named in honor of that Duke of York and of Albany who afterwards became

ăle; câre; ăm; ärm; ēve; ĕnd; makēr; īce; ĭll

King James II; **Binghamton** (bǐng′hăm-tǒn) memorializes William Bingham, a prominent Philadelphian who settled the city in 1787; **Cooperstown** was named for the father of James Fenimore Cooper who wrote *The Deerslayer*, a story you no doubt have read, and other splendid Indian tales. **Elmira** was named after the daughter of Nathan Teall, a tavern keeper; **Glens Falls** is a memorial to one John Glenn. **Johnstown** in New York is named after its founder, Sir William Johnson of Colonial fame, but **Johnstown** in Pennsylvania has no such noble ancestry; it was named for an early settler, Joseph Yahn. A Mr. Ogden was the original proprietor of **Ogdensburg** (ŏg′dĕns-bûrg), as was Col. Nathaniel Rochester of **Rochester** (rŏch′ĕs-tẽr). Away back in Anglo-Saxon days a chap named *Hfrofes* founded a settlement, a *ceaster*. Little did he dream that *Hfrofesceaster* would some day furnish the name for the big city of Rochester. But it did. His settlement became a city in England, from which the Colonel got his name, and he in turn brought the name to New York.

Pennsylvania has a varied lot of city names. There is only one Indian name of importance, **Shamokin** (shă-mō′kǐn), from *Schahamoki* = 'the place of eels,' or from *Shumokenk* = 'where antlers are plenty.' **Philadelphia** (fǐl-ă-dĕl′fǐ-ă) is a place name which has been thoughtfully given, one of the few such that exist. William Penn called it after the Greek city *Philadelphos,* which meant 'loving one's brother.' The history of the founding of his colony explains why he chose this name. **Altoona** (ăl-tōō′nă) has a lofty name, and it fits, because Altoona is high up in the Allegheny mountains. It is from the

ōld; ôrb; ŏdd; ūse; ûrn; ŭp; fōōd; fŏŏt; out; oil

Latin *altus* = 'high.' **Bradford** was named after William
Bradford, Penn's printer colonist, but his name was in
turn originally the Anglo-Saxon *bradanford* or 'broad
ford.' William Penn named **Chester** for a friend from
Chester, England. That was once a *Lega-ceaster,* or the
'legion camp' (Latin, *castra*), because a legion, or regiment, of Roman troops was stationed there. **Lancaster**
(lăn'kăs-tẽr) is named after the English Lancaster or
**Lancashire** (lăn'kă-shẽr). In these words we have
again *ceaster,* as before, and *shire,* a 'share' or a division
like a township, and the old name of the stream *Lune.*

**Bethlehem** (bĕth'lē-hĕm) was named on Christmas
day, 1741, after the birthplace of Christ. In Hebrew
*beth* is a 'house' and *lechem* = 'bread.' Thus Bethlehem
is equivalent to 'bread house.' The idea was that this
place was on the fruitful, fertile plain of Judea. **Home-
stead** is named after the steel company which laid out
the site, but *stead* in Old English meant 'place.' **Hazelton**
is so called on account of the abundance of hazel shrubs
at that locality.

**Reading** (rĕd'ing) is from *Readingas,* an Anglo-
Saxon family name, which may account for the way in
which it is pronounced. As elsewhere, we have a long
series of names in Pennsylvania that recall founders and
other persons. **Braddock** (brăd'ŭk) marks the place
where General Braddock was defeated and fatally
wounded in 1755. **Easton** (ēs'tŭn) was named by the
founder in 1738 after the estate of an English friend who
later became the Earl of Pomfret. **Allentown** recalls
William Allen, chief justice of Pennsylvania for the
quarter-century following 1750, and **Harrisburg,** John

āle; câre; ăm; ärm; ēve; ĕnd; makẽr; īce; ĭll

Harris, storekeeper who founded it in 1785, a Friend, or Quaker, of whom it was said he could go anywhere among the Indians unaccompanied and unarmed, so well was he liked by them. **Pittsburgh** (pĭts'bûrg) was named by George Washington after William Pitt the elder, whom we have met before; **Norristown,** after Isaac Norris, who bought the land for the town site from William Penn; **McKeesport** (mă-kēz'pôrt), on the Monongahela, after David McKee who there kept a ferry; **Williamsport,** on the Susquehanna, after William Hepburn, a county judge. The term "port" added to these names of towns on rivers had a real significance when it was first applied, for rivers, before the time of railroads, were much used to transport goods and people. At Williamsport, not many years ago, several of the old river steamers were still in use for local movement of men and merchandise.

The important anthracite coal cities all bear the names of men. **Scranton** (skrăn'tŭn) recalls Joseph H. Scranton, the founder, who settled there in 1847 and developed the coal industry of that section; **Wilkes-Barre** (wĭlks' băr-ĭ) is made up of the names of two members of the British Parliament who sympathized with the American Revolutionists, John Wilkes and Colonel Barré; **Pottsville** is a memorial to John Potts, who founded the town, and **Connellsville** (kŏn'nĕls-vĭl) to Zachariah Connell, for the same reason.

Two place names in New Jersey are purely of Indian origin; a third is a mixture of English and Indian. **Passaic** (pă-sā'ĭk) is an Indian word meaning 'valley'; **Rockaway** (rŏck'ă-wā) **Beach** is what we have made

ōld; ôrb; ŏdd; ūse; ûrn; ŭp; fōōd; fŏŏt; out; oil

of the Indian word *regawihaki,* meaning 'sandy land.'
How easily one might go wrong in explaining that name
if the record of its origin had not been preserved. There
is a **Perth** in Scotland and in Australia and a **Perth
Amboy** (pûrth ăm′boi) in New Jersey. *Perth* is the
Welsh word for 'brambles'; the original Indian name of
the New Jersey city was *Ompage,* of which the meaning is
lost, apparently.

There is a small harbor in France near the Pyrenees
which has the same name as **Bayonne** (bā-yōn′) in New
Jersey. Hence it is probable that Bayonne is made up of
the Basque words *ona* = 'good' and *baia* = 'haven.'
The Basques are responsible for the article of feminine
dress called a "basque." **Long Branch** is so called after
a long branch of the Shrewsbury River.

New Jersey does not lack personal names. **Trenton**
(trĕn′tŭn) is a memorial to Col. William Trent, speaker
of the New Jersey House of Assembly in 1720, but his
name may be a short form of the Roman place name
*Tridentum,* that is, 'three teeth' or 'three-pointed rocks.'
If the Trenton people can find about their city three con-
spicuous pointed rocks, they may accept these as a sure
sign that their city is rightly named. **Elizabeth** was the
name of the wife of Sir George Carteret, to whom the
province of New Jersey was ceded after its seizure from
the Dutch, and gave her name to the first English settlement made in 1665; most other Elizabeths about the
country are memorials to Queen Elizabeth of England.
**Camden** (kăm′dĕn) recalls that Lord Camden was a
friend of the Colonies in the British Parliament in Revolutionary days; William Paterson was a senator from

āle; câre; ăm; ärm; ēve; ĕnd; makēr; īce; ĭll

New Jersey in the First Congress of the United States, and later governor of the state, hence **Paterson** (păt'ĕr-sŭn), the city.

**New Brunswick** (brŭnz'wĭk) was incorporated in the time of King George III, who was a member of the House of Brunswick; Brunswick means 'Bruno's village'; and Bruno was a duke in Saxony in the year 861. **Annapolis** (ă-năp'ō-lĭs), Maryland, is from Anne (Queen of England, 1702-1714) and *polis*, Greek for 'city.' **Baltimore** (bôl'tĭ-môr) in Maryland has a very noble name. In the first place it is named after Lord Baltimore, to whom Maryland was granted in 1632. In the second place his title is from the Celtic words *baile-an-tighe-mhoir*, that is 'town of the great house.' It is, indeed, quite near to Washington where the Capitol, or 'great house' of the nation, is located. **Wilmington** (wĭl'mĭng-tŭn) in Delaware was formerly Willington, and was named after Thomas Willing, who settled it in 1732; **Wilmington** in North Carolina recalls the Earl of Wilmington, patron of Gabriel Johnston, the royal governor of North Carolina when the town was incorporated in 1739.

Now, as the last of this list, we come to the most interesting, in our country, of all personal place names, that of **Washington, D. C.**, named after George Washington, the great general and first president. Washington's name goes back to a little place in England, where, in Anglo-Saxon times, there was found *Hwessingatun,* that is the *tun* or 'enclosure' of the Hwessing family. One can be sure that when the Hwessings sat around the fire and talked, after hunting the wild boar with arrow

ōld; ôrb; ŏdd; ūse; ûrn; ŭp; fōōd; fŏŏt; out; oil

and spear in the oak forests of Britain, they never had any idea that one of their descendants would be the Father of a Country. And how those family names do change in form! But if one's name is not true to its earliest origin, sometimes one might prefer it as it is.

The state of Washington as well as the city is a memorial to Father George, though a better name for it would have been one relating to its wonderful scenery or to those hardy explorers who first reached it.

# CHAPTER VII

## THE GRAIN STATES

IN geography books the Grain States are called the North Central States. But it seems that it would be worth while to remember this group as the one in which grain-growing is the predominant agricultural feature. These states might also be called the Pioneer States, for in them did true Americanism first develop. The settlers in New England and in the states along the Atlantic Coast generally were, it is true, a hardy lot, "sot," as we sometimes say, in their ideas, and adventurous in spirit. But they were, after all, a homesick group, as is made clear by the names they gave their settlements. The first really brave and true Americans—not here because they could not "get along" in England, nor here simply to make money—were the men and women who crossed the mountains to make American homes for themselves in the wilderness of the West. Hence, in the Grain States or the Pioneer States we find many Indian names, and the English personal and other names that occur have little to do with ancestral homes and people. The pioneers lived in and were part of America, and their wilderness homes were part of them.

**Indiana** (ĭn-dĭ-ăn′ă) was so named because it was purchased by the United States from the Indians in 1795.

ōld; ôrb; ŏdd; ūse; ûrn; ŭp; fōōd; fŏŏt; out; oil

77

That was a fitting enough name, but **Indianapolis** (ĭn-dĭ-ăn-ăp'ō-lĭs), name of the capital city of Indiana, mixes up Indian with Greek, for *polis* is the Greek for 'city,' and the combination, though it sounds all right, is not a happy one. **Illinois** (ĭl-ĭ-noi') was had from the Indians who lived there, and who called themselves *Iliniwek*, that is, 'true, admirable men.' People who hail from Illinois consider the idea still to apply. The Dakota Indians called their neighbors who lived in **Iowa** (ī'ō-wă) *Ayuhba* or *Iowa*, that is, 'the sleepy ones.' Possibly this was because the Dakotas once caught the Iowans napping, off guard, and killed almost all of them. **North Dakota** and **South Dakota** (dă-kō'tă) are named after these fierce warriors, and their name meant 'the allies' or 'the friends.' Their enemies, the Algonquins, did not, however, share the good opinion the Dakotas had of themselves, for the Algonquins called them *Nadowe-isi-weg,* that is, 'the little snakes.' Usually they did not bother to speak the whole phrase, but snorted only the abbreviation *isi-weg,* and the French explorers made this into *Sioux.* Hence, to-day we have **Sioux** (sōō) **City,** Iowa, and **Sioux Falls,** South Dakota. The name of the state of **Kansas** (kăn'zăs) is that of the *Akansea,* one of the tribes of the Sioux or Dakota confederacy, which meant 'people of the South Wind.'

**Nebraska** (nē-brăs'kă) is an Indian word meaning 'flat, shallow, broad water,' that is, the **Platte** (plăt) **River,** for in French 'flat' is *plat.* We see, then, that the French trappers simply translated the Indian word *nebraska.*

**Minnesota** (mĭn-ē-sō'tă) combines the Indian word

āle; câre; ăm; ärm; ēve; ĕnd; makĕr; īce; ĭll

for 'water,' *minne,* and the word *sota,* 'sky color.' Hence Minnesota is the 'land of the sky-blue water.' As there are nearly ten thousand lakes in Minnesota, some of which "decorate the open prairies, others glitter in the dark of forests, and still others lie, like crystal jewels, in rocky clefts," this name is very appropriate. One recalls also **Minnehaha Falls,** 'the laughing water.' **Minneapolis,** like Indianapolis, is, however, a faulty mixture of languages.

**Wisconsin** (wĭs-kŏn'sĭn) was called *Mishkonsing* by the Indians, but the French, who came there early, thought this ought to be *Ouesconsin,* that is, 'at the west,' from the French *ouest* = 'west' and the Indian *ing* = 'in' or 'at.' Some say the original Indian word meant 'wild rushing channel,' and referred to the Wisconsin River. If that is true, the French might better have left it as it was. The other two of this group of the Grain States are Ohio and Missouri, names which have already been explained above.

The natural features of this part of the United States, with the exception of those great ones already considered, are not especially striking. Perhaps it would be more true to say that they are so numerous that it is not possible to list them all. The ten thousand lakes in Minnesota are an example. However, in North Dakota there is an area that was once a lake but is now only a dry lake-bottom, and as such is an exceedingly level place. On account of this flatness of the land the memory of the one-time lake is preserved in the name **Ancient Lake Agassiz** (ăg'ă-sē), so called after the famous naturalist, Louis Agassiz. There are many interesting things written

ōld; ôrb; ŏdd; ūse; ûrn; ŭp; fōod; fŏŏt; out; oil

about his life and what he made clear about the geography of our country.

In South Dakota are found the **Bad Lands.** When the French explorers described these as *"mauvaises terres pour traverser,"* that is, 'difficult country to travel across,' they were quite right, and we should have translated 'Difficult Lands.' The third and last land feature that needs to be mentioned is the **Keweenaw** (kē-wē'nô) **Peninsula** in Michigan. *Keweenaw* is the Indian word for 'canoe carried back,' that is, 'portage place.' The map will show reasons why they called it that.

The most poetical of the river names here to be noted is that of the **Wabash** (wô'băsh). The Indians called the river *Wauaubache,* which meant 'cloud borne by an equinoctial wind.' Another explanation is that the Indian word was *Wabashiki* = 'gleaming white,' because of the bright white limestone in the upper course of the stream.

The **Red River of the North** is a long name because white people translated in full its Indian name, *Misqui sakiegan.* It was a mild translation, however, for the Indian words are really 'bloody river.' They called it that because so many battles were fought along it that its waters often ran red with blood. The **Menominee** (mē-nŏm'ĭ-nē) river and city in Michigan have a more peaceful name; it means 'wild rice here abundant.' The **Niobrara** (nī-ō-brăr'ă) **River** in Nebraska is the Indian way of saying 'broad water.'

When the pioneers came into Ohio, most easterly of this group of states, they seem still to have been thinking occasionally of the lands and the history of the past. Thus the capital is **Columbus.** They named **Cincinnati** (sĭn-

āle; câre; ăm; ärm; ēve; ĕnd; makĕr; īce; ĭll

sĭ-năt′ĭ) for an organization made up of officers who had
fought in the Revolutionary War.  These men took the
name of Cincinnatus, a Roman patriot, who dropped his
plow in the field and hurried away to become dictator of
his country in time of need.  The pioneers, too, had all
left their old homesteads when they came out into the
wilderness to forward the growth of their nation.  **Steu-
benville** (stū′bĕn-vĭl) is also a Revolutionary War name,
for it recalls Baron von Steuben, the Prussian soldier
who helped George Washington.  **Lorain** (lō-rān′) similarly is a memorial to the help the French gave us in
those days and recalls the name of the French province
Lorraine.

**Akron** (ăk′rŏn) is a Greek word which means 'the
summit,' and Akron is situated on the highest land in the
northern part of the state.  **Toledo** (tō-lē′dō) is named
after Toledo in Spain, which was *Toletum* in Roman
days.  Perhaps *Toletum* was derived from the Hebrew
*toledoth* = 'genealogies,' hence, 'city of generations.'  If
so, the Toledans at any rate expressed confidence that
their city would endure.  One more ancient name given
to an Ohio town we must include for two reasons.
**Xenia** (zē′nĭ-ă), Ohio, is not a large place, but it is
one of very few places in the world that has a name
beginning with X.  *Xenia* is Greek and means 'friendly
hospitality.'  But the second reason for including Xenia
is not that the Xenia folk are hospitable; it is because
William D. Howells, one of America's great writers,
lived near Xenia in pioneer days and mentions it in his
little book *My Year in a Log Cabin*.  That is one of the
finest accounts we have of the life in those regions after

ōld; ôrb; ŏdd; ūse; ûrn; ŭp; fōōd; fŏŏt; out; oil

the Indians were gone but in times when conditions were still very primitive.

Only two Ohio cities of importance have Indian names—**Ashtabula** (ăsh-tă-bū'lă), meaning 'fish river,' and **Conneaut** (kŏn-ē-ôt'), meaning 'many fish.' If you will go back over the pages you have already read in this book and set down all the Indian names you find that have to do with fish, you will probably say, after completing this list of names, that fish were important to the Indians.

**Cleveland** (klēv'lănd) was named for Gen. Moses Cleveland who mapped its site in 1796; **Dayton** (dā'tŭn), after Jonathan Dayton, one of the first land owners, as was **Youngstown,** after John Young for the same reason; Dayton and Youngstown were founded in the same year, 1799. **Zanesville** (zānz'vĭl) bears the name of Ebenezer Zane, a celebrated pioneer of the Ohio Valley in Revolutionary times.

**Terre Haute** (tĕr'ē hōt'), Indiana, has a French name, *terre* = 'land' and *haute* = 'high,' because the city is built on a bank that rises sixty feet above the Wabash River. Four other Indiana cities that we learn about have personal names. **Bloomington** (blōōm'ĭng-tŭn) recalls an early settler, William Bloom; **Evansville** is a memorial to Gen. Robert M. Evans, who laid it out in 1817; **Fort Wayne** was a fort in 1794 and was named after Gen. Anthony Wayne, often called "Mad Anthony," because he was brave to the verge of rashness. **Gary** (gā'rĭ), one of the newest large towns in the United States, is named for Judge Elbert H. Gary, president of the United States Steel Corporation. The reader may be familiar

āle; câre; ăm; ärm; ēve; ĕnd; makĕr; īce; ĭll

with the controversy concerning the educational ideas originated there and known as the "Gary plan."

**Chicago** (shĭ-kä'gō), the largest city of Illinois, has an Indian name which is explained in two ways, but neither translation is very complimentary. One authority says it is from the Indian words *she-kag-ong* = 'wild-onion place,' and that the Indian word for onion also carries with it the suggestion 'bad smell.' Another student of the Indian languages says Chicago is from *shekagua,* that is, 'skunk.' Is it because the name of the city is so thoroughly connected with 'bad smells' that Chicago has great stockyards which smell so bad? **Peoria** (pē-ō'rĭ-ă), the name of a tribe, is the only other large place in Illinois that has an Indian name. This tribal name was obtained from an Indian personal name *Piware* = 'he who comes carrying a pack on his back.'

**Aurora** (ô-rô'ră) is Latin for 'dawn,' and **Moline** (mō-lēn') is from the Latin *molina* = 'a mill.' **Rockford** is situated on both sides of the Rock River, and **Rock Island** has that name because there is a rocky island in the Mississippi River at that place.

The French were the earliest explorers of the interior parts of the United States. Two city names in Illinois are witness of their presence, **Joliet** (jō'lĭ-ĕt), who was first in Illinois, and **La Salle** (lă săl'), who first sailed down the Mississippi. **Decatur** (dē-kā'tûr) is named after Commodore Stephen Decatur, the hero of the war with Tripoli; **Evanston,** after John Evans, a governor of Colorado; **Quincy** (kwĭn'sĭ), for President John Quincy Adams. **Elgin** may consider itself "elegant," for it was named after the Earl of Elgin, a British nobleman, and

ōld; ôrb; ŏdd; ūse; ûrn; ŭp; fōōd; fŏŏt; out; oil

he got his title from a Scotch word *elga* = 'noble.'
**Pullman** (pŭl'măn) in Illinois, like Gary in Indiana,
is quite modern, and is named for George Pullman, who
invented sleeping cars.

**Des Moines** (dē moin') in Iowa is a name with a
complicated history. It was first an Indian word *moin-
gona,* which meant 'a place on the road.' The French
explorers shortened this to *moin,* and called the river
*Rivière des moins.* In that form it was 'river of the
road.' Later, however, the Indian origin of *moins* was
forgotten, and the words were written *Rivière des
moines,* that is, 'the river of the monks.' **Dubuque**
(dōo-būk') is named for a French trader, Julien
Dubuque, who founded the city in 1788. **Council
Bluffs** recalls that Lewis and Clark, the great explorers
of the West, took council of the Indians whom they
there met. **Keokuk** (kē'ō-kŭk) is an Indian chief's
name, and meant 'watchful fox' or 'one who moves
about alert.' **Cedar Rapids** explains itself, a cedar tree
at a rapids, and one other important place in Iowa,
**Davenport** (dăv'ĕn-pôrt), was named after Colonel
Davenport, an early settler.

All the places in Missouri seem to be named after
persons. They begin with **Hannibal** (hăn'ĭ-băl), a
famous Carthaginian general who almost overcame Rome;
next follows **Jefferson City,** after Thomas Jefferson,
third president of the United States; then **Clarksville** for
Capt. William Clark of the famous Lewis and Clark expedition; followed by **Joplin** (jŏp'lĭn), after Rev. H. G.
Joplin, who lived nearby; then **St. Louis,** the big city,
named after Louis IX of France, who was made a saint;

and finally, **St. Joseph,** named to honor Joseph Robidoux, the first white settler (1826), but in form after St. Joseph, the husband of the Virgin Mary.

In Nebraṣka, also, we have two personal names for the prominent cities. **Lincoln** was named for President Lincoln, and **Logan** for Logan Fontanelle, a friendly Indian chief who had taken a French name. **Omaha** (ō'mă-hä), however, is an Indian word and meant 'upstream people.'

In Michigan are found several Indian names. Of these, **Kalamazoo** (kăl-ă-mă-zōō') often makes people laugh; it started as *negikanamazo* and meant only 'otter tail.' **Saginaw** (săg'ĭ-nô) was *saginawa* and meant 'mouth of a river'; it is on **Saginaw Bay,** as is **Bay City** also. **Escanaba** (ĕs-kăn-yä'bă) is Indian for 'flat rock,' whereas **Flint** is the translation of the Indian word *pawonnuk-ening* = 'the river of flint.' One can hardly blame the people of Flint for translating it. **Battle Creek** recalls an Indian fight on the banks of the creek of the same name; **Grand Rapids** calls attention to the rapids of the Grand River.

In the northern states, of which Michigan is the most easterly, the French influence is indicated much more frequently in place names than in the states to the south. Thus **Calumet** (kăl'ū-mĕt) is a corruption of the French word *chalemel,* meaning 'little reed,' and refers to the smoking of a pipe (reed) of peace here by the Indians. **Marquette** (mär-kĕt') recalls Father Marquette who discovered the mouths of the Ohio and Missouri in 1673. **Detroit** (dē-troit') in French means 'strait' or 'narrow place.' **Sault Ste. Marie** (sōō sănt mä-rĭ') translates 'falls or leap of Saint Mary'; referring to the **St. Mary's**

ōld; ôrb; ŏdd; ūse; ûrn; ŭp; fōōd; fŏŏt; out; oil

**River.** People soon tired of saying all that so now the place is commonly called **the Soo.**

Of personal names in Michigan we have **Ann Arbor,** because two settlers both had wives named Ann, and the place was a pretty grove, that is 'an arbor.' **Jackson** in Michigan, and also in Mississippi, and **Jacksonville** in Florida are places named after Gen. Andrew Jackson, seventh president of the United States, whereas **Houghton** (hou′tŭn) is named after Douglas Houghton, the first state geologist of Michigan.

**Milwaukee** (mĭl-wô′kē) is our way of writing *miloaki,* the Indian word for 'good land,' as **Sheboygan** (shē-boi′găn) is for *jibaigan* = 'an object with a hole in it.' The Indians needed to make holes in many of the tools they used because they lacked nails and screws, hence had to tie the parts to each other. **Oshkosh** (ŏsh′kŏsh) was an Indian chief whose name meant 'the claw.'

**La Crosse** (lă krôs′) is a name the French gave to a ball game that the Indians played, and it is said that the flat on which the town is built was one of their favorite meeting places for the sport. **Racine** (rā-sēn′) is a French word meaning 'root,' and it was the name of a great French dramatic poet. **Madison** (măd′ĭ-sŭn) commemorates James Madison, our fourth president, and **Ashland** is a place where many ash trees grew.

**St. Paul** and **Minneapolis** are important Minnesota cities a short distance apart on the Mississippi River; hence they are called the **Twin Cities.** We find the same idea in **Two Harbors,** Minnesota. The river at Minneapolis is broken by **St. Anthony's Falls,** so called by Father Hennepin, who discovered it when a prisoner of

āle; câre; ăm; ärm; ēve; ĕnd; makẽr; īce; ĭll

the Indians in 1680, because "the Saint had got him many favors." Duluth (doo-looth') is named for one of the first of the French explorers whose full name was Sieur Daniel Greysolon du Luth.

In North Dakota, Bismarck (bĭz'märk) is named for the German Chancellor, Otto von Bismarck; his name originally meant 'bishop's mark,' that is, 'the bishop's land.' Fargo (fär'gō), also in North Dakota, bears the name of William G. Fargo, one of the founders of the Wells-Fargo Express Company. Back in the early days, letters and small packages were carried across the Great Plains by "pony express." Men on horses rode at a gallop as fast as they could from post to post, changing horses and changing men at each post in a few seconds of time. Thus a letter literally galloped west. On the way the riders had to fight Indians, brave storms, ford flooded rivers, and dodge prairie fires, never stopping. There are many stories of the pony express, very exciting tales. Pierre (pĭ-yâr'), in South Dakota, recalls Pierre Chouteau who established a fur-trading post where the city now stands.

Wichita (wĭsh'ĭ-tô), in Kansas, is the name of an Indian tribe. Topeka (tō-pē'kă), also in Kansas, and the last name in our list of those found in the Grain States, is an Indian word for 'potato.' The potato we use, however, was not meant, though our potato is also a food that was first used by American Indians. The *topeka* potato, rather, was the bulb-like root of a wild bean.

---

ōld; ôrb; ŏdd; ūse; ûrn; ŭp; fōod; fŏot; out; oil

# CHAPTER VIII

As we called the preceding group of states the Grain States, we might call this, the group of southern states, the Cotton States. Cotton is grown in all but one of them, and is their most distinctive product.

New England was settled by people from England who were poor and religious; some of the southern states along the Atlantic Coast were colonized by other people from England with rich and lordly leaders. Accordingly we find that names of kings, queens, lords, and ladies are common in those states.

Thus **Virginia** (vĭr-jĭn'ĭ-ă) was named after the unmarried, or virgin Queen Elizabeth. The discoverers brought back so handsome an account of the country that the queen was willing to have it so named in her honor. **West Virginia** was part of old Virginia, hence may be regarded as a daughter Virginia. **North Carolina** (kăr-ō-lī'nă) and **South Carolina** both derived their names from King Charles IX of France, in whose honor the first French settlers, led by Jean Ribault, named the country in 1562. After the English got the country, the name still fitted, for Charles I and Charles II were then, in turn, kings of England. **Georgia** (jôr'jĭ-ă) was separated from the Carolinas in 1732 by King George II and

 āle; câre; ăm; ärm; ēve; ĕnd; makēr; īce; ĭll

was given his name. The king gave the land to be "a colony for the poor and helpless." **Louisiana** (lōō-ē-zĭ-ăn'ă) originally was taken possession of by La Salle in the name of King Louis XIV of France. So we see that six of the southern states are named in honor of kings and queens.

**Florida** (flŏr'ĭ-dă) was named by Ponce de Leon, who landed on its coast in his search for the Fountain of Youth on Easter Day, March 27, 1513. This day is the Spanish *Pascua Florida* or 'Feast of Flowers.' Possibly Ponce also thought, when he called it that, of the pleasing flowery aspect which the country showed. Florida still attracts people because of its flowers, and people do renew their youth in visiting it, but not in the way old Ponce had in mind.

All the rest of the Southern States have Indian names. **Alabama** (ăl-ă-bă'mă) was originally *Alibamu,* which probably meant 'burnt clearing,' whereas **Tennessee** (tĕn-ĕ-sē') was, in Cherokee, *Tanasse,* that is, 'the bend of the stream,' though some say that *Tanasse* was only the name of the tribe living there. The Tennessee River is truly a very winding one. **Arkansas** (är'kăn-sô) got its name from the *Akansea* tribe. We have already noted these people as giving their name to Kansas. *Akansea* is also explained as meaning 'handsome men'; rather vain, that! **Oklahoma** (ō-klă-hō'ma) is the name of a Choctaw tribe and meant 'red people.'

The Spaniards, it will be remembered, made a mistake in regard to the name of Yucatan. In **Texas** (tĕks'-ăs) they made another like it. A Spanish missionary visited the Texas coast in 1688; he asked the Indians whom he

ōld; ôrb; ŏdd; ūse; ûrn; ŭp; fōōd; fŏŏt; out; oil

met, it is said, "What is your name?" and they answered in Indian *"Texia."* The good father then said in Spanish, "All right, Texas it is." But it wasn't all right, for what the Indians had said was "We are good friends." Their real name, as was found out later, was *Hasinai.*

**Kentucky** (kĕn-tŭk'ē) was formerly spelled *Kentaki.* The Indian word was originally *Kantuckkee.* *Kantuckkee* meant 'bloody ground,' because the Indians, from both the north and the south, came here to hunt; and if two rival hunting parties met, they fought. There were no Indian villages in this region; accordingly, Daniel Boone found across it a not too dangerous route over which he led the pioneers to new homes in the west. In the form *Kentaki* the word meant 'meadow land'; on such areas the pioneers liked to settle.

Wherever possible the settlers followed river routes. Thus in Virginia they went up the **Potomac** (pō-tō'măk), originally *Potomeck,* the name of an Indian town which was a short way of saying 'where something is brought'; and up the **Shenandoah** (shĕn-ăn-dō'ă), 'the river of the spruces.' They floated down the **Cumberland** (kŭm'bĕr-lănd) into Kentucky, and gave it this Welsh name which means 'land of the fellow countrymen.' The **Rappahannock** (răp-ă-hăn'ŭk) **River,** in Virginia, is the Indian way of saying 'place where the tide ebbs and flows,' and, in Georgia, **Chattahoochee** (chăt-ă-hoō'chē) **River** is in the Indian language 'painted stone.'

There are a number of rivers in the Southern States that have been given European names. The language of these names and the places where they occur give clues about the early settlement of such areas. Thus, in Vir-

āle; câre; ăm; ärm; ēve; ĕnd; makĕr; īce; ĭll

ginia, we find the **James River** and **Jamestown,** named
for James I of England. The **Perdido** (pâr-dĭ'dō) **River**
in Florida has a Spanish name which means 'lost' or
'doomed.' A Spanish ship was sunk at its mouth. In
Louisiana is the **Sabine** (să-bēn') **River** with the French
name for the 'cypress' tree. The **Brazos** (brä'zōs) **River**
in Texas has, again, a Spanish name; originally, this was
*Brazos de Dios,* that is, 'the arm of God.'

There are no big fresh water lakes in the South.
**Lake Pontchartrain** (pŏnt-chär-trän') in Louisiana is
not a lake but a branch of the sea. It was named for
Count Pontchartrain, a minister of Louis XIV of France.
There are, however, many swamps, of which **Dismal
Swamp,** in Virginia and North Carolina, is perhaps the
largest. Its "dismalness" was once much greater than it
is now, for much of the swamp has been reclaimed into
farm lands. At the south end of Florida are found the
**Everglades,** a vast, grass-grown, clear-water swamp,
from which the water outflows underground. The water
escapes by underground passages from the Everglades
because the rock-floor is limestone, which dissolves. Similarly the **Luray** (lōō-rā') **Caverns,** in Virginia, were dis-
solved out of limestone, but the passages are now dry.
Because of the beauty and whiteness of these caverns the
name Luray is appropriate, for the word is a corrupted
pronunciation of the French *la reine,* that is, 'the Queen.'

When Alexander the Great conquered all the known
world, he founded cities in every part which he called
"Alexandria." There were, no doubt, people who thought
that there ought to be Alexandrias in the New World too,
hence one reason for **Alexandria,** Virginia. Besides, a

ōld; ôrb; ŏdd; ūse; ûrn; ŭp; fōōd; fŏŏt; out; oil

prominent family of the name of Alexander lived in those parts in the early days. **Charlottesville** (shär'lŏts-vĭl), Virginia, and **Charlotte,** North Carolina, were both named for Queen Charlotte, the wife of George III. Other place names in Virginia that recall the home shores of the colonists are **Norfolk** (nôr'fôk), which was in Anglo-Saxon *Northfolc,* that is, the 'northern folk'; **Hampton** derived from *Huntenatun* == 'the camp of the huntsmen.' **Richmond** is a corruption of *Riche-mont,* that is, 'rich or fertile mountain.' This last was a French term, brought into England by the Norman conquerors, and referred to a fruitful part of the territory of York.

The rest of the Virginia names to be listed smack of the native soil. Thus **Danville,** also Danville in Missouri, was named for Daniel M. Boone, the famous scout; **Lynchburg** (lĭnch'bûrg), for John Lynch, its founder, a brother of the Revolutionary Col. Charles Lynch, who is said to have been the originator of "lynch law" by his practice of severely flogging without trial persons suspected of Tory sympathies; **Petersburg,** for Peter Jones, one of the founders in 1733; and **Mount Vernon** (vûr'nûn) for Adm. Edward Vernon of the British navy, under whom George Washington's elder brother Lawrence served in 1741. Lawrence named in his honor the estate which he bequeathed to his more celebrated brother. **Newport News** has no connection with news or newspapers, for it is named after two English navigators, Christopher Newport and William Newce. It was Captain Newport who commanded the three ships that landed the first colonists in Virginia in 1607. He is responsible also for the pleasing name,

āle; câre; ăm; ärm; ēve; ĕnd; makĕr; īce; ĭll

**Point Comfort.** He called the landing place of the expedition that because he found safety there in a severe storm. **Roanoke** (rō-ă-nōk') is the only one of these Virginia names that is of Indian origin; it started as *rarenawok* = 'smoothed shells,' and it designated a kind of shell bead which the Indians used for money.

**Raleigh** (rô'lǐ) in North Carolina recalls Sir Walter Raleigh, who sent out the ill-fated expedition that colonized Roanoke Island in 1587. **Winston-Salem,** in the same state, bears the name of Joseph Winston, a Revolutionary soldier; Salem, like Salem in Massachusetts was so named because the group of religious folk who first settled there hoped to live in peaceful security. **Durham** (dŭr'ăm) is named after a place in England which was originally *Dunholm, dun* = 'a hill' and *holm* = 'a river island.'

South Carolina presents a similar group of names. **Charleston** was named for Charles II of England; **Asheville,** for Samuel Ashe, governor of the state in 1796. **Spartansburg** (spär'tăns-bûrg) was so named, however, because its inhabitants denied themselves everything in order to save and thus to help win the Revolutionary War.

**Macon** (mā'kŏn), in Georgia, is a memorial to Nathaniel Macon, a prominent member of the United States Senate, 1815-1828. **Atlanta** (ăt-lăn'tă), in Georgia, is a proud name, for the people called it that to show that they were connected with the Atlantic Ocean by railroad when the city was incorporated in 1847. **Savannah** (să-văn'ă), Georgia, is what we have made of the Indian word *Shawano,* which meant 'the Southerners.'

ōld; ôrb; ŏdd; ūse; ûrn; ŭp; fōōd; fŏŏt; out; oĭl

Florida has three interesting Indian names. **Pensacola** (pĕn-să-kō′lă) was originally *Pan-sha-okla,* and this meant 'hairy people.' **Tallahassee** (tăl-ă-hăs′ē) combines the Indian words *talua* = 'village' and *hasi* = 'old'; hence, 'old village,' because this was a very ancient settlement before the white men came. **Tulsa** (tŭl′să), in Oklahoma, is a shortened form of the same word. **Tampa** (tăm′pă) was *Itimpi,* that is, 'close by' or 'near it,' but near what we do not know. What would you guess?

**Key West** is the Florida name that has probably the most curious history. Originally it was *Cayo Hueso,* that is, in Spanish, 'bone reef.' It was so called because the Spaniard found Indian skeletons there. The English who said *Cayo Hueso* (kā-yō hwĕ′sō) did not know what the words meant, so gradually they twisted them to Key West, which made sense in English, and fitted for a reason the map will show. **St. Augustine,** as may be guessed, was so called because a Spanish expedition arrived there on St. Augustine's Day, August 28, 1565. The Saints' Calendar must have been a very handy book for those old Spanish and French explorers. Every time they came to a new place all they had to do, seemingly, was to say, "What saint's day is this?" and name the place accordingly. But **Fernandina** (fĕr-năn-dē′nă) bears the name of plain Fernando, or Hernando, De Soto, the Spanish discoverer of the Mississippi in 1542, who, perhaps, was not very saintly.

De Soto in 1540 had a desperate fight with the Indians at **Mobile** (mō-bēl′), Alabama, for this, *Maubilia* = 'palisaded town' in the Indian language, was no doubt a difficult place to capture. **Montgomery** (mŏnt-gŭm′-

āle; câre; ăm; ärm; ēve; ĕnd; makēr; īce; ĭll

ĕ-rĭ), in Alabama, recalls Gen. Richard Montgomery, the Revolutionary soldier who was killed in 1775 in an attack on Quebec, also a very strongly fortified town. It is quite a coincidence that both these Alabama cities are memorials to similar events.

Way back in the ancient days of Egypt there was a city on the Nile after which **Memphis** (mĕm'fĭs), Tennessee, is named. Memphis is the Greek way of saying the Egyptian term *Ma-m-phtah*, that is 'the place of Phtah.' Phtah was the god of fire. It is noteworthy that both the ancient Memphis and the modern one are on sites that are quite similar; also, that another city on the Mississippi has an Egyptian name, **Cairo** (kī'rō), Illinois. When you look up the place names of Egypt you will find what Cairo meant. **Natchez** (năch'ĕz), in Mississippi, was derived from the Indian word *naksh*, which meant 'a hurrying man.' That seems strange, but can easily enough be appreciated when one understands that what the Indians had in mind was 'one running to a fight' or 'a warrior.' Natchez, then, was once 'the place where the people were spoiling for a fight.' **Vicksburg** (vĭks'bûrg), another important place in Mississippi, is tamer. It was named for a Mr. Vick, who founded it in 1826. One is always led to wonder, however, what kind of men these first citizens of towns were.

The French remained long enough in Louisiana to pin French names on its two most important cities. **Baton Rouge** (bă-tŏn rōōj') is 'red staff.' There are two explanations as to why this name was given. One is that a great, red, cypress tree, free of branches, marked the boundary between the French settlers' and the Indians'

ōld; ôrb; ŏdd; ūse; ûrn; ŭp; fōōd; fŏŏt; out; oil

lands; the other is that the Indians massacred the first settlers on this spot. **New Orleans** (ôr'lē-ănz) carries us back to the old French city of Orleans, which bears a name shortened for *Civitas Aurelianorum,* that is, 'city of the Emperor Aurelian.' **Bogalusa** (bō-gă-loo′să) probably begins with the Indian word *bogue* = 'creek,' though there are persons who insist that the name is derived from the exclamations of an excited Italian who was a laborer in that vicinity. One day his boss tied some sort of wild animal to a tree, and a little later the Italian discovered the beast escaping. The Italian could not speak English very well so he shouted "Broka-loosa! Broka-loosa!" **Shreveport** is named for Henry M. Shreve, who invented an improved steamboat in 1817 and devoted many years to developing the navigation of western rivers.

Texas abounds in cities named after people. Thus, we note **Austin** for Stephen F. Austin, who in 1822 established there the first permanent American colony in Texas; **Dallas** (dăl'ăs), for George M. Dallas, Vice-President of the United States in the administration of President Polk (1845-1849); **Fort Worth,** originally a fort, named for Gen. William J. Worth, prominent in the Mexican War; **Galveston** (găl'vĕs-tŭn), for Don José de Galvez, who in 1779 colonized the valley of Sonora in Mexico; and **Houston** (hūs'tŭn), after Gen. Sam Houston who won the independence of the Republic of Texas from Mexico in the battle of San Jacinto in 1836 and became its first president. Houston's name was originally 'Hugh's town' in England; hence, perhaps, the way it is still pronounced.

**Beaumont** (bō'mŏnt) is French for 'beautiful mountain,' which scarcely describes the surroundings of the Texas town. **El Paso** (ĕl păs'ō) in Spanish means 'the pass' or 'the gap,' and refers to the gap made by the Rio Grande River. **San Antonio** is named after a Spanish mission of that name at that place; the mission itself is now called *Alamo*. Everyone should know the story of the Alamo.

**Texarkana** (tĕk-sär-kăn'ă) is the largest of a number of new towns in the United States that have names formed in a like way. It is quite evident that Texarkana combines Texas and Arkansas, the state names, into a city name. This in turn suggests that the name has its origin in the location of the place. The idea of composing names in this way is one that seems to please very much, for already there are thirty places in the United States so named. Some of these are: Arizmo, Calada, Calexico, Kanorado, Mondak, Sylmar, Wissota, Arkla, Wyuta, and Kenova. It is something of a problem to work out from the names only where each of these places will be found. Kenova may prove to be particularly puzzling. Most such towns are as yet too small to be placed on the maps of the school geographies.

Place names in Arkansas explain themselves. There are hot springs on the site of the city of **Hot Springs**; **Little Rock** is built on solid rock; and **Fort Smith** is on the site of a fort built by Gen. Persifer F. Smith, a soldier in the Mexican War.

In Oklahoma, **Muskogee** (mŭs-kō'gē) is an Indian term for 'open marshy land,' whereas **Guthrie** (gŭth'rē) was probably named for the brothers Guthrie, who were

ōld; ôrb; ŏdd; ūse; ûrn; ŭp; fōōd; fŏŏt; out; oil

early settlers in the state of Missouri.  Tennessee has two prominent "villes": **Knoxville,** named for Gen. Henry Knox, Revolutionary soldier and friend of George Washington, and **Nashville** for Abner Nash, a governor of North Carolina during the Revolution.  The Indian name for the site of **Chattanooga** (chăt-tă-noo'-gă) was *A-tla-nuka* = 'hawk hole.'

Kentucky also has a "ville," **Louisville,** named for King Louis XVI of France.  **Paducah** (pă-doo'kä) was the name of an Indian chief who lived there.  **Covington** (kŭv'ĭng-tŭn) is a memorial to Gen. Leonard Covington, who fought under Wayne during the Revolution and was killed in action in the War of 1812.  The most romantic of the Kentucky names, however, is that of **Lexington** (lĕk'sĭng-tŭn).  On its site a party of hunters, one night in the year 1775, were sitting about their campfire, when a stranger came out of the forest and gave them the news of the Battle of Lexington.  This so enthused the hunters that they, then and there, decided to found a settlement on the spot and call it Lexington.  It must be admitted that it was a well conceived plan, for Lexington, Kentucky, thrives until this day.

**Wheeling** (hwēl'ĭng) in West Virginia is not a name that would appear to have much of a story.  It is explained in two ways, neither of which would be suspected from its form.  The nicer explanation is that the name is derived from the Indian word *whilink,* meaning 'at the head of the river.'  The other, and creepy one, is that the Indian word was *weal-ink* and meant 'place of the human head.'  It is said that back in pioneer times the Indians put the head of a white man on a long pole and

āle; câre; ăm; ärm; ēve; ĕnd; makēr; īce; ĭll

set up this gruesome thing on the river bank. **Huntington** (hŭnt'ĭng-tŭn) is named for Collis P. Huntington,
a railroad promoter who built the Chesapeake and Ohio
and many other important railroads. His name, however, harks back to England, where it started its career
in Anglo-Saxon times as *Huntandun,* that is, *hunta* = 'a
hunter' and *dun* = 'a hill,' hence 'hunter's hill.' At
**Harper's Ferry,** West Virginia, in 1734, Robert Harper
started a ferry, and the name keeps alive not only the
memory of him but even of his enterprise.

Much of West Virginia and eastern Kentucky, and
wide areas in Tennessee, North and South Carolina,
Georgia, and Alabama are mountainous, rough, forested
country. The reader will do well to examine maps
showing relief to gain true appreciation of how large
this area of high land and no large cities is, and where
it extends. The region is not only elevated and rough, but
is also very difficult to travel in, or across, for even short
distances. Nevertheless it was settled at an early date
by white people, those families which, for one reason or
another, did not succeed in the more fertile and level
lowlands. When they first moved into the mountain lands,
these white people were quite as intelligent as settlers who
went elsewhere. But because of the difficulty of travel
and by reason of poverty, the mountain dwellers became
very much cut off from the world. Education was
neglected. Only small crops were raised on the few acres
of land level enough to be cultivated.

In consequence, the mountain people became, like the
Indians who were there before them, very skilful hunters
and fishermen. Their minds in other respects, however,

ōld; ôrb; ŏdd; ūse; ûrn; ŭp; fōōd; fŏŏt; out; oil

were less and less capable, and though they remained white people, they grew to be as simple and ignorant as the savages whose lives they were copying. In fact, they were not even as able as the Indians to make up names for places. It will be recalled that Indian names are for the most part descriptive, like 'fish river' and 'great hill.' The mountain whites in some districts became so ignorant that they could think only in names of one syllable, and in some instances they could not even manage that. Accordingly, names like Ho, Aunt, Rest, Ged, Bud, Mae, and Tom are found in these parts of Tennessee, and, in Kentucky, Odie, Trixy, and Pearlie. It is interesting to search out in a *Postal Guide* the numerous simple and odd names given to post offices in the parts of these and adjoining states occupied by the mountain whites. One will be surprised how many such there are. It would seem that any well taught child could find much better names than these grown men and women have been able to give their settlements. Yet some few, like Cut Shin Creek, lead us very directly to an understanding of the home country of the mountain folk.

Moreover, these mountain people have preserved many old customs and speak words no longer used elsewhere and do many things in quite ancient fashion. Therefore, an account of their lives and homes is like a story book, only better, because it is a real and true tale. Horace Kephart has lived with the mountain people and has put in his book, *Our Southern Highlanders,* a very entertaining and informative account of their personalities and ways.

āle; câre; ăm; ärm; ēve; ĕnd; makẽr; īce; ĭll

# CHAPTER IX

## THE WESTERN STATES

ONE explanation of the name of the state Arizona is grasped immediately the word is thought about. So we will pass Arizona for the moment, and also **New Mexico, Colorado,** and **Washington** because they are names that we have already considered. **Nevada** we also understand. Thus we manage to pass over quickly many of the names of the Western States and ought to be willing to take on a hard one for a real start. **Wyoming** (wī-ō′mǐng) was originally *Mcheuwomink*. Try to pronounce that and you will understand why white people were satisfied with Wyoming. Anyhow, the Indian word meant 'extensive plains,' and that fits well much of the territory of Wyoming. However, *Mcheu*—and the rest of it—was not a word used by the Indians of Wyoming, but one that was brought there by the white people from Pennsylvania who had learned it from Indians resident in the east of the United States. **Montana** (mǒn-tä′nä), likewise, is an imported word; it was built up in a rather hit-or-miss fashion from the Latin *mons* = 'mountain.' The people in Montana wanted to make clear that theirs was a state that had high mountains, as well as wide plains.

ōld; ôrb; ŏdd; ūse; ûrn; ŭp; fōōd; fŏŏt; out; oil

If the reader has not already solved it we are now ready to finish with **Arizona** (ăr-ĭ-zō'nă). The apparent explanation, is, of course, 'arid zone,' for much of the state is very dry. Some persons, however, insist that the name is really from the Indian words *ari* = 'small' and *son* = 'spring,' and that would also be appropriate in an arid region. Finally, still others say that the word is of Aztec origin, and was at first *arizuma,* that is, 'silver-bearing.'

The names of all of the Western States are interesting Consider **Idaho** (ī'dä-hō), which the Indians called *E-dah-hoe* = 'the jewel of the mountains.' What could be prettier than that? **Utah** (ū'tä) is named for the Ute tribe of Indians, and their name translated is said to mean 'mountaineers.' **Oregon** (ôr'ē-gŏn), also, is a tribal name, but seems to be one that was made up by the Spaniards, who called the natives living there *Orejones,* that is, 'big-eared men.' The Oregon Indians cut and pulled their ears so that these organs became monstrously large. **California** (kăl-ĭ-fŏr'nĭ-ă or kăl-ĭ-fŏrn'yă) is explained in two ways. It may be from the Spanish words *calida fornax,* which meant 'hot furnace.' Although parts of California are quite hot, other parts, those where most Californians live, are only pleasantly warm; in fact, some parts of the state are not hot at all. So Californians probably prefer the other explanation, which is that California is the name that a Spanish storybook writer made up for an imaginary island he described. On this island much gold and precious stones were found. That does very well for California even if it is not an island.

In California are several great natural features with

interesting names. The **Yosemite** (yō-sĕm'ĭ-tĭ) **Valley,**
with its tremendous cliffs and waterfalls, was, to the
Indians, 'the valley of the grizzly bear.' They said it a
little differently from our way, for the Indian word was
*osoamit.* We have also done things to the Indian words,
*homok-avi,* which meant 'tribe of the three hills,' for
it is from these words that we got the name **Mohave**
(mō-hä'vä) **Desert.**

**Yellowstone National Park** in Wyoming has its name
from the Yellowstone River, and truly the rocks along
the upper part of that river are surprisingly yellow. But
personal names were used in the Western States, as well
as in the East, for places and things: thus **Mt. Rainier**
(rā-nēr') was so named by Captain Vancouver in honor
of a British admiral, and **Juan de Fuca** (wăn dā fū'kă),
the strait which separates the state of Washington from
the Canadian Vancouver Island, after the Greek navigator
who found it in 1592. People who live in **Tacoma** (tă-
kō'mă) insist that Mt. Rainier should really be called
*tacoma,* the Indian word for 'mountain,' and to satisfy
both those who wish it Rainier and those who wish it
Tacoma, it has been called "Rainier-Tacoma." That is
fitting enough, for it then means 'Rainier Mountain.'

Western names of importance include an unusually
large number of rivers. That is not because all of these
streams are so large, but rather because quite small ones
mean much to people living in certain parts of the
Western States. Many of the rivers are used to water
crops by irrigation.

The **Snake River** of Idaho is the translation of the
Indian word *shoshone,* originally *shishinoats hitaneo* =

ōld; ôrb; ŏdd; ūse; ûrn; ŭp; fōod; fŏŏt; out; oil

'snake people,' by which the falls, **Shoshone** (shō-shō′nē) **Falls** are known. A **Salt River** in Arizona and another in Kentucky acquired notoriety in the nineties (1890-1900) as the river up which defeated candidates for the Presidency were supposed to row; its waters are probably "bitter." The **Gunnison** (gŭn′ĭ-sŭn) **River** was named for Capt. John W. Gunnison, an engineer who was murdered by Indians in 1853 while surveying a central railroad route to the Pacific. Three quite unusual names of rivers are of Indian origin. In Colorado we note the **Uncompahgre** (ŭn-kŏm-pä′grä), a name made up of *unca* = 'hot,' *pah* = 'water,' and *gre* = 'spring.' The **Willamette** (wĭl-lä-mĕt′) **River** of Oregon was in the Indian tongue, *wallamet* = 'beautiful running water.' The **Chehalis** (chē-hä′lĭs) **River** in Washington bears a tribal name that denoted 'the inlanders,' or 'people on the sand.'

California river names are Spanish. The **Sacramento** (săk-rä-mĕn′tō) has for its full name *Rio del San Sacramento* = 'river of the Holy Sacrament.' **Merced** (mârthĕd′ or mĕr′sĕd) is the Spanish word for 'mercy.' The **Yuba** started as *Rio de las uvas* = 'river of the grapes,' and of course there is a stream with a saint's name, the **San Joaquin** (săn wä-kēn′) **River.** No one seems to know what the Spanish name of the **Gila** (hē′lä) **River,** in Arizona, means.

Speaking of rivers, **Riverside,** the California city, is one of a number of places in the Western States that have descriptive names in plain English. **Oakland** is another such in California. **Goldfield** in Nevada, **Silverton, Leadville,** and **Telluride** in Colorado, advertise the mineral wealth of those states. Watery names are **Glen-**

āle; câre; ăm; ärm; ēve; ĕnd; makĕr; īce; ĭll

wood Springs in Colorado, **Salt Lake City** in Utah, and **Great Falls** in Montana; hot springs fixed the name of the first, the saltness of Great Salt Lake that of the second, and the third is at a great falls in the Missouri River.

**Albuquerque** (ăl-bū-kẽr′kē) in New Mexico is from the Spanish *quercus* = 'oak,' and *albus* = 'white.' There are no white oaks at the place, but a Spanish Duke of Albuquerque visited the spot in 1703. **Santa Fé** (săn-tă fā′), in New Mexico, means 'holy faith' in the Spanish language. **Phœnix** (fē′nĭks), in Arizona, is a name of distinction. This city is built on the site of prehistoric ruins, at a place where a city had stood, not only before the white men came, but even before the Indians occupied the region. The name Phœnix, therefore, is intended to predict a new life, a new growth, to this old place. This is because the phœnix was a fabled bird of Arabia which, after living five or six hundred years, burnt itself to ashes in a great bonfire, and then rose from its own ashes, with renewed youth, to live another five hundred years. A clever bird—an enterprising city. **Tucson** (tū-sŏn′), in Arizona, is Indian for 'black creek.' **Prescott** (prĕs′kŭt) was named for William H. Prescott, the historian of the Spanish conquests in the New World.

**Cheyenne** (shī-ĕn′), Wyoming, is an Indian term meaning 'people of a foreign language,' a name given to the Indians living in the Cheyenne region by their neighbors. **Laramie** (lăr′ă-mē), named for Jacques Laramie, a French fur trader, and **Sheridan** (shĕr′ĭ-dăn), named for Gen. Philip H. Sheridan, are two other Wyoming cities. Almost every American is familiar with the story of "Sheridan's ride."

ōld; ôrb; ŏdd; ūse; ûrn; ŭp; fōōd; fŏŏt; out; oil

In Colorado, **Denver** (dĕn'vẽr) was named after James W. Denver, governor of Kansas in 1858, because Colorado was then part of Kansas. **Durango** (dū-răn'-gō) is the name of a Spanish family of that place. But **Ouray** (ōō'rā) is the really choice, personal, place name in Colorado, and perhaps the best one anywhere. The Ute Indians, who lived there, had a chief who wanted to be called "Willie," after a white man whom he admired. But when the chief's followers tried to say "Willie," the best they could do with the name was to pronounce it "Ouray."

**Pueblo** (pwĕb'lō), Colorado, has a Spanish name which means 'village.' Rightly spelled, it should be *puebla* and in Mexico there is a **Puebla** (pwĕb'lă), of which the full name is *Puebla de los Angeles* = 'village of the angels,' because it is said that when a cathedral was being built there, angels each night added as much to the structure as the workmen had been able to do during the day. One would judge that the men worked feverishly under those circumstances.

In French *butte* means a 'small hill' or 'knoll,' and an elevation of this kind overlooks the site of **Butte** (būt), Montana. **Helena** (hĕl'ĕn-ă) in the same state was thought by some to have been named for Helen of Troy, but on looking up the history of the founding of the city it was found that **St. Helena,** an island in the Atlantic, famous as the place of Napoleon Bonaparte's exile and death, was in mind when the name was given. The island, in turn, was named for St. Helena, the mother of the Roman Emperor Constantine the Great, because it was discovered on her day in 1502. **Billings** (bĭl'ĭngz),

āle; câre; ăm; ärm; ēve; ĕnd; makẽr; īce; ĭll

in Montana, however, brings us back to modern times, for it was named in honor of Parmley Billings, son of the first president of the Northern Pacific Railroad.

In Idaho we have two French names to consider. **Boise** (bwŏz'ā) means 'woody,' because there were fine trees along the river of the same name; **Cœur d'Alène** (kûr dă-lān') means 'heart of an awl.' One realizes immediately that this is a name with a story, and the story is a good one. The name was given by the French fur traders, because they found the Indians here very "sharp" in making bargains. This makes us chuckle, because in most instances the white traders gave only cheap strings of beads for a valuable fur. It does one good to think that some of the Indians were smart enough to have "awl hearts."

**Lewiston** (lū'ĭs-tŭn), Idaho, is named for Meriwether Lewis, of the Lewis and Clark Expedition; **Bingham** (bĭng'ăm), Utah, for a congressman of that name; **Ogden** (ŏg'dĕn), Utah, for an old mountaineer, Peter Skeen Ogden, who was associated with the Hudson's Bay Company; and **Provo** (prō'vō), Utah, for a man named Provost. In this last the French pronunciation was kept in an honest, English spelling. **Carson** (kär'sŭn) **City**, Nevada, was named after Kit Carson, the famous scout, and **Reno** (rē'nō), Nevada, was so called in honor of Gen. Jesse L. Reno, a Federal soldier in the Civil War.

We are not truly advised as to how **Tonopah** (tŏn'ō-pä), Nevada, got its name, but perhaps the persons who called it so "happened on" both the place and the name, for the name comes to that if one spells it backwards—

ōld; ôrb; ŏdd; ūse; ûrn; ŭp; fōōd; fŏŏt; out; oil

hap-on-ot. An Indian word, *ton,* means 'trunk of a tree'; possibly Tonopah got its start from that.

Washington presents place names quite varied in origin. Starting in Greek times, we find **Olympia** (ō-lǐm'pǐ-ă), also the **Olympic Mountains,** named after the Greek Mt. Olympus on which the gods were supposed to dwell. The word suggests this, for it means 'shining heights.' In **Bellingham** (bĕl'ĭng-hăm) we have a record of the early explorations, for this place probably was named after Sir Henry Bellingham by Captain Vancouver. Bellingham, a Commissioner of the British Navy, checked over Vancouver's supplies at the start of the voyage. The explorers, of course, found Indians in possession, and some of the Indian names have been retained. **North Yakima** (yä'kē-mă) preserves in its second part the Indian word for a 'runaway'; **Seattle** (sē-ăt'l) was *Se-a-thl,* the name of an Indian chief, resident in those parts when the first settlers came. **Spokane** (spō-kăn') is located in a region where the skies are usually bright and clear, and its name tells this fact, for according to it the residents of Spokane are 'children of the sun,' as the Indians before them were also called. **Walla Walla** (wä'lä wä'lä) is a most unusual name, one that many persons find it fun to pronounce. More than that, it probably had its origin in a sound, for it means 'rushing stream.' If one has ever stood on the banks of a deep, swift river and listened to the gurgling of the water, it may be recalled that the sound was somewhat like "walla-walla-walla."

Oregon has three important personal names. **Eugene** (ū-jēn') is the given name of a first settler, Eugene F. Skinner; **Astoria** (ăs-tō'rǐ-ă) is a memorial to John

āle; câre; ăm; ärm; ēve; ĕnd; makēr; īce; ĭll

Jacob Astor who founded the fortune of the Astor family in the fur trade during the first quarter of the last century; **Pendleton** (pĕn′dĕl-tŭn) is named for George H. Pendleton, a candidate for the Vice-Presidency in 1864. At **Portland,** two settlers, one from Boston, Massachusetts, the other from Portland, Maine, each wanted to name the place after his home town. They tossed a coin. Oregon has also a very fine Spanish name **Corvallis** (kôr-văl′ĭs), a word meaning 'heart of the valley,' because the place is situated in the center of the productive Willamette Valley.

It would not be fair to say that it is because of jealousy of the beautiful name Corvallis, in Oregon, that California's one important Indian name has about the same meaning. Still, the Western States are great rivals of one another, and this may account for **Pasadena** (păs-ă-dē′nă), the 'crown of the valley.' Other California cities are **Bakersfield,** named for Col. Thomas Baker, a prominent California pioneer who donated the site of the town in 1870; **Berkeley** (bĕrk′lē), after Bishop George Berkeley, an English divine whose efforts to found a college in America about 1730 are thus honored; and **Stockton** (stŏk′tŭn), for Commodore Robert F. Stockton, who took part in the conquest of California as commander-in-chief of the Pacific squadron during the Mexican War.

However, the most characteristic of the California names are the Spanish ones. Naturally, under those conditions "the saints have it," with **San Francisco** (săn frăn-sĭs′kō), **San Diego** (săn dē-ā′gō), really *Saint Iago,* and **San Jose** (săn hō-sā′). There is, further, an important San Jose in Costa Rica. The angels, also, were not forgotten; indeed, **Los Angeles** (lōs ăn'gĕl-ĕs) in its original, full name was 'town of the queen of the angels.' It would be difficult to surpass that. But the Spaniards once in a while did pay attention to earthly scenes, though even then they were evidently looking above, for the worldly place names of California have to do with trees. **Fresno** (frĕz'nō) means 'ash tree'; **Palo Alto** (pă'lō ăl'tō) ïs 'high timber'; and **Alameda** (ă-lă-mā'dă) is the Spanish for 'poplar grove.' As it was used in everyday language, however, *alameda* meant 'a promenade'—a stroll under the trees, as it were.

āle; câre; ăm; ärm; ēve; ĕnd; makēr; īce; ĭll

# CHAPTER X

In an earlier chapter the making of a "picture-name" map of one of the groups of states was described. Now that the study of the place names of all the United States is completed, those who were successful with the smaller picture-name map may wish to try something much more ambitious. That will be to make a picture-name map of the whole United States, big enough so that all the different places we have described can be made to show.

To do that well the map will need to be so big that one could walk around and over it! But where, the reader will ask, would one find a place for so large a map? Well, there are several possibilities. If the weather is going to be fine when one plans to set up such a map, the proper spot will, perhaps, be part of a smooth lawn somewhere near. If the making of the map will need to be done indoors, a portion of a large room such as part of a gymnasium floor, or a large hallway, may serve. It will be much better, however, if one can make the map somewhere out of doors.

The outlines of the country and of the different states may be made either with flour sifted along the pattern, or with white cord held in place at the corners and bends

ōld; ôrb; ŏdd; ūse; ûrn; ŭp; fōōd; fŏŏt; out; oil

with long wire nails, driven into the gound up to their heads. Indoors, chalk lines will, of course, serve.

It will be a good problem in map making and the scale of maps to develop the large representation of the United States that will be needed. Quite a little figuring will need to be done before the actual work of drawing the map is started. It will be necessary to decide just how large a scale will be possible in the space available. If the project is undertaken by a geography class of some size, different pupils may be made responsible for both the position and outline of a certain state or states. After the outline of the country has been drawn, measure in from each of the four boundary lines of the United States as a whole, to determine just where the boundary lines of a given state should come. Here, again, figuring will be necessary and the use of map scales also, before one can begin measuring. When the outlines have been prepared, the map will be ready for the picture part. Some names will, of course, be easy to represent; to make others show rightly will require much cleverness. The branch of a tree with the twigs lopped off nearly to the main stem, the bark peeled away and then painted red would do very nicely for Baton Rouge. New Orleans would be more difficult, but a cardboard model of an old French castle, made after a picture in an encyclopedia or found, perhaps, in an illustrated French book, might do. Use modeling clay, wood, cardboard, cloth, any and every kind of material, to give form to the idea that will best picture the name it is planned to show. Anyone who is familiar with work in manual training can fashion some especially good pieces.

āle; cȃre; ăm; ärm; ēve; ĕnd; makēr; īce; ĭll

When the figures are all completed, each one of them must be inserted at its proper location on the big map. To place those of cities will, of course, be easy. But rivers will need to be marked with blue yarn, or blue chalk; mountain ranges with jagged cardboard and so on. Also, it should be planned to have the various figures stay in place, once they are set up. Thus, for example, if one is doing a city that has a personal name, of, let us say, Kit Carson, then one should have a stick on the back of the scout figure that will make Kit stand up stiffly where he is put on the map.

Many good ideas will occur to those who try such a map as the explanations of the different names are thought over. Perhaps if each of a number of persons has his state to do, everyone will want to work harder. Each person will wish to have his state look better than those of others in the group. Take the city name, Texarkana. That might seem impossible to picture. But suppose, for this, one drew on stiff white cardboard, two maps, one of Texas, the other of Arkansas, and then labeled each of these maps with the proper state name in printed letters. Next these state maps might be placed one over the other so that they overlapped. Then it would be possible to cut across and through both maps in such a way that when the pieces were taken up one piece of Arkansas could be made to fit exactly into the "cut across" piece of Texas. If the printing had been cunningly arranged, it might even be possible to manage so that part of the word "Texas" and part of "Arkansas," on the cut pieces, would come together to form the word "Texarkana."

What could be finer than such a map for a school

ōld; ôrb; ŏdd; ūse; ûrn; ŭp; fōod; fŏŏt; out; oil

exhibit? Everybody would be glad to see it and have it explained to them; they would probably learn a lot of geography that they had never known before. Or, different schools in a city might each make up a map, and then school classes could go to see where a rival school map was not so good as the one their school had made, where better, and where one person had hit on exactly the same notion that some one in another school did.

Of course, teachers would wish to save the best specimens from each map. In another year such specimens could be used either to help out on a map of the United States for that year or a class might be permitted to use all of last year's things for the United States map, and be expected to make new ones for a map of South America, or for that of a country in Europe.

The authors of this book will be delighted to see photographs of such maps well done, photographs both of the whole map and of special states. There will be a chance here to use cameras to good purpose. Send the prints on to us, at our addresses given in the front of the book. Perhaps we can use the best photograph we receive as a frontispiece in future editions.

āle; câre; ăm; ärm; ēve; ĕnd; makẽr; īce; ĭll

# CHAPTER XI

The important names in Alaska, so far, are those of the great natural features. It is a country in which there are many small settlements where gold diggers, miners, and fishermen live, but of only few large cities.

Sailing to the north and west we come to the **Gastineau** (găs-tĭ-nō′) **Channel,** which was named after a steamer belonging to the Hudson's Bay Company. A little beyond this channel we come to the coast where the great glaciers of North America are found. The most famous of these is the **Muir** (mūr) **Glacier;** named for John Muir, the eminent explorer and naturalist, who discovered it in 1879. There is a little book by Muir called *Stickeen.* It is the story of a little dog on a glacier, and all dog lovers will find it a delightful tale. Another big glacier nearby, as large as the whole state of Rhode Island, is the **Malaspina** (mä-lä-spē′nä), named for an Italian who sailed a ship into these parts in 1791.

The **Copper River** is so named because of the immense masses of copper ore that are found in its upper valley. **Kodiak** (kŏd-yăk′) **Island** is one of those names that repeat the native word for the kind of place it is: the Eskimo for island is *kikhtah,* hence, Kodiak. Another mistake, not quite the same, was made in the case of the

**Aleutian** (ă-lū'shän) **Islands.** When the white people first came there, the natives kept saying *"Alikuaia, Alikuaia,"* meaning 'What is all this? What is all this?' But the strangers thought the natives were trying to tell them the name of the place, hence they called the islands Aleutian. But it may be true that the Russian explorers only applied a Siberian word *aliuit* = 'island people' to the natives of the Aleutians.

If the results were not quite so unusual, the explorers were on safer ground when they used personal names in their own languages for their discoveries. Of this kind are the **Pribilof** (prē-bĕ-lŏf') **Islands,** named for the Russian explorer, Pribilof, who discovered them in 1786; **Cook Inlet,** because this was the most northern point reached in 1778 by Capt. James Cook, who was killed in Hawaii the following year, in his search for a northerly route home to England; the **Seward** (sōō'ärd) **Peninsula,** named for William H. Seward, who bought Alaska from Russia for the United States in 1867; and **Point Barrow** (băr'ō), which was named for an English geographer, Sir John Barrow, who as secretary to the British Admiralty (1804) promoted many voyages of exploration to the Arctic.

**Nome** (nōm), the cape and the city, altogether by chance have this odd name. Anyone might think, especially after reading so far in this book, that it is easy to give satisfactory names to geographic objects. Well, one of the authors of this volume had a chance to try it himself in Alaska, and he can tell you it is not so easy as it seems. When one has, on all sides of one, unnamed peaks, glaciers, streams, and bays, and is expected to

āle; câre; ăm; ärm; ēve; ĕnd; makẽr; īce; ĭll

mark them on a map with names that other people will say are good, one thinks, and thinks, and thinks. Often one does not know what would do, even after considering a long while. Let the reader make an attempt if he will. Mark different places about the home, mountain number 1, number 2, and so on; stream number 1, number 2, and so on; do the same for cities, capes, and other features; assume that these geographical items are in Alaska, or in Ohio, or in Africa, and then go around with a paper and write down a fitting name for each. It is a fair guess that before the experimenter comes to the fifth one he will be thinking of the silliest things, and at about the tenth he will be ready to give up. That must have been about the state of mind of the men who discovered Cape Nome. They marked its outline on the map, but because they could not think of a good name, they put down "? *name.*" Later on it was forgotten that the cape had not been named, and when the draughtsmen were given the map to copy for engraving, they saw this "? *name*" and decided that it was meant for "C. Nome." They put it down so, and so it has remained.

On the other hand, good names were given to some places in Alaska by the natives, but the meaning of the names was later forgotten. That is true of **Ketchikan** (kĕch′ĭ-kăn), **Sitka** (sĭt′kă), and **Nenana** (nē-nä-nä′). But we do know that *ket,* or *quet,* means 'narrow strait,' and Sitka may be 'on Shi,' that is, 'on the island, *Shi.*' In Nenana we also know that the final *na* means 'river,' for we find this likewise in **Tanana** (tä-nä-nä′), which is made up of *tanan* = 'mountain men' and *na* = 'river'; hence, the Tanana is the 'river of the mountain men.' It

ōld; ôrb; ŏdd; ūse; ûrn; ŭp; fōōd; fŏŏt; out; oil

is the more disappointing that the full meaning of these native names has been lost, for those like Tanana and **Skagway** (skăg'wā), which are known, are very attractive. Skagway means 'home of the North Wind.' The **Klondike** (klŏn'dīk) is, perhaps, the 'deer river.'

**Juneau** (jū'nō), the capital of Alaska, recalls Joseph Juneau, a prospector; **Fairbanks** (fâr'bănks), the largest city, was named for Senator Charles W. Fairbanks, later Vice-President in President Roosevelt's second administration (1905-1909); and **Dawson** (dô'sŭn), the important point on the Yukon in Canada, was named for George M. Dawson of the Canadian Geological Survey, in memory of his geological explorations during the fixing of the Alaskan boundary in 1873.

It is a long way from Alaska to Hawaii, but that is where we go next for names. It surprises most people to learn that the shortest route from Seattle to Hawaii by steamer is to go around by way of Alaska, instead of straight across the Pacific. If the reader is not ready to believe that, let him measure the two distances with a string over the globe map. To understand just why this is true, it will be necessary to learn about "great-circle sailing," a topic which will probably be found under the heading "Navigation" in most encyclopedias.

**Hawaii** (hä-wī'ē) was formerly *Owhyhee*, which, translated, is 'the hot place.' The group of islands of which it is one was at first called the **Sandwich Islands**. When the authors were at school, that was the geographic name which most aroused our curiosity. How did a lot of islands out in the Pacific get a name that we thought of most as food for a picnic? Well, Captain Cook, who

āle; câre; ăm; ärm; ēve; ĕnd; makēr; īce; ĭll

discovered the group in 1778, named them for an English nobleman, the Earl of Sandwich. His name meant 'sandy abode,' *wic* being Anglo-Saxon for 'abode' or 'village.' The Anglo-Saxons borrowed *wic* from the Latin *vicus* = 'a village.' But that does not help us much to understand the foodstuff. However, the old lord was in the habit of playing cards, and when so engaged, he munched slices of bread with meat between—and that arrangement came to be known as a "sandwich."

**Honolulu** (hŏ-nō-lōō′lōō or hŏn-ă-lōō′lōō) is the largest city of Hawaii and the seaport. The native word *hono* means 'harbor,' *lulu* is 'fair'; hence, 'fair' or 'fine harbor.' The great feature of Hawaii is the immense volcano, **Mauna Loa** (mō′nă lō′ă), from the native *mauna* = 'mountain' and *loa* = 'long.'

Continuing across the Pacific we come to the **Philippine** (fĭl′ĭ-pēn) **Islands,** so named by the Spanish who took possession of the islands in 1565, in honor of Philip II of Spain. As the Spaniards wrote the name it was *Islas Filipinas;* hence we are not wrong in speaking of the natives as **Filipinos** (fĭl-ĭ-pē′nōs). The largest island of the group is **Luzon** (lōō-zŏn′), a name which comes from the native word *losong,* 'a wooden bowl' in which rice is pounded to flour. A promontory that shows boldly as one approaches the island has the shape of such a bowl, hence the name. **Mindanao** (mĭn-dä-nä′ō), another large island, derives its name from *min* = 'land' and *danu* = 'lake,' hence, 'lake land.' This is fitting because there are many lakes filling craters of extinct volcanoes in Mindanao. **Manila** (mă-nĭl′ă), the capital city, has a curious name, the form of which, it might be thought, is one that savage peoples would have used more commonly. The word is built up of *mairon* = 'to be,' 'is,' and *nila,* a kind of bush. Hence Manila means 'Here is nila bush.'

Starting back east now, we arrive next at **Guam** (gwäm), a small island possession of the United States; the first part, *gu,* is an East Indian term for 'waters.' Journeying south from Guam we find **Samoa** (sä-mō'ă) with a name corrupted from the native *Sa-ia-Moa,* that is, 'sacred to Moa.' Moa was the ancient hero chief who, according to the natives, led their people to these islands.

Next comes a long trip to, and through, the Panama Canal. Here we see the **Chagres** (chä'grĕs) **River,** so called by the Spaniards because of the *chagres* fish which they reported it to contain, and which were "like crocodiles and eat men." **Colon** (kō-lŏn'), the city, recalls our old friend Christopher Columbus, who had to change his name to *Colon* when he became a Spanish citizen.

Now we are back into the Caribbean, where we have already noted Porto Rico. Recently the United States has also bought the Danish group of the **Virgin** (vûr'jĭn) **Islands.** These consist of a swarm of small islands, about 100 altogether, discovered by Columbus on his second voyage, in 1493. When Columbus saw how many there were, he gave up the idea of naming each one and called them *Las Virgenes,* that is, 'the maidens.' They do look young, fresh, green, and attractive as one sails over the seas toward them, so the name was well chosen. To make up for neglecting religion for the ladies, however, Columbus did stop long enough to name the three largest islands of the group **Saint Thomas, Saint John,** and **Saint Croix** (sănt krwoi'), that is, 'the holy cross.'

āle; câre; ăm; ärm; ēve; ĕnd; makẽr; īce; ĭll

# CHAPTER XII

CANADA is divided into provinces in much the same way that the United States is made up of different states. The origins of the names of some of the Canadian provinces we already know: **New Brunswick,** from that of the city in New Jersey; **Ontario** from Lake Ontario; **British Columbia, Saskatchewan,** and **Yukon,** from the names of those rivers.

Nearly all those that remain have names that are different enough to make them worth while. **Nova Scotia** (nō'vă skō'shă), for example, has a double interest. In the first place, it was King James I's (who though himself very learned) Latin way of saying 'New Scotland.' Then the term Scotland itself is unusual in its original form and meaning. It was the Celtic *scuit,* and denoted 'wanderers'; but whether these wanderers were nomadic herdsmen or fugitives fleeing from a conquering invader is not clear.

**Quebec** (kwē-běk'), the name both of a province and its capital city, is an Indian word meaning 'the narrows.' It was originally *keb-bec.* At Quebec, the city, the St. Lawrence River first becomes narrow, or choked and impeded, in distinction from its wide lower course. **Manitoba** (măn-ĭ-tō'bă) is a province which takes the Indian name of a great lake that lies within it. This name refers

old; ôrb; ŏdd; ūse; ûrn; ŭp; fōod; fŏot; out; oil

121

to *Manito,* 'the great spirit,' and may have been, originally, the combination *Mana-tuopa,* that is, 'where the great spirit lives.'  There are sea caves in the cliffs at the northern end of a big island in the lake, and at times the waves rush into these caves in such a way as to cause a sound like distant church bells.  If church bells were to begin to ring on a week day and at a time when you were doing something naughty, you probably would feel rather guilty.  You can imagine that the ignorant Indians were quite solemn when they heard sounds so unusual to them.

**Alberta** (ăl-bûr'tă) was named for Prince Albert, the husband of Queen Victoria, and **Prince Edward Island** for the Prince Edward who was in 1798 commander of the British forces in North America.  **Cape Breton** (brĕt'ŏn) **Island,** nearby, a part of Nova Scotia, probably is a memorial of the Brittany (Breton) fishermen who voyaged there in early days.

In the case of the **Saguenay** (săg'ē-nā') **River** we just miss knowing the meaning of the name because the explorers who recorded it apparently did not stop to ask. Their account reads:  "And it is that (river) which leadeth and runneth into the country and kingdom of Saguenay as by the two wild men of Canada it was told us."  But perhaps the Indians only meant to tell the French that the place was *saginawa* = 'the river mouth.' The **Fraser** (frā'zẽr) **River** in British Columbia is named for Simon Frazer, the first white man to cross the Rocky Mountains in that latitude.  The **Nelson** (nĕl'sŭn) **River,** and **Port Nelson** at its mouth, were named for an officer on the ship which followed up Hudson's discoveries.

āle; câre; ăm; ärm; ēve; ĕnd; makẽr; īce; ĭll

Nova Scotia not only has an interesting name itself but also has done well in the name of its chief city, **Halifax** (hăl′ĭ-făks). Rude persons have been known to say "Go to Halifax," intending to convey that they wished to be rid of you and also that you should go to a place not very comfortable.[1] But in this they make a great mistake, for the name Halifax probably means, in the Anglo-Saxon original, *haligfax* = 'holy hair.' It is an English place name, and the story goes that a maiden was murdered there. A lock of her hair was found hanging on the branch of a tree. Later it was discovered that the underside of the bark of trees growing at that spot had a fine, hair-like webbing, like a cobweb, and this was thought to be the hair of the murdered girl. Those who may have observed such webbing on the inner bark of trees will appreciate this idea. Another explanation is that the word means 'holy face' because of an image of St. John the Baptist kept at that place. **Sydney** (sĭd′nē), in Nova Scotia, and also in Australia, is in origin an Anglo-Saxon word, *sudanie* = 'the south island.' However, it was in honor of Lord Sydney, a member of the Cabinet of the younger Pitt (1783), that the name was used for the Canadian and Australian places.

---

[1] Perhaps this expression got its vogue from a piece by John Taylor, 1580-1653, entitled "A Very Merry-Wherry-Ferry Voyage," in which these lines occur:

"There is a Proverb and a prayer withal,
That we not to three strange places fall:
From Hull, from Halifax, from Hell, 'tis thus,
From all these three, good Lord deliver us."

It would be a very interesting project to search out in old books just why Hull and Halifax had such an evil reputation in Taylor's day.

ōld; ôrb; ŏdd; ūse; ûrn; ŭp; fōōd; fŏŏt; out; oil

New Brunswick names are commonplace: **Fredericton** (frĕd′rĭk-tŭn) for the Prince of Wales, son of George III and who was the father of George IV, and **St. John.** But the metropolis of Canada, **Montreal** (mŏnt-rē-ôl′), in the Province of Quebec, has a name that is splendid, both in form and meaning. It translates to 'Mount Royal,' and refers to the position of the city at the base of a great volcanic hill which rises very steeply from the level plains of the river lowlands.

**Toronto** (tō-rŏn′tō), in Ontario, is an Indian word variously explained. Some say it means 'gathering place,' others, 'oak rising from the lake.' Best of all is the explanation which makes the original form *te-o-ron-to,* which translates 'here the waves begin to die.' This will be better understood if one has watched waves coming in, breaking, and "dying" on the beach. **Ottawa** (ŏt′ă-wä) has a more practical name. It is an Indian word also, and means 'he trades.' One may picture the Indians meeting in the woods and talking about a fur trader at Ottawa to whom they planned to take their skins. Other Ontario cities of importance are **Sudbury** (sŭd′bēr-ĭ), made up of the Anglo-Saxon *suth* ='south' and *bury* = 'a walled town'; **Hamilton** (hăm′ĭl-tŭn), named for a George Hamilton, who laid out the city in 1813; **Brantford** (brănt′-fōrd), named after Joseph Brant, the Mohawk leader of the Revolutionary War; and **Cobalt** (kō′bôlt), so named because of the cobalt ore found there.

**Winnipeg** (wĭn′ĭ-pĕg), in Manitoba, takes its name from the lake on which it is situated. The Indian word means 'dirty water' from *wi* = 'muddy' or 'dirty' and *nipi* = 'water.' The Saskatchewan River, which empties

āle; câre; ăm; ärm; ēve; ĕnd; makēr; īce; ĭll

into the lake, brings in its current much whitish mud which discolors the lake waters. The Indians, however, have a very comical story to explain the dirtiness. It seems that a bad fairy, a boy goblin, who liked to play jokes on men, was once caught at his tricks by an old Indian woman. She grabbed him, and with the help of all the other Indian women gave him first a terrible licking, and then smeared him over with mud so completely that he needed all the water of the lake to wash himself clean again. The name of this goblin was *Weesakootchaht,* and he corresponds to the English Puck.

The western provinces have as yet only few large cities. **Regina** (rē-jī′nă), in Saskatchewan, is probably so called because it is the 'queen' of prairies; **Edmonton** (ĕd′mŭn-tŭn), in Alberta, is derived from the Anglo-Saxon personal name, *Eadhelm,* and *tun,* that is, 'Eadhelm's farm home.' **Dunvegan** (dŭn-vē′găn) repeats the name of a Scottish *dun,* or fortified 'hill.' **Vancouver** (văn-kōō′vēr) island and city in British Columbia were named after Capt. George Vancouver, who with Captain Cook discovered British Columbia in 1778. **Victoria,** the capital of the province, was so named by special permission of Queen Victoria of Great Britain. Whether the queen also gave her special permission to use her name for a lake and a waterfall in Africa and a province in Australia is not said; nevertheless, these also are named Victoria for her. Vancouver Island is separated from the mainland by **Queen Charlotte Sound,** and off the coast are the **Queen Charlotte Islands,** both named by Vancouver for the wife of King George III.

ōld; ôrb; ŏdd; ūse; ûrn; ŭp; fōōd; fŏŏt; out; oil

# CHAPTER XIII

## THE LANDS AND ISLANDS OF THE SPANISH MAIN

THE "Spanish Main" is a poetical way of speaking of the high seas on which the Spaniards were for a long time dominant after the discoveries of Columbus. The lands and islands of the Spanish Main are, therefore, Mexico, Central America, and the West Indies.

The names of the different countries on the continent itself we have already considered. We also know about the most important of their natural features. There remain, however, four of these natural features that must not be passed by without notice. Balboa gave the name **Darien** (dā-rĭ-ĕn′) to the isthmus (a gulf nearby is also called Darien) he crossed over when he got his first view of the Pacific Ocean in 1513. He was trying to preserve a native word, *Tarena,* the name of a river, but failed to note it exactly.

**Tehauntepec** (tā-wän-tā-pĕk′), the Mexican isthmus, has an Indian name, derived from *tecuani* = 'a beast of prey' and *tepetl* = 'mountain.' Jaguars would probably be the animals that the Indians feared.

The ocean shore line in Nicaragua is known as the **Mosquito Coast.** We ought to be clear on this term because it implies that the name is due to the abundance of mosquitoes there. Mosquitoes are abundant, but the

āle; câre; ăm; ärm; ēve; ĕnd; makẽr; īce; ĭll

name is of other origin. In Spanish, *mozo* is 'fellow,'
as we say, "lazy fellow." In Nicaragua are found people
whose ancestors are in part negro, in part Indian, and
those persons are called *Mosquitos,* which means no-
account, 'little fellows.' In the island of Martinique is
found the volcano **Mont Pelée** (môn pē-lā'), which
is French for 'bare' or 'bald mountain.' This is the volcano which caused such tremendous destruction by its
eruption in 1902.

Mexico has a number of comparatively large places,
some of which have the old Aztec names, whereas the rest
are, of course, Spanish. **Acapulco** (ä-kă-pūl'kō) is Aztec
for 'destroyed' or 'conquered town.' **Tampico** (täm-
pē'kō) probably combines the Aztec *tam* = 'place' with
the portuguese *pico* = 'a peak.' **Mazatlán** (mä-zä-
tlän') was originally *mazatl* and meant 'where deer are.'

**Manzanilla** (män-sä-nēl'yä) begins like Mazatlan but
is a Spanish word derived from the Spanish term *man-
zana* = 'an apple.' It is the name of a poisonous tree,
abundant at that place, but found all over these regions,
which has a fruit like an apple. But to eat those apples
is to die; even the juice of the tree is poisonous; it raises
blisters on the skin as poison ivy does. In **Vera
Cruz** (vā'rä krōōs') the Spaniards are true to form, in
that it is another of their religious names. Cortez called
the place *Villa Rica de la Vera Cruz,* that is, 'rich city of
the true cross.' But the site he picked was unhealthy, so
they had to move the city some miles farther south, re-
gardless of Cortez's name for the spot first chosen. **Leon**
(lä-ōn') is named after the city in Spain, and that was
originally *Legion,* because of a 'legion,' or regiment, of

old; ôrb; ŏdd; ūse; ûrn; ŭp; fōōd; fŏŏt; out; oil

Roman soldiers, at one time there stationed. **Progreso** (prō-grä′sō) is one of the Mexican harbor cities from which sisal, the hennequen fiber used for binder twine, is shipped. *Progreso* is Spanish for 'progress,' and everyone hopes the Mexicans will make progress in the next few years, for they have been sadly lacking in that quality recently. In any case, the name Progreso is like **Sonora** (sō-nō′rǎ), the name of one of the Mexican provinces, 'fine sounding.' **Guadalajara** (gwä-thä-lä-hä′rä) is named after a river in Spain which got its name from the Arabic *Wad-al-hajarah,* that is, 'river of stones.'

**Belize** (bě-lēz′), the capital of British Honduras, may be a corruption of the French word *balise* = 'a beacon.' But more likely it is an attempt on part of the Spaniards to say Wallis, or Wallace. A Scotch adventurer of that name, in 1610, tried to make himself master of Honduras, and the town name seems to be the only result of his efforts. **Greytown** (grā′toun), at the boundary line between Nicaragua and Costa Rica, is named for Charles (later Earl) Grey, a British soldier who commanded the land forces in the attack on the French West Indies in 1794. **Nassau** (năs′ô), in the Bahamas, was originally a Dutch town, and gets its name from the words *nass* = 'wet' and *aue* = 'meadow.'

Now we are ready to make stepping stones of the islands of the West Indies for a journey east and south, stopping on each long enough to become acquainted. Previous to acquaintance one must have introductions, and introductions mean learning names—so it appears we are doing quite the proper thing.

**Cuba** (kyū′bǎ) was the native Indian word for 'dis-

āle; câre; ăm; ärm; ēve; ĕnd; makēr; īce; ĭll

trict.' **Havana** (hă-văn'ă) or **Habana** (hă-bă'-nă) was probably the name of a Cuban Indian tribe, but no one seems to know now what this meant. One writer, though, simply translates Havana as 'the harbor.' **Santiago** (sän-tē-ä'gō), also in Chili, is a form of *St. Iago,* that is, in Spanish, 'St. James,' who is the patron saint of Spain. Away back in the year 835 the Spaniards became very much excited because Bishop Theodmir of those days asserted that he had found, buried near Iria in Spain, the bones of St. James. The Bishop said a star had guided him to the place. Thousands of Christians made pilgrimages to the spot and were given a certain kind of shell to prove they had made the trip. These tokens were so highly prized that their possession was shown by picturing them on family coats-of-arms. The Spanish government put on a tax of one bushel of grain from each acre harvested all over Spain, the proceeds to be used to keep up the place where the bones were found. At one time as much as $1,000,000 per year was collected through this tax for that purpose. The tax was stopped in 1835, but these facts show the state of mind which made the Spaniards so possessed to give religious names to every new place they discovered.

At **Matanzas** (mä-tän'säs), in Cuba, the Spaniards went to quite the other extreme, and with good reason. Matanzas is from the Spanish word *matanza* = 'murder,' 'bloodshed.' Spanish sailors, shipwrecked there, were massacred. Of a whole ship's crew and passengers only one woman and her daughter survived, and they were found eighteen years later, wandering about in the woods, naked, except for clothes made of leaves.

ōld; ôrb; ŏdd; ūse; û͞n; ŭp; fōŏd; fŏŏt; out; oil

Haiti or Hayti (hā'tē) was the Indian name for the island of **Santo Domingo** (săn-tō dō-mĭn'gō) and meant 'rough, sharp, craggy,' as indeed much of it is. The name the Spaniards gave the island means 'Holy Sunday.' **Port au Prince** (pôrt ō prăns') is French for 'Port of the Prince' and is a name given when the French held the island, which they did from 1697 to 1803. **Puerto Plata** (pwĕr'tō plä'tä), also in Haiti, is Spanish for 'Port Silver.' Columbus saw a silvery cloud at the summit of a Haitian mountain and called it *Monte de Plata,* and this name is preserved in the name of the harbor city. The republic at the east end of the island is named, after the island, the **Dominican** (dō-mĭn'ĭ-kăn) **Republic.**

**Jamaica** (jă-mā'kă) has a native Indian name, originally *Yamaca,* which means 'abounding in springs.' This island is much better watered than some of the other islands of the West Indies. **Porto Rico** (pôr'tō rē'kō) is named for its chief harbor, the 'rich port of St. John,' that is, **San Juan** (săn wôn'). **Ponce** (pŏn'thā), another large city in Porto Rico, recalls Ponce de Leon, whom we met in Florida.

Passing by the Virgin Islands with a bow, because we are already acquainted, we come next to **Antigua** (ăntē'gwä). Columbus, on his second voyage in 1493, named this island for a chapel in the cathedral at Seville. A week earlier he had named **Guadeloupe** (gwä-dēlōōp') for a convent in Andalusia, because he had promised the monks at that place to name one of his new discoveries for their institution. The day before was Sunday, so he called the island at which he was stopping *Domingo* = 'Sunday.' We now use the form **Dominica**

āle; câre; ăm; ärm; ēve; ĕnd; makĕr; īce; ĭll

(dŏm'ĭ-nē'kă). This was the first land sighted on the second voyage, and its discovery appears to have excited the old sailor not a little, for it seems that he must have skipped from island to island, like a tourist, after that.

Columbus did not, though, get around to **Martinique** (mär-tĭ-nēk') until 1502. The name originally seems to have been *Matigno,* perhaps an Indian term, the meaning of which is unknown. On the same voyage he found St. Lucia (loō-sē'ă) on the day of that saint (Lucy). **Barbados** (bär-bā'dōz), however, escaped him, because it lies so far out to the east. But the Spaniards discovered it later and called it *Los Barbados,* that is, 'the bearded ones.' This was because the island was then covered with wild fig trees having branches that end in brown fibers, and these fibers hang down like hair in a long beard.

The supply of saints was still good in 1498, so Columbus used up another for **St. Vincent** (vĭn'sĕnt). When he arrived at **Trinidad** (trĭn'ĭ-dăd) in the same year, he rested on the saints, for the three, distinct, flat summits that rise up out of the sea there immediately suggested the 'trinity' to him. Although one cannot well find fault with this, it would have been much prettier if he had used the native name of the island, which is *Iere,* and means 'the land of the humming birds.' Our old friend Vespucius beat Columbus to **Curacao** (Koō-ră-sä'ō), and, possibly because of this fact, it escaped a religious name and kept its native one, which was *Curasaote* and meant 'the great plantation.' Nearly all of the West Indian islands have become great plantations, and in saying good-by to them and their names, we can think of them sweetly, for they supply us with much of our sugar.

ōld; ôrb; ŏdd; ūse; ûrn; ŭp; foōd; foŏt; out; oil

# CHAPTER XIV

## SOUTH AMERICA

AFTER all, even though we do not know what each one of them means, we are familiar, through use, with the names of places in North America. We see the North American names so often, in newspapers, for example; we hear people say they have been to this or that place; we have cousins who come to see us from distant states. Accordingly, we say and remember those names easily, though many are queer-sounding when we stop to think about them.

But, as we found when we were sailing around the Spanish Main, once one leaves the more familiar regions behind, the places one comes to have names that are not only meaningless but are also strange in form and stranger still in pronunciation. Hence, though it was interesting and worth while to learn how our home place names originated, and what they mean, it is *important* to understand those of foreign lands. For if one does not understand such names, they are little more than senseless jargon, as if one put together "bxylmth" and called it a name.

So we begin with the names on a new continent, South America, knowing that these are names which it will well repay us to understand.

āle; câre; ăm; ärm; ēve; ĕnd; makĕr; īce; ĭll
132

Let us consider first the different countries of South America. **Brazil** (bră-zĭl′) is the largest of these countries, and its name, right at the start, supplies us with an example of an unusual origin. Brazil is derived from the Portuguese word *braza,* meaning 'live coal.' Not long after the country was discovered, it was found to contain a wood which gave a bright, red dye. This was called 'brazil wood,' that is, 'live-coal' wood. By and by the country from which the dye-wood was had itself became known as Brazil.

The British, the French, and the Dutch have each a colony named **Guiana** (gē-ä′nă) in South America. And Guiana, as a name, is not less unusual than Brazil. It is a South-American Indian word and was spelled by those people *Guaya-na.* It came from *na* = 'we' and *guaya* = 'the esteemed people.' Of course, when white people pronounced this phrase, not knowing what it meant, it soon was slurred off to the single word *Guiana.* That often happens to names, as we have already found out.

We try next **Venezuela** (věn-ā-zwē′lă or vā-nä-swä′lä), and again hit on an origin quite unlike those that we met with in North America. Venezuela is Spanish for 'little Venice.' Now Venice is a city in Europe which was first built on posts in a swamp. When the discoverers, who knew all about the old Venice, came to the coast of Venezuela, they found there an Indian village built on posts over the water. So of course they exclaimed at once, *"Venezuela!"*

**Colombia** we know all about, it is true, but was it to be expected that **Ecuador** (ĕk′wä-dôr) is the Spanish word for 'equator'? If one will look at a map to see

ōld; ôrb; ŏdd; ūse; ûrn; ŭp; fōōd; fŏŏt; out; oil

where the capital of Ecuador is located, one will understand why they called the country that. To say that "Peru (pĕ-rōō′) is peculiar" is an odd phrase. But it is just as odd that so compact a name does not have a sure and certain origin. The Spanish conquerors had a fight with a chief whose name they thought was *Piru,* and all the country has since then been known by the name they thought was his. And we will probably never know now whether it was or was not. But **Bolivia** (bō-lĭv′ĭ-ă) is in a different class. Still, one would never guess the origin of its name any more easily than those we have already considered. Bolivia is named after Simon Bolivar (bō-lē′vär), a native of Venezuela, the great liberator of the South American republics from Spanish rule.

Not only different, but also quite unlike each other, are these names of the countries of South America, you will admit. But are they all so various? **Chili** (chĭ′lĭ) comes next, as we go south. How about that name? It is just as surprising as the others. A kind of thrush abundant in Chili has a note which sounds like *tschili,* hence the name of the country. Some authorities are unwilling to accept that explanation and say that Chili was originally *Chili mapu,* that is, in the Peruvian language, 'chilly land.' But that seems too like English to be believable.

**Argentina** (är-jĕn-tē′nă) has a name from the Latin *argentum* = 'silver.' But Argentina is a country in which very little, if any, silver is mined. The explanation is that when Argentina was first known, it was thought to have silver deposits, because the natives brought silver

āle; câre; ăm; ärm; ēve; ĕnd; makẽr; īce; ĭll

down its river from the mountains, far to the west, in Bolivia.

Uruguay (ū'roŏ-gwā) has an Indian name, made up of *uru* = 'bird' and *guay* = 'tail,' hence, 'bird's tail.' That certainly is a funny name for a country. And the more so because it was not actually a bird's tail that gave rise to the name. Rather it was because a great waterfall in that country resembled the outspread tail of a bird. It required some imagination certainly to name Uruguay.

Finally we come to little **Paraguay** (păr'ă-gwā). It is so modest, is Paraguay, on account of its littleness and "tucked-awayness" perhaps, that it has a name that is more like average names than those of any of the other South American countries. To begin with, it copies its *guay* from the *guay* of Uruguay. In the second place its name is really the name of a river, and to take the name of a river is to pattern after the names of many other places. But the **Paraguay River** was perhaps the *Paraguacu* river, that is, 'the great water.'

Now we shall go around the continent again. This time we shall start at the north, go through the Panama Canal, then down the west coast, past the south end and up the east coast, stopping to take note of the islands about South America and the land features of the continent itself

We first encounter on this trip **Gallinas** (gäl-yē'näs) **Point,** projecting from Colombia into the Caribbean Sea. *Gallina* is the Spanish word for 'hen,' and the name probably was given because the point has the shape of a chicken's head.

Once we are in the Pacific the tremendous heights of

ōld; ôrb; ŏdd; ūse; ûrn; ŭp; foōd; foŏt; out; oil

the **Andes** (ăn'dēz) **Mountains** are found to be the most impressive feature of the continent, and these mountains continue all along down the west coast. Andes is possibly derived from the Peruvian word *anta,* meaning 'copper,' and much copper is obtained from the southern ranges of these mountains. If Andes is not from *anta,* we do not know its origin. So, also, we lack much information about the names of the very lofty volcanoes that surmount the Andes. These peaks are very prominent landmarks, so that, of course, they were named at a very early time, even before the Inca people came into the country. These ancient names, moreover, survived, though their meaning was forgotten. However, **Chimborazo** (chĭm-bō-rä'zō) is apparently derived from the word *chimpa,* meaning 'opposite shore.' The idea of the whole word Chimborazo evidently was that 'the snow of the mountain is seen from the village of the opposite shore.' **Cotopaxi** (kō-tō-păk'sē) is from *ccota* = 'pile' and *pasca* = 'shining' or 'brilliant'; hence, 'shining pile.' The above two volcanoes are in Ecuador. **Illimani** (ēl-yē-mä'nē) is nearby in Peru. Its name comes from *illi* = 'snow' and *mani,* probably meaning 'mountain.' Thus it was the snow on their summits, or the brilliance of that snow, that evidently determined the names of each of these peaks. Why should this snow have so much impressed the primitive peoples of these parts?

High up in the Andes, at the southern end of Peru, is one of the most famous lakes in the world, **Lake Titicaca** (tē-tē-kä'kä). Part of its fame is no doubt due to its unusual name. The best explanation of this name is that it is made up of two Indian words, *titi* = 'wild cat'

āle; câre; ăm; ärm; ēve; ĕnd; makēr; īce; ĭll

and *kaka* = 'rock'; hence 'wild-cat rock.' Out in the lake there is a rocky island and the markings of the rock (veins) make a drawing like the face of a wild cat or puma; the name of the lake, then, is really after the name of this rock.

If we had actually climbed over the Andes to see their features, we should have found it a long, hard trip and should be glad to return to our ship for easier traveling. For a time we should then sail in the **Humboldt** (hŭm'-bōlt) **Current,** named for Alexander von Humboldt, a very celebrated German naturalist, who, as early as 1799, visited these regions. But we must sail off to the west, right along the equator, for a way in order not to miss the **Galápagos** (gä-lä'pä-gōs) **Islands.** Their name is a Spanish word meaning 'giant tortoises,' and it certainly fits the islands, for everyone agrees that the Galápagos fairly swarm with turtles of peculiar varieties and with one kind, especially, which is of huge size. Far to the south of the Galápagos Islands, and nearer to the continent than they, we encounter the **Juan Fernandez** (hwän fĕr-nän'dāth) **Islands.** These are named for a Spanish pilot, who discovered them about 1563, but they are famous because a sailor, Alexander Selkirk, was put ashore on them in 1704 and lived there alone for more than four years. Selkirk's adventures are supposed to have given Daniel Defoe the idea for *Robinson Crusoe.*

At the southern tip of the continent is **Cape Horn.** This was named by the Dutch navigators who first doubled it in 1646 for a village in Holland, *Hoorn,* on a 'horn' or 'spit,' projecting into the Zuyder Zee. But instead of trying to go around the Horn we will use the

ōld; ôrb; ŏdd; ūse; ûrn; ŭp; fōōd; fŏŏt; out; oil

**Strait of Magellan** (mă-jĕl'ăn) because, as we are going from west to east, we shall have the wind with us. Magellan, however, while on the first voyage completely around the world in 1520, went the other way, and it took him thirty-seven days to make that little stretch of his great trip. No wonder he was pleased with the Pacific Ocean when he finally reached it and sailed over its calm waters.

While Magellan was striving to get through the strait, he had plenty of time to observe the land to the south, **Tierra del Fuego** (tyĕr'rä dĕl fwā'gō). Evidently the Indians were watching him and his strange ship also, for the natives built so many fires along the shore that Magellan called this land the 'Land of Fire.' But in so doing he created an altogether wrong notion about Tierra del Fuego, for people think of it as a land of volcanoes, of which there are none on that island. Before sailing through the strait Magellan had spent some time on the mainland to the north and east, the region of **Patagonia** (păt-ă-gō'nĭ-ă). Here his sailors found footprints in the snow resembling those of a large, clumsy beast. Later it was discovered that these prints were made by men who wore great, ungainly moccasins, made of guanaco skins. Accordingly, Magellan called these people *Patagones,* that is, in Portuguese, 'paw-footed men.'

Off the coast of Patagonia are found the **Falkland** (fôk'lănd) **Islands.** These were named for Lord Falkland who helped an English explorer, Strong, who sailed into a strait between the islands in 1690. Strong called this strait after his patron, and later the name of the strait was made to apply to the islands themselves.

Between the mountains and the uplands of South

āle; câre; ăm; ärm; ēve; ĕnd; makēr; īce; ĭll

America are vast, level plains, known by the Spanish and Portuguese words for those land forms, *campos* and *llanos*. Over these lowlands flow the great rivers of the continent, one of which, the **Amazon** (ăm'ă-zŏn), is the largest river in the world. Its name has two possible explanations. One is that the Spanish explorer Orellana thought he saw women warriors on its banks. Hence he called the river Amazon, for *Amazon* was the Greek word for fabled, warlike women of a certain people who cut off their right breasts in order that they might better be able to handle a bow. The other explanation is that the word is a native term, *amassona,* meaning 'boat destroyer.' This name was given because the tide rushes up the Amazon so violently that the wave often destroys the native's boat. It is possible that both explanations are correct, for the explorer, thinking he saw women fighting and hearing the natives say *"amassona,"* probably said to himself, "Aha, here at last are found Amazons!" For the Greeks had this idea about women warriors, Amazons, but they could never prove it.

As Argentina is from the Latin for silver, so is also **Rio de la Plata** (rē'ō dä lä plä'tä) from *plata,* the Spanish word for silver, hence 'river of silver.' We already know about this silver being obtained from regions far from the river, but we should understand also that to call the stream "River Plate," as has been done in English, is to add another mistake to the first one. The Indians along the **Orinoco** (ō-rĭ-nō'kō) **River** called it the *Orinucu,* that is, simply, 'the river.' But the **Parana** (pä-rä-nä') **River** has a more distinctive name, its meaning in the Indian language being 'relative of the sea.' The

ōld; ôrb; ŏdd; ūse; ûrn; ŭp; fōōd; fŏŏt; out; oil

Indians called it that because the stream was so broad and big.

The **Magdalena** (mäg-dä-lä'nä) **River** has a romantic name. On the holy day of St. Mary Magdalene in 1523, a group of pretty Indian girls, who had never before seen white men, were brought into the camp of the first Spanish explorers on the river. They were united with the Spanish soldiers on that same day; hence the leader of the Spaniards, Andagoya, thought Magdalena a very fitting name for the stream.

The **Rio de Janeiro** (rē'ō dä zhă-nä'rō), 'River of January,' is not a river at all. The name was given to a bay, discovered by a Portuguese navigator on January 1, 1531, which was thought to be the mouth of a river. Now Rio de Janeiro is also the name of the great city on the bay.

Along the coast of Brazil we find, besides Rio de Janeiro, a number of other large cities. To the south lie **Sao Paulo** (sou pou'lōō), Portuguese for 'St. Paul,' and **Santos** (sän'tōōs), 'all of the saints.' To the north of Rio de Janeiro we note **Bahia** (bä-ē'ä), Portuguese for 'bay,' on a bay of the same name, hence 'bay bay.' Next north is **Pernambuco** (pûr-näm-bū'kō), which combines the native *parana* = 'river' with *buco* = 'branch' or 'arm.' Another writer translates Pernambuco as the 'mouth of hell' because of the violent surf at the mouth of the harbor.

**Para** (pä-rä'), still farther north, is the root form of *paraguacu, parana,* and *pernambuco,* and means simply 'water' or 'rain.' There is plenty of water and of rain, both, at Para, for the city is at the mouth of the Amazon and receives the equatorial rains. Going up the Amazon

āle; câre; ăm; ärm; ēve; ĕnd; makẽr; īce; ĭll

we find **Manaos** (mä-nä'ōs), the last of the Brazilian cities to be noted. This has the name of an Indian tribe that lived there. The Manaos Indians intermarried with the whites, and their descendants still occupy the region.

In the Guianas we find the three capital cities the only important places. The French one, **Cayenne** (kī-ĕn'), is simply another way of saying and spelling *Guaya-na,* 'we, the esteemed people,' the name of the province itself. In **Paramaribo** (păr'ă-măr'ĭ-bō), Dutch Guiana, we encounter again our old *para,* this time linked up originally as *Paramachire,* that is, 'dwellers in the sea.' The Indians called the Dutch that, for the Dutch, when they came, immediately set to work to reclaim the coastal lowlands. Why the Dutch should have been so possessed to do that when there was plenty of dry land farther back may be understood only when it is remembered that in Holland much of the best land has been similarly reclaimed from the sea. **Georgetown**, in British Guiana, was named for King George III of England.

**Caracas** (kä-rä'käs), in Venezuela, has a "crackly" sound and was the name of a warlike tribe that held this area. **Maracaibo** (mä-rä-kī'bō) was the name of one of their chiefs. **Puerto Colombia** (pwěr'tō), in Colombia, we understand at once. But **Barranquilla** (bär-rän-kēl'yă) is harder. *Barranca* is Spanish for 'gorge,' *quilla* for 'keel'; hence this would be 'keel-like gorge.' **Bogota** (bō'gō-tä'), a third Colombia city, is named after Bogotta, an Indian chief, vanquished here by the Spanish conqueror, Quesada, who founded the city in 1538.

Passing around to the Pacific countries once more, we

ōld; ôrb; ŏdd; ūse; ûrn; ŭp; fōōd; fŏŏt; out; oil

note **Guayaquil** (gwī-yă-kēl′), the Ecuadorian seaport, with an Indian name, perhaps from *Guaycuru* = 'the fast runners,' as a tribe living in Brazil was called. **Quito** (kē′tō), the capital of Ecuador, also preserves a tribal name, *Quitis,* but the meaning of this has been lost.

**Lima** (lē′mä), the capital, and also the seaport city of Peru, was originally *Pimac,* meaning 'he who speaks.' Indian priests had a great idol at this place. The idol was hollow and the priests would conceal one of their number inside it. At the proper moment, when great multitudes were assembled to worship, this hidden priest would shout out warnings to the people in a terrible voice. Of course, then the people would do just as the "god" said, which was exactly what the priests wanted.

**Arequipa** (ä-rä-kē′pä), Peru, is a city on the route between the coast and **Cuzco** (kōōz′kō), a city in the interior. Arequipa is from *are-quepai,* the Inca term meaning 'yes, rest here.' Cuzco, the ancient capital of the Incas, retains its original name, which meant 'the central place.'

**Cerro de Pasco** (sĕr′rō dā päs′kō) is another Peruvian town. *Cerro* in Portuguese, like *sierra* in Spanish, means 'saw-tooth mountain,' and the Portuguese *Paschoal* is 'Easter Day'; hence 'Easter Mountain.' But **La Paz** (lä päz′), in Bolivia, a name that sounds somewhat like Pasco, is from the Spanish words *la* = 'the' and *paz* = 'peace.' La Paz was founded to commemorate a peace made between rival Spanish conquerors in 1548. **Potosí** (pō-tō-sē′), in Bolivia, is how the Indian word *potosci* = 'he who makes a noise' has been preserved. It refers to a mountain which, when the Incas commanded that it be

āle; câre; ăm; ärm; ēve; ĕnd; makẽr; īce; ĭll

dug into for silver, made a tremendous noise, as if to say, "this silver is reserved for others." Nevertheless, this mountain was the source of the silver that resulted in the names of Argentina and Rio de la Plata, and the amount mined from it in 400 years probably was worth over $20,000,000,000. That is a lot of silver. No wonder that another silver-mining city, in Mexico, **San Luis Potosi,** was named after this great deposit at Potosi in Bolivia.

In Chili the best name is that of **Valparaiso** (văl-pă-rīs'ō, or, as the natives pronounce it, văl-pă-rä-ē'sō), that is, 'the Vale of Paradise.' So in 1544 the Spanish expedition of conquest coming from the dry, hot regions of Peru, in the north, called this cool and fresh, green valley as it first met their eyes. The leader of this expedition was Pedro de Valdivia. About **Valdivia** (väl-dē'vyä), which he founded a few years later, the story is not so pleasant. Valdivia was a very cruel man, and he wanted always gold and yet more gold. He treated the natives very badly to force them to give him tribute. But one day the natives captured Valdivia. Then they prepared a great feast and made Valdivia a guest. At the end of the meal they told Valdivia, "Now you will get your fill of gold also." Then they brought out a saucer full of melted gold and poured it down his throat. "And so they killed him," says the old narrative.

We need to draw a long breath after that story, so we will go to **Buenos Aires** (bwā'nōs ī'rās), Argentina, for its name means 'good airs.' They had fine weather at Buenos Aires when Pedro de Mendoza started the city, away back in 1535, and really it has a fine climate all of

ōld; ôrb; ŏdd; ūse; ûrn; ŭp; fōōd; fŏŏt; out; oil

the time. Now that we feel better we can go back to
**Punta Arenas** (po͞on′tä ä-rä′näs), in Chili. Its name is
the Spanish for 'sandy point.' **Rosario** (rō-sä′rē-ō), in
Argentina, also has a Spanish name, which is the word
for 'rosary.' **Mendoza** (mĕn-dō′sä), Argentina, is
named for the Spanish explorer who founded Buenos
Aires.

Finally, to complete our round of South American
names, we must consider the capitals of Uruguay and
Paraguay. **Montevideo** (mŏn′tē-vĭd′ē-ō) is one of the
names for which Magellan is responsible, and, as in this
case, he usually gave interesting ones. As he sailed up
the Plata River, in 1520, he noticed a hill, in the otherwise flat lands, at the place where the city now is, and he
put down *Mont-vide-eu* = 'a mount saw I'—so there you
are, Montevideo. **Ascuncion** (ä-so͞on′syōn), however, is
more true to the Spanish ideas of place names, for it
remembers in its name that it was founded by a lieutenant
of Mendoza on the feast day of the 'Assumption' of the
Virgin Mary in 1535.

# CHAPTER XV

"Go West, young man, go West!" was the good advice once given by a famous American to a youth who aspired to win a fortune. By "West" the man who gave the advice meant the western section of our United States. At a little earlier time, "West" would have meant anywhere in the New World, and in truly ancient days, the advice would have been, "Go to Europe, young man, go to Europe!" Nowadays Europe is where many Americans go to spend a fortune, but only seldom to make one.

But, as has been suggested, **Europe** (ū′rŭp) anciently was 'west,' that is, its name is from the Semitic or Hebrew word *ereb* = 'to the west,' 'the land of the setting sun,' or 'darkness.' *Ereb* also meant 'barter' or 'trade,' and the Phœnicians called their trading settlement in the west *Ereb*. And it was because of trade and commerce that people spread westward, as indeed people now go to all parts of the world for business. In the Greek form *Europe* the word means 'broad-faced' and referred to a wide plain. That fits much of Europe, too. For a long time, however, European peoples remained close to the shores of the **Mediterranean** (mĕd-ĭ-tē-rā′nē-ăn) **Sea,** a name which means 'middle-of-the-land' sea. The Romans called this sea, also, *Mare Internum,* which is 'sea internal' or the 'inside-of-the-land sea.' Still another name they had for it was *Mare Nostrum,* or 'our sea.' From all this one will understand that the ancients had quite an affection for the Mediterranean; in fact, they were so fond of it that one of their authors wrote, disgustedly, "Like frogs around a pond we cling to the shores of this sea." Did you ever stop to think how, in modern times, the peoples of European origin have clustered about the North Atlantic Ocean? It seems that, in so doing, we have been acting much as the ancients did, only our pond is slightly larger.

The Mediterranean is divided into several parts, to each of which a different name was given. Thus **Adriatic** (ā-drē-ăt′ĭk) possibly refers to a very ancient town, Hatria, on that sea, built on a 'black,' or *hatrian,* soil. The **Ægean** (ē-jē′ăn) has a name derived from a Latin word *æga* = 'a goat.' It seems that there was formerly an island in the middle of this sea which had the form of a goat lying down, hence the name. But island, goat, and all have since sunk beneath the waves. Connected with the Mediterranean, at its eastern end, is the **Black Sea.** That name does not need to be translated, for it is a translation of the Greek and the Turkish names which have the same meaning. The Greek is *Mauri Thalassa,* 'black sea' simply, but the Turkish name, *Fanar Kara Dengis,* is more expressive: it means, 'bad, black sea.' All peoples in those regions seem to have been agreed that "black" was the Black Sea's rightful name, for its skies are black and stormy by contrast with the clear and cloudless skies of the nearby Mediterranean.

The Mediterranean and the Black Seas are not joined

up by a single strait. Between the two larger seas is another smaller sea, the **Sea of Marmora** (mär'mō-rä). Its name is the Latin word *marmor* = 'marble,' and it was so called because fine marble was obtained from an island in it, even in very ancient times. At the west end of the Sea of Marmora is the strait called **Dardanelles** (där-dă-nĕlz'), named after an old Greek city, *Dardanus,* and at its east end, the strait of the **Bosphorus** (bŏs'pôr-ŭs). This also is a Greek word, *Bosporos,* made up of *bos* = 'ox' and *poros* = 'a ford.' Far to the east, beyond the Black Sea, and not connected with it, is another great body of inland water, the **Caspian** (kăs'pĭ-ăn) **Sea**. This seems to have been so named by the Greeks for a tribe, the *Caspii,* who lived on its shores, much in the same way that we have named lakes and rivers after Indian tribes.

On looking at a map of Europe it will be noted that the continent is really a great peninsula of Asia. More than that, it is a peninsula made up of peninsulas. One is reminded of the old riddle: "A duck in front of a duck, a duck behind a duck, a duck, a duck, a duck! How many ducks?" Thus Europe is a peninsula, a peninsula, a peninsula! The Mediterranean and the other seas help to make it that on the south side; on the north side other seas play a like part. The largest of these is the **North Sea**, or *Noord Zee* (nōōrd zē'), as the Dutch call it, to distinguish it from their little **Zuider Zee** (zī'dĕr zē') or 'south sea,' which lies just south of the North Sea. Branching off from the North Sea we note the big **Baltic** (bôl'tĭk) **Sea,** so called because of the white rock cliffs on islands in it, for the Lithuanian word *baltas* means 'white.' The **White Sea** of Russia—the name is a translation of

ōld; ôrb; ŏdd; ūse; ûrn; ŭp; fōōd; fŏŏt; out; oil

the Russian words *Biel Osero,* having the same meaning—
is, however, so called because in winter it freezes over and
becomes covered with a sheet of glistening, white snow.

We have made so much fuss about the peninsulas of
Europe that it would hardly do to pass these by altogether
in this chapter. So we will consider a few of them here
and reserve the rest for chapters to come. The most
prominent of all the peninsulas is that known as the
**Iberian** (ī-bē'rĭ-ăn) **Peninsula.** Its name is from a
Basque word *ibarra,* meaning 'stream valley'; the stream
valley referred to is that of the **Ebro** (ē'brō) **River,** and
that name is simply another form of *ibarra.* At the south
tip of the Iberian Peninsula we note the great rock of
**Gibraltar** (jĭ-brôl'tēr). This has an Arabic name *Gibel-
al-Tarik* = 'the mountain of Tarik.' Tarik was a one-
eyed Berber chief who captured the rock in 711 and thus
founded the Moorish power in Spain. The other peninsula we will take up here, the **Balkan** (bôl'kăn) **Peninsula,** has a Turkish name meaning 'wooded heights.'
An old Turkish word *balak* means simply 'high' or 'big.'
Perhaps, assuming that all mountains are wooded, *balkan*
means simply 'mountains,' hence the **Balkan Mountains.**
But the Balkan Mountains are not very high mountains
compared with the **Alps** (ălps) in Europe. When we
mention that the ancients quarreled about the origin of
this word *Alps,* it will not be found surprising that no
one is sure to-day as to how it first started. The Romans
thought the name was related to their word *albus* =
'white,' on account of the snow on the Alps. But perhaps it really always was *alp* = 'a mountain,' or, as the
Swiss say now, *alb.* In the form *alb,* the high, shelf-like

āle; câre; ăm; ärm; ēve; ĕnd; makēr; īce; ĭll

pastures found in the Alps are meant. Geography texts quite generally include a picture of one of these *alb*-pastures.

The Alps are high mountains, but the **Caucasus** (kô′kă-sŭs) **Mountains** are higher. Originally, their name was *Graucasus,* a combination of the old Russian word *grau* = 'rock' and *casus* = 'white,' and, as in the case of the Alps, they were so called on account of the snow cover. Perhaps the reader will recall another word through which *casus* = 'white' has been made quite familiar. While we are so far east we may as well consider the **Ural** (ū′răl) **Mountains.** By contrast with the Caucasus and the Alps, these are the lowest of the European mountains, but they are as much of a separating line as there is between "peninsular Europe" and the truly continental land mass of Asia. Hence their Turkish name *ural* = 'a belt' or 'girdle' is quite appropriate for these boundary mountains. If, however, one thinks of the map of Europe and Asia as a person wearing a belt, the waist line made by the Urals reveals a rather ungainly figure.

Two other mountain ranges in Europe have names of the same meaning but of different form, because the names are from different·languages. The **Carpathians** (kär-pā′thĭ-ănz) derive their name from the Slavonic word *chrb* = 'a ridge'; the **Pyrenees** (pĭr′ĭ-nēz), from the Celtic word *byren* which also means 'ridge.' The **Vosges** (vōzh) **Mountains** have an odd name, but one so old that all record of its origin, both as to language and as to meaning, seems to have been lost.

Two rivers of Europe are sufficiently great and sufficiently international that they need to be considered here

ōld; ôrb; ŏdd; ūse; ûrn; ŭp; fo͞od; fo͝ot; out; oil

rather than under any country. The **Rhine** (rīn) was anciently *Renos,* and this form was built up from a Celtic root word, or syllable, *ri* = 'to flow.' The name of the **Danube** (dăn'yūb) is similarly derived from a Celtic root form *dan* = 'strong.' Thus the Danube must have impressed the early barbaric peoples of Europe as a 'strong' or 'swift' stream.

Now we will consider the names of the countries in Europe.

We will find, in connection with these, and also later as we take up the place names in each country separately, that we have here a much greater variety of origins in names than we had in North America, or even in South America. In the New World there were, to be sure, people of a number of European nationalities, besides the Indians, all furnishing names. But the result, even so, was not very complicated. A name may be English, French, or Spanish, but is usually simple to translate or understand, if those languages are known. Our Indian names have more of the nature of the European names. We have adopted some of the Indian names without change, but more often we have modified them to suit our habits of pronunciation, or made them shorter so that we would not need to waste too much time on them. Now, suppose people with some language other than English took possession of our country and added their ideas of how these Indian names ought to be spelled and pronounced—what resemblance to the original Indian words would be left? Exactly that has happened again and again in most places and place names of Europe. Hence many of the names are difficult to unravel, and when

āle; câre; ăm; ärm; ēve; ĕnd; makēr; īce; ĭll

traced back, often show the effects of a series of language shifts.

Consider **Great Britain** (brĭt'ăn). It has the prefix Great to make it distinct from Brittany, in France, which once had exactly the same form. The first part of Britain may be the Celtic word *bro* = 'region,' whereas the last part is perhaps the Basque word *etan,* meaning 'those who are in.' Accordingly, the combination would refer to the 'people who are in that region,' that is, in the British Isles. We have this Basque word *etan* also in Aquitania and Mauretania, names now of ships, but used first as Basque place names. Another explanation derives Britain from the Irish word *Cruithneck,* which meant 'the painted or tattooed men,' for the ancient Britons painted their bodies as did our North American Indians. The Irish *c* changes to a *p* in the Welsh language, and there are other similar letter changes, which together mold the Irish *Cruithneck* gradually to *Pretanicos,* from which the form Britain is readily enough derived.

The new **Irish** (ī'rĭsh) **Free State** was originally *Erin,* which meant 'the west-lying.' When the Romans came, they immediately made *Hibernia* out of *Erin,* for *Hibernia* in Latin meant 'winterland,' and Ireland was to the Romans cold enough to deserve such a title. Perhaps the form Ireland was had through the Celtic *iar* = 'back of' or 'behind,' hence, like *Erin,* = 'to the west.'

**France** (frăns) is easier. It was named after a confederation of Teutonic tribes who called themselves *Franken,* that is, 'freemen.' **Germany** (jûr'mă-nĭ) was the Roman *Germania,* or 'land of the Germani tribes.' *Germani* may have meant 'hill men,' or may be derived

ōld; ôrb; ŏdd; ūse; ûrn; ŭp; fo͞od; fŏŏt; out; oil

from the word *ger* = 'a spear,'. hence 'spear men.'  Still
another explanation connects the tribal name with *germe*
= 'thick woods,' hence 'woodland people.'  **Switzerland**
(swĭt'zēr-lănd) is named for the small region called the
*Schwyz,* about which the Swiss Republic was built up.
*Schwyz* may be from the Old High German word *suedan*
= 'to burn' and, if so, indicated a place where a forest
fire had destroyed the woods.  Another guess, among
many, is that *Schwyz* is the German *schweiz* = 'sweat,'
and that this name was fitting because of the numerous
springs which appear at the base of the steep slopes of
the mountains.

The **Netherlands** (nĕth'ēr-lăndz) are the 'low lands'
or 'Low Countries'; the form is the English of the Dutch
*Neerlands.*  The Low Countries formerly included both
Belgium and Holland.  Now the term Netherlands applies
only to Holland.  **Belgium** (bĕl'jŭm) is named for the
Gallic tribe of the *Belgæ,* meaning, perhaps, 'the fighters.'
Since the World War that name certainly fits.  Another
explanation derives Belgium from the Celtic *bol* =
'swamp' and *gai* = 'forest,' hence 'swampy forest.'  That
would make Belgium similar to **Holland** (hŏl'ănd), which
was at first *Holtland,* that is, 'woodland.'  **Denmark**
(dĕn'märk) is sometimes considered with the Low Countries, but is more commonly reckoned a Scandinavian
country.  There is an old Saxon word *marca* = 'district'
and an old Norse word *mork* = 'forest.'  Denmark,
accordingly, is the 'forested district of the Danes.'

If Denmark be excepted, then **Scandinavia** (skăn-dĭ-
nā'vĭ-ă) consists of the great peninsula between the Baltic
and the North Seas.  The word Scandinavia is had, prob-

āle; câre; ăm; ärm; ēve; ĕnd; makēr; īce; ĭll

ably, from the Teutonic *skadino* = 'dark,' hence 'the land of darkness'; and the northern part of the peninsula does have six months of very short days. On the peninsula are two countries, Norway and Sweden. **Norway** (nôr'wā) is from the Anglo-Saxon *Norweg,* that is, 'northern way,' and this meant the north route over which the Vikings came to ravage the English coast. **Sweden** (swē'dĕn) in Swedish is *Sverge,* as you see it spelled on postage stamps. *Sverge* is probably compacted from an original *Zwerijke* = 'two realms,' for Sweden was made up of what had been two separate countries, one in the north, the other in the south.

**Russia** (rŭsh'ă) was originally *Routsi* = 'the rowers.' By this name the Finns called the Viking oarsmen and warriors who came over to help a besieged Russian city and who, after driving off the attackers, turned around and made themselves the city's masters. Since the World War a number of small countries have been newly established or reëstablished along the western border of Russia. One of these, **Ukraine** (ū-krān'), not altogether independent of Russia, has the very appropriate Polish word *ukraina,* that is, 'border' or 'frontier,' for a name. Another, **Lithuania** (lĭth-ōō-ā'nĭ-ă), has its name from *lytus* = 'rain,' hence 'land of rain'; **Latvia** (lăt'-vĭ-ă) is possibly a name derived from *Livonia,* and that term goes back to *liiw* = 'sand.' Its capital city, **Riga** (rē'gă), has a name which was first *Rialin* and meant the *lin* = 'fortress' of the Rugii. **Esthonia** (ĕs-thōn'yă) is 'the land of the people of the East'; its capital, **Reval** (rā'văl), spelled also Revel, gets its name from the Swedish word *rafvel* = 'sandbank.' The Esthonians now

ōld; ôrb; ŏdd; ūse; ûrn; ŭp; fōōd; fŏŏt; out; oil

desire the city to be called **Tallinn** (tăl'ĭn), derived from the ancient Esthonian *Tani Linn* = 'town of the Danes.' **Finland** (fĭn'lănd) is a translation of *suoma laiset,* or 'swamp men,' as the Finns called themselves. This was first translated into Gothic, when *suoma* became *fani,* and then into English, when *fani* became *fen.* *Fen* still means swamp in English, and from *Fenland* to *Finnland* was an easy transition. **Helsingsfors** (hĕl'sĭng-fôrs), the capital of Finland, was the *fors,* or 'waterfall' of the *Helsings,* a Swedish tribe. **Ladoga** (lă-dō'gă), the largest fresh water lake in Europe, is found in Finland; it is shallow, hence its name from *laddo* = 'marsh' and *ga* = 'water.'

Another new-old country is **Poland** (pō'lănd). Its name is the English way of saying *Polska,* 'the country of the plain,' from the Slavic word *pole* = 'a plain.' Poland now possesses most of the basin of the **Vistula** (vĭs'-tū-lă) **River,** which has its name from the Polish word *wisla* = 'hanging water' or 'waterfall,' and the river does have a very great waterfall near its source in the mountains. At the mouth of the Vistula is the **Free City of Danzig** (dăn'zĭg), with a name derived from an original form *Godanske* = 'town of the Goths.'

**Spain** (spān) is the rabbit country, for its name is the Phœnician word *shaphan* = 'rabbit.' In ancient times there were so many rabbits in Spain that people could not grow crops as fast as rabbits ate them up. **Portugal** (pôrt'ū-găl) is a relic of the Roman name for the harbor of Oporto, *Portus Cale,* that is, the 'entrance' or 'harbor' of Cale. **Oporto** (ō-pôrt'ō) itself is simply the Portuguese way of saying 'the port,' since their ō corresponds

āle; câre; ăm; ärm; ēve; ĕnd; makẽr; īce; ĭll

to our *the*.  **Italy** (ĭt'ă-lĭ) is from the Greek *italos* = 'ox'
and was apparently derived from the numerous cattle
which roamed the peninsula in ancient times.  River,
translated into Italian, is *fiume,* hence **Fiume** (fē-
ōō'mā).  **Austria** (ôs'trĭ-ă) was originally *Ostar-
rike* = 'the eastern realm' of the Franks, the modern
German form of which is *Oesterreich;* whereas **Hungary** (hŭn'gă-rĭ) was *Hungarvaria* = 'the land of the
Huns.'  **Czechoslovakia**  (chĕk'ō-slō-văk'ĭ-ă)  means
'the land of the first Slavs,' from the word *czech* = 'be-
ginners.'  The idea is that these were the first Slavs to
settle on Teutonic lands.  **Jugoslavia** (yū'gō-slä'vĭ-ă)
means 'the Southern Slavs,' or perhaps 'river Slavs,' from
the Finnic word *jogi* = 'river,' or perhaps the 'yoked
Slavs,' from the Latin *jugum* = 'yoke.'  **Albania** (ăl-bā'-
nĭ-ă) may have its name from the Latin *albus* = 'white'
on account of the snow cover on its mountains.

**Greece** (grēs) seems to have obtained its name from
a root word *gar,* which meant 'the ancient ones' or 'the
honorable ones.'  At any rate the ancient Greeks are the
"honorable ones" of our civilization.  **Bulgaria** (bŭl-gā'-
rĭ-ă) has a Turkish name, originally *bulga-mak* = 'to re-
volt,' hence 'the rebels.'  **Turkey** (tûr'kē) itself is from
*Turkur* = 'a robber,' and that is the part the Turks
played in Europe.  Turkey still has left of its former
large possessions in Europe the great city of **Constantinople** (kŏn-stăn-tĭ-no'p'l), that is, the 'City of Constantine,' named for Constantine the Great, the first Christian Emperor of Rome, who established his capital there
in 330 A.D.  The Turks, who are Mohammedans, prefer
the name **Istambul** (ĭs'tăm-bōōl), which is a corruption

ōld; ôrb; ŏdd; ūse; ûrn; ŭp; fōōd; fŏŏt; out; oil

of *islam* = 'true believing,' and *bul* = 'copious,' hence 'abounding in the true faith'—that is, the Moslem religion. The Rumanians of **Rumania** (rōō-mä′nĭ-ă), also spelled earlier, Roumania, and, very modernly, Romania, were originally colonists from Rome and were proud of their ancestry, hence called themselves *Romani* or 'Romans.' They speak a language which is similar to the old Latin of the Romans.

Finally, to make the round of European countries complete, we need to mention **Luxemburg** (lŭks′ĕm-bûrg), from *Lutzelburg,* or 'little castle'; **Monaco** (mŏn′ă-kō), from the Greek word *monœcus* = 'settlers'; and **Liechtenstein** (lĭk′tĕn-stīn), or 'the shining stone'; These are all little countries tucked away between much larger ones in Europe. **Andorra** (än-dōr′rä) and **San Marino** (mă-rē′nō) are two independent republics which are so small that it is difficult to find them on a general map of Europe. Of the origin of the name Andorra nothing seems to be known, but San Marino is said to have been founded early in the fourth century A.D. by St. Marinus, a Christian stone-mason who escaped from Rome during the persecutions of the Emperor Diocletian.

āle; câre; ăm; ärm; ēve; ĕnd; makẽr; īce; ĭll

# CHAPTER XVI

**Scotland** (skŏt'lănd), as was noted in considering Nova Scotia, is derived from the Celtic *scuit,* meaning 'wanderers,' perhaps 'fugitives,' perhaps 'nomadic shepherds.' It was noted, too, that *Wales* (wālz) is from the Anglo-Saxon *wealas* = 'foreigners.' Possibly Wales has an even more ancient derivation from the Sanskrit word *mlechha* = 'one who talks indistinctly.' The Welsh would, of course, consider that an insult. **Ireland** (īr'-lănd) is now in part the Irish Free State, and hence was taken up as one of the separate countries of Europe. There remains to be considered, accordingly, only **England** (ĭn'glănd) of the chief subdivisions of the British Isles.

England is a corruption of the earlier form *Englaland,* that is, 'the land of the Angles,' who invaded Britain in the middle of the fifth century A.D. and, with the Saxons and Jutes, conquered the island after a century and a half of warfare. The Angles dwelt originally in the region of the south part of Denmark, and their tribal name is formed from the word *angar* = 'a pasture'; hence the Angles may be thought of as 'natives of the meadow lands.' Besides the British Isles and Gibraltar, Great Britain also holds in Europe the islands of **Malta** (môl'-tă) and **Cyprus** (sī'prŭs) in the Mediterranean. Malta is a corruption of the Phœnician word *melita* = 'the refuge,' and was so called because the island has excellent harbors. Cyprus is also a Phœnician word meaning 'island of the tree or herb.'

The **Strait of Dover** (dō′vẽr) is the branch of the sea that separates Great Britain from the continent of Europe. Hence it is quite proper that Dover is the direct descendant of the Celtic word *dubr* = 'water,' for it is a water separation. Two bays very nearly pinch off part of Scotland from the rest of Great Britain. Both of these bays are called **firths** (fûrths), a Middle-English word that was used in the same sense as our word estuary. The **Firth of Clyde** (klīd), on the west side, into which the River Clyde empties, has its name from the Welsh word *clywd* = 'warm,' hence, probably, 'the bay of the warm river.' Perhaps, however, it was only the Celtic *cluyd* = 'water.' The **Firth of Forth** (fôrth) name has a more complicated history. The **Forth** is also a 'river,' and the name is derived from an old Gaelic word *fortail* = 'strong.' The general sense of the term, then, seems to be that a strong current sets into the *firth*.

Adjacent to the larger of the British Isles are smaller islands and island groups of some importance. Off the south coast of England the **Isle of Wight** (wīt) gets its name from the Welsh word *gwyth* = 'channel.' This term was used first for the strait between the smaller island and the British coast. But as the meaning of the word was forgotten, Wight came to be used as a name for the small island itself. The **Scilly** (sĭl′ĭ) **Islands** are quite small, but as you pronounce their name, you will surely want to know its meaning. The explanation, however, is disappointing, for Scilly means only 'cliff,' the original being the Irish word *sceilig* = 'a sea cliff.' North of Scotland are the **Shetland** (shĕt'lănd) **Islands,** which we think of in connection with Shetland ponies. The name, however, comes from the Old Norse word *hjalt* = 'the knob' or 'hilt of a sword'; indeed, our word *hilt* is the same word in its modern form. Later *hjalt* became *Hetland,* and the change from that to Shetland was easy. The "knobs" of Shetland are the great, round masses of rock that stick up all over the islands. The **Faroe** (fä'rō) **Islands,** still farther to the north, do not belong to Great Britain but are part of Denmark. Faroe, more correctly *Faroer,* is Norwegian for 'sheep islands.' Hence when we call them Faroe Islands we say 'sheep islands islands.'

The **Pennine** (pĕn'nīn) **Mountains** in Great Britain get their name from the Celtic word *pen* = 'mountain.' **Mt. Snowdon** (snō'dŭn) is the highest summit in England and Wales, and its name is made up of the Anglo-Saxon words *snaw* = 'snow' and *dun* = 'hill.' Snowdon does have snow on its top long after the rest of the winter's fall has melted away, but not so long as **Ben Nevis** (bĕn nē'vĭs) in Scotland, which is the highest peak in all the islands. Ben Nevis, moreover, has a very satisfactory name, one of the few splendid place names in the world. It is Gaelic, and in full was originally *Beinn-nimh-bhathais* = 'the mountain with the cold brow.'

Rivers on islands cannot well be large or long, but those of Great Britain are, nevertheless, among the most famous in the world. Most celebrated of the British rivers is the **Thames** (tĕms), which has a Celtic name,

ōld; ôrb; ŏdd; ūse; ûrn; ŭp; fōōd; fŏŏt; out; oil

originally *Tamese* = 'the tranquil river.' The **Humber**
(hŭm'bĕr) also harks back to the sea, its first syllable,
*hum,* being the old Norse word for 'the sea.' The name
was given on account of the dark color of the water, and
the Humber is more of an estuary than a river. So we
turn to the **Tyne** (tīn) to find a proper river, for Tyne
was formerly *Teign,* and before that *Tain,* and *tain* is the
ancient British word for 'stream.'

It is not improbable that the first discussion in the
English language concerning place names had **London**
(lŭn'dŭn) for its subject. In any event the matter has
been much argued since. All the trouble, however, has
to do with the syllable *lon.* Among many possibilities
two are especially favored. One of these is that the
original syllable was *llyn,* the Welsh word for 'pool';
the other that it was the name of the Celtic war god
*Llud.* The successive changes were from *Llud-dun* to
*Lud-dun,* then to *Lun-dun,* and finally to London. The
'dun,' as in other instances, is 'hill.' In the one case we
have, therefore, London, the 'hill above the pool'; in the
other the 'hill' or 'temple site' of 'Llud.'

As this is the most famous example of *dun,* it may be
added here that in the days when people spoke of hills
as 'duns,' they said *a-dun* when they meant going down
hill. But, by and by, *dun,* the word for hill, was forgotten, the while people were still using *a-dun.* Then
the *a* was omitted, and thus the original word for hill
now survives only as *down.* Not in other words, but
by the same word, what was up is now down. Many
other simple words in our language have histories just
as curious.

āle; câre; ăm; ärm; ēve; ĕnd; makĕr; īce; ĭll

**Greenwich** (grĕn'ĭtch), where the great astronomical observatory is located, is situated quite near London; its name means 'green bay.' **Bristol** (brĭs'tŏl) was originally *Bricgstow* = 'the place at the bridge.' **Southampton** (south-ămp'tŭn) was the Anglo-Saxon *Suth Heantune,* that is, the 'south, high enclosure.' **Portsmouth** (pôrts'-mŭth) explains itself; cities in New Hampshire and Virginia are named after it. **Lands End** also explains itself, as you will see by looking at the map. **Yarmouth** (yär'mŭth) gets the first part of its name from the Celtic *garw,* meaning 'rough' or 'mighty,' and this term referred to the river now called Yare. **Liverpool** (lĭv'ĕr-pōōl), like London, is in difficulties on account of its first syllable. Perhaps the most interesting explanations are that the original word was the Welsh term *llathr,* meaning 'smooth gleaming pool,' that is, 'swampy pool,' or the Welsh *llyr-pwl* = 'the sea pool.' **Holyhead** (hŏl'ĭ-hĕd) was the Welsh *Pen Caer Gybi* = 'the hill of the fort of St. Cybi,' a name which, as people became tired of saying all of it, was eventually shortened to 'holy,' for the saint; and 'head,' for the hill. **Hull** (hŭl) is the name of a small stream on which the city is located. **Grimsby** (grĭmz'bĭ) was originally 'Grim's house,' because the end syllable *by* in the Scandinavian means 'house.' **Newcastle** (nū'kăs'l) marks the site of a "new castle" built in 1080 A.D. to replace one destroyed by William the Conqueror. All these are important seaport or harbor sites of England, and from their number one gets an idea of the importance of the sea to English commerce.

Newcastle is one of the great centers, also, of the coal

ōld; ôrb; ŏdd; ūse; ûrn; ŭp; fōōd; fŏŏt; out; oil

industry of England, as is **Cardiff** (kär′dĭf) in Wales. The name Cardiff, like Newcastle, refers to a strong place, for it is made up of the Welsh word *caer* = 'fortress' and a contraction of Didius, the name of the Roman who built this fortress. From these and from other coalfield regions fuel is supplied to the industrial cities of England. **Birmingham** (bēr′mĭng-h′m), which has a namesake in Alabama, was, presumably, once the *ham*, or 'home,' of the 'Boerings.' **Sheffield** (shĕf′fēld) started as *Scafeld*, and this name referred to the 'field' at the River *Shaef*. **Leicester** (lĕs′tēr) was the Anglo-Saxon *Ligora-ceaster* = 'town on the river Ligera.' *Ligora* itself was named for a Celtic water god, *Llyr*, and Shakespeare's play *King Lear* preserves the name of this god in another form. Notice how careless these ancient peoples were about using the double *l*, difficult to pronounce. They must have liked to twist their tongues. **Leeds** (lēds) reminds us of the *Loidis*, a kingdom and people who tried to keep the Angles out of Britain. **Oxford** (ŏks′fôrd) was the Anglo-Saxon *Oxnaford*, or 'ford of the oxen.' Another place in Europe with a name of the same meaning, but in a different language was noted on a preceding page.

The large cities of Scotland are all harbor sites. **Glasgow** (glăs′gō) in 1301 was *Glas-gu*. Now this may have been made up of the British words *glas* = 'cold' or 'grey' and *gu* = 'woods'; hence 'grey woods.' But another and pleasing explanation is that hereabouts there dwelt long ago, an old monk, St. Mungo. Mungo was so well liked that people called him affectionately *munchu* = 'dear dog.' Then, not satisfied with that pet name, a

āle; câre; ăm; ärm; ēve; ĕnd; makēr; īce; ĭll

pun on his real name, they changed it to *Glaschu,* that is, 'grey dog,' on account of his white hair. Both these explanations may be wrong, but they have the merit of being entertaining. **Edinburgh** (ĕd′ĭn-bŭ-rō) was *Edwin's burg,* or 'fortress,' named after Edwin, an Anglo-Saxon king of Northumberland who occasionally made it his residence. **Leith** (lēth), the port of Edinburgh, was originally *Inverleith* = 'place at the mouth of the Leith,' and Leith was the British word *llith,* meaning 'flood.' The Celtic form of *inver* was *aber;* hence **Aberdeen** (ă-bĕr-dēn′) means 'at the mouth of the **Dee** and **Don** rivers,' where *don* was simply 'water' and *dee* seems to have meant 'divine stream.'

**Belfast** (bĕl′făst) is the large city in the north of Ireland; its name in Irish was *Bel-feirsde,* which, however, translates very prosaically to 'ford of the sand bank.' **Dublin** (dŭb′lĭn), on the east coast, the other large Irish city, was anciently *Duibh-linn,* that is, the 'black pool,' *dub,* or *duv,* being the Celtic for 'black.' The dark color of the river water at Dublin is responsible for the name. **Londonderry** (lŭn′dŭn-dĕr-ĭ) is the *daire* or 'oakwood' of London, because King James I gave the place, originally called Derry, to London merchants because of the resistance of the inhabitants to English rule. **Queenstown,** an important port of call for steamships, was so named in honor of the visit of Queen Victoria to the place in 1849.

ōld; ôrb; ŏdd; ūse; ûrn; ŭp; fōōd; fŏŏt; out; oil

# CHAPTER XVII

We now cross over the English Channel to consider how the French have identified the features and the places in their country.

We have several times mentioned the Basques. They are a people who live in the mountainous country on the south border of France. The Basque word for 'man' is *vasok.* The Romans modified this word to *Vascones* for use in their Latin language. In consequence of this change in the Latin, we now have **Gascon** (găs′kŏn) and **Gascony** as the names of a group of people and a region of southern France. The Spanish had a different idea about how *vasok* should be changed for their purposes; they made it *Viscaya* = 'the land of the Basques' or *Vasoks* or *Gascons.* And from *Viscaya* we have **Bay of Biscay** (bĭs′kā), which is the name we have been aiming at, really, in all this paragraph.

The explanation of **Mt. Blanc** (blŏnk) need not be so roundabout as that of Biscay, for the *blanc* is French for 'white,' and refers of course to the mountain's snow cover. The **Ardennes** (är-dĕn′) **Mountains** get their name from the Celtic word *ard,* which meant 'hilly,' or 'high.' This leads us to infer that the Forest of Arden, known to most readers for its connection with the charm-

 āle; câre; ăm; ärm; ēve; ĕnd; makēr; īce; ĭll
164

ing Rosalind in Shakespeare's *As You Like It,* but really
of much importance historically as the playground of
kings, is also hilly and high.    In the south-central part
of France we find the **Auvergne** (ō-vûrn′) **Mountains,**
named for a Celtic people, the *Arverni,* a title which also
is thought to mean 'highlanders.'    The edge of the Auvergne region is called the **Cévennes** (sā-vĕn′); from
another Celtic word, *cefn* = 'a ridge.'    There is a delightful book which tells of the quaint people and life
of this region.    It is by Robert Louis Stevenson, and
its title is *Travels with a Donkey.*

Many French streams have Celtic names.    The **Seine**
(sān) and the **Saone** (sōn) are named from Celtic words
similar in form, which also have like meanings.    The first
is derived from *seimh-an,* and means the 'soft,' or 'smooth
river'; the second comes from *soghan,* the 'quiet river.'
On the other hand, the **Garonne** (gă-rōn′) is from *gar-
van,* the 'swift river,' and the **Rhone** (rōn), which was
the *Rhodan,* is the 'violent stream.'    Note the consistent
use of the syllable *an* in the Celtic, and how this, which
was like *river* with us, has been incorporated in the
proper name later.    One other large French stream, the
**Loire** (lwär), takes its name from that of a Celtic tribe,
the *Ligures,* a word which is thought in its earliest form
to signify 'water.'

France is divided into a number of provinces or districts.    We should know about the names of two of these
at least.    **Brittany** (brĭ′tăn-ĭ) is a form of Britain, and
since the fifth century the district has been so called because British tribes fled there from the Saxon invaders
of England.    The name **Brest** (brĕst) of the chief city

ōld; ôrb; ŏdd; ūse; ûrn; ŭp; fo͞od; fo͝ot; out; oil

of this region is still another modification of Britain. **Alsace** (ăl-zăs'), however, is more complicated. The word conveys the idea that Alsace is the 'land of those who settled on the other shore.' The origin of the term may be the German *sassan* = 'strangers,' and the Germans did call the region *Elsass;* or the first form may be *alisazo,* that is, 'the other seat of the Allemanni.' In both cases the "other" part refers to the far shore of the Rhine.

At least half a dozen French cities have names that recall the tribes which, like the Indians in North America, once dwelt in France in barbarism. Included among these tribal names is that of the largest city, **Paris** (păr'ĭs). The tribal name was *Parisii* and denoted 'the strong ones.' **Amiens** (ăm'yän) recalls the *Ambiani,* 'the wealthy' or 'the numerous people,' or, perhaps, 'the people dwelling on the water'; we are not sure which. **Rheims** (răns) is from *Remi*; they were a proud lot, for they called themselves 'princes' or 'rulers.' **Limoges** (lē-mōj') was the territory of the *Limovices,* that is, 'those who dwelt among elms.' **Nantes** (nänt) is where the *Nametes* (as Cæsar called them) lived; they, like the *Parisii,* asserted that they were 'strong ones.' **Tours** (tōōr) is so called after the *Turones,* but it does not seem to be known what the Turones asserted to be their fine quality. These French names, and many others, since the World War have been commonly pronounced in America as the English spellings would indicate. But it is quite probable that the French pronunciations will be preferred again in the future; indeed that is true now.

Then there are a number of places not directly named

āle; câre; ăm; ärm; ēve; ĕnd; makēr; īce; ĭll

for tribes, which are, however, marked by Celtic words. Of these, the name of **Boulogne** (boō-lōn´) is perhaps most fundamental, for it is derived from an earlier form *Bolonia,* and this comes directly from the Celtic *bona* = 'a town.' **Bologna** (bō-lō´nyă), in Italy, and **Bonn** in Germany, also follow this form. **Namur** (nă-mûr´) was once *Namuco* = 'the sacred grove'; **Calais** (kă-lā´) was *Caletes* = 'the men of the inlet,' that is, of the inlet of the Seine. **Rouen** (rwän) was *Rotomag* = 'the crossing place,' perhaps 'the cross roads'; and **Toulouse** (tōō-lōōz´) is the form that the Celtic *tulach* = 'a small hill' now has. **Dieppe** (dē-ĕp´) is Scandinavian; it comes either from the word *diep* = 'the deep' or from *diupa* = 'water.'

The Celtic tribes were overcome by the Romans, who then dominated France.. **Verdun** (vâr-dŭn´) is a name that gives us a record of the time of transition. Verdun was originally *Virodunum,* and thus combined the Latin *vir* = 'man' and *dunum,* a Celtic word meaning 'hill fortress.' Brave men they were, too, who held this hill fortress in the World War. **Metz** (mĕts) may also be classed as a transition name. Originally, Metz was called *Mediomatrici,* in which *medio* meant 'central place of' and *matrici,* ' javelin throwers.' The javelin throwers were forgotten later on, the while *medio* became *mettis,* and, finally, Metz.

**Marseille** (mär-sâ´ē) in Roman days was *Massilia,* a word which is thought to be of Greek origin and to mean 'where the breasts join.' **Bordeaux** (bôr-dō´) has a very humble name; it is derived from the Low Latin word *bordigala* = 'a fish tank.' A small stream there formed

ōld; ôrb; ŏdd; ūse; ûrn; ŭp; fōōd; fŏŏt; out; oil

a tidal pool in which fish congregated, hence comes the name.

**Lyon** (lē-ôn') has a short name, but one with a curious history. It is a survival of *Lugudunum,* and this longer form was thought to be comprised of the Celtic *lugon* = 'a raven' and *dunum* = 'a hill fortress.' It was related that at the founding of Lyon ravens came and filled all the trees about. More recently, however, it has been determined that the name really refers to 'the hill fortress' of the Celtic sun god *Lugus.* **Cherbourg** (shĕr'bûrg) is easier; it was *Cæsaris-burgus,* that is, 'Cæsar's castle.' So also is **Sèvres** (sâ'vr') easy, if derived from the Latin *silva* = 'woods'; but it may be had from an older name, *Savara,* applied to a stream and meaning 'the boundary river,' because it divided two tribes. **Nice** (nēs) was anciently the Greek Nicæa = 'the city of victory.'

The French language developed from the Latin, which the Romans introduced into the country, and by and by the French also found opportunity to name a place or two. Thus **Havre** (äv'r') is French for 'harbor,' but it is a word which goes back to the Low Latin *habulum* having the same meaning. **Lille** (lēl) was originally *L'île,* that is, 'the island,' from the Latin *insula.* Its first buildings were erected between two brooks which, when in flood, made the region of Lille look like one of many islands. **Dunkirk** (dŭn'kĕrk) in the French form *Dunkerque* is the 'church among the dunes'; and **Belfort** (bĕl'fôrt) is the French way of saying 'pretty fort.'

Of course, in a French country there must be at least a few places with saints' names, so we mention **St. Nazaire** (nă-zâr') and **St. Etienne** (ā-tyĕn').

āle; câre; ăm; ärm; ēve; ĕnd; makĕr; īce; ĭll

Finally, there are two places with names that are important, not of themselves, that is, as to origin or meaning, but because their names now have a world-wide recognition for another reason. **Cambrai** (kăm-brā′) has given a name to cambric, and **Tulle** (tōōl), without any change in form, to the fabric known as *tulle*. It is interesting to note that French cities especially are famous for particular products.

# CHAPTER XVIII

THE German people were misled and perverted by the Prussians, and the catastrophe of the World War was the result. **Prussia** (prŭsh'ă) is a district of north Germany, and the people who lived there were originally called *Pruzzi*. The name *Pruzzi* may have been derived from the Polish word *protza* = 'a sling,' as this was the weapon that the *Pruzzi* used in preference to bow and arrows. If the Prussians knew that derivation, it may have helped to give them the idea that they were so wonderful in a military way. On the other hand, the world hopes now that they will see the point to another explanation of the origin of their name. According to this Prussia comes from a word in the Prussian language itself, *pruta,* which means 'come to one's senses again.'

If derivations of names count, the people of **Saxony** (săks'ōn-ĭ), as well as the Prussians, may be held in part responsible for the German outbreak. The *Saxones* formerly lived farther to the north than where the present state of Saxony is located, and they were known by their weapon, a *sahs,* that is, a 'short sword.' The Romans called this weapon *saxum,* which suggests that the blade was made of stone; the modern Saxon and Saxony are forms that have resulted from the gradual change of the Latin word.

**Bavaria** (bă-vā'rĭ-ă), too, is said by some to have a name leading directly to bloodshed. According to this explanation the term is based on the Celtic *bagh* = 'battle' and the ending *ire,* denoting 'those who engage in battle,' hence 'warriors.' It is, however, only fair to add that his explanation is discredited, and that the Bavarians of the province of Bavaria are now considered to be only 'men from Bohemia,' that is *Bauivarii.* Still, the earliest name of this tribe, when it lived in Italy, whence the tribe was driven by the Romans, was *Boii* = 'the terrible ones.'

The **Black Forest,** or **Schwarzwald** (schvôrtz'vôlt) in German, is the one mountain region in Germany deserving mention; it gets its name from the dark pine woods that cover all its slopes.

River names in Germany, though of different forms, have nearly all of them the simple significance of "stream" or "water." Thus the **Elbe** (ĕl'bē) is from the Anglo-Saxon term *alf,* or *elf,* = 'river'; and the **Oder** (ō'd'r) has a name probably based on the Sanskrit root *udra* = 'water,' in the form *odora* = 'a flow.' Two smaller German streams have more interesting names. The **Weser** (vā's'r) was once the *Wisaraha;* this changed to *Wisara,* and then to the present form. As *Wisaraha* the name was made up of *wis* = 'west' (or possibly *visuri* = 'rich in meadows') and *aha* = 'water.' The **Isar** (ī'sär) combines *is* = 'ice' and *ar* = 'flowing,' hence is the 'ice-flowing,' or 'ice-cold stream,' which perhaps meant that it was a glacial stream.

As in the case of London, a great variety of explanations of **Berlin** (bĕr-lĭn') have been suggested. The two

ōld; ôrb; ŏdd; ūse; ûrn; ŭp; fo͞od; fo͝ot; out; oil

most fitting are that the name is had from a Wendish tribal word *berle* = 'uncultivated ground,' or from a Slavic word *brljina* = 'a pool.' Both conform to early conditions around Berlin, for the city is built in what was once a swampy tract of land. Near Berlin is **Magdeburg** (măg′dē-bûrg), or the 'Maiden's town.' The "Maiden" in the case seems to have been a heathen idol, the statue of a beautiful girl with golden hair holding a rose between her lips. This statue was hauled about in a golden wagon and represented the goddess of love.

Before the World War Germany had very large shipping interests and an important group of cities developed on the basis of these. Of such **Hamburg** (hăm′bûrg) and **Bremen** (brăm′ĕn) were the leaders. Hamburg was anciently *Hammaburg,* that is, 'forest fortress.' *Hamma* meant 'extensive woods' then, but still earlier it had the meaning 'hemmed in,' and we have our word *hem* from this term. Curiously enough, the term *bram,* from which Bremen is derived, also gave us an English word, *brim.* The reason for this is apparent when we learn that the original significance of *bram* was 'wave,' 'flood,' or 'the sea.' **Stettin** (stĕt-tēn′), another seaport, combines 'to flow,' with *ing,* thus *steting* = 'a place where water flows together.' **Lubeck** (lōō′bĕk) is named for the Slavic prince *Liuby,* who founded the place. The **Kiel** (kēl) **Canal** has a Dutch name, *kiel* meaning 'bay.'

The coal and iron industry of Germany centers about the Saar and Ruhr districts adjacent to the Rhine. **Saar** (sär) is from a Sanskrit root *sru,* or *srava,* meaning 'to flow'; **Ruhr** (rûr) likewise has to do with water. Ruhr, however, is Celtic; its original form was *Rubro-gilum,*

āle; câre; ăm; ärm; ēve; ĕnd; makēr; īce; ĭll

which meant 'red brook.' The Ruhr stream, it seems, is formed by two brooks, one red because of swamp water, the other also red because of red sandstone sediment. In these districts are a number of city centers of which we note: **Köln** (kĕl'n) or **Cologne** (kō-lōn'), the latter the French form of the Roman *Colonia Agrippina,* so called because the Emperor Claudius founded a colony there in 51 A.D., which he named in honor of his wife. **Dusseldorf** (dŭs'sĕl-dôrf), the *dorf* or village on the *Düssel* stream; **Essen** (ĕs'ĕn), which was *Astenidum,* a term of which the meaning is lost; **Barmen** (bär'mĕn), perhaps from the Celtic word *bar =* 'an enclosure' (or *barr-meon =* 'little summit'), a term from which we get our English word *barrier.* **Elberfeld** (ĕl'bĕr-fĕld) is the *feld* or 'field' beside the Elber stream. **Aachen** (ä'kĕn) the French call **Aix la Chapelle** (ā lă chä-pĕl'). Aachen and Aix are both contractions of the Latin *ad aquas =* 'at the waters,' which were hot sulphur springs; *chapelle* is the 'church' founded there by the Emperor Charlemagne in 796.

Before the World War Germany had a population of nearly 70,000,000 people, and as the whole country was then scarcely larger than Texas, there had to be numerous large cities to contain them all. Hence, south of the iron and steel districts, we find **Frankfort** (frănk'fôrt) **on the Main** (mān) = 'the ford of the Franks,' where the great Emperor Charlemagne was shown a way across the river by a deer—so runs the story. **Strassburg** (strŏs'bûrg) was the *burg* or 'castle' on the *strass* = 'road' or 'street' which here crossed the Rhine and was a very important highway in Roman times. Farther

ōld; ôrb; ŏdd; ūse; ûrn; ŭp; fōōd; fŏŏt; out; oil

east is **Stuttgart** (stŭt'gärt), or the 'horse garden,' because the city grew up about a great pen in which many horses were kept. **Munich** (mū'nĭk) is a variation from the Latin *monachus* = 'a monk,' and was so called because monks at one time owned the land. **Augsburg** (ougs'bûrg), near Munich, was the 'castle' or 'fortress' of the Emperor, because the two, castle and city, usually grew together. Our English adjective *august* remains still the best term to express just what it was intended the Latin *augustus* should convey.

Going north again, we come to **Nuremburg** (nū'rĕmbûrg), which was perhaps formerly *Neronberg,* because the Roman Emperor Tiberius Nero was said to have founded the place on a *berg* or 'hill'; possibly, however, Nuremburg was named for the *Norici,* a tribe which settled there after having been dislodged from their old home by the Huns. Still farther north is **Chemnitz** (kĕm'nĭts), which gets its name from the German word *kamen* = 'a stone,' because the city is located on a cliff. **Leipzig** (līp'zĭg) is a German corruption of the Slavic word *lipsk* = 'linden wood.' **Halle** (hŏl'lē) is the Celtic word *hal* = 'salt'; Halle is a place where salt has been mined for hundreds of years. **Dresden** (drĕz'dĕn) is derived from *Drjezd janje,* a Wendish phrase meaning 'forest inhabitants.' Finally, there is **Breslau** (brĕs'lou), named after *Wrateslaw,* a king of Bohemia, who is said to have founded the city about the year 1000 A.D.

āle; câre; ăm; ärm; ēve; ĕnd; makẽr; īce; ĭll

# CHAPTER XIX

THE outstanding and "upstanding" feature of Switzerland is its mountains. To be sure, Swiss cities do not cling to steep mountain slopes; like other cities they are situated on level or gently sloping land. But the low land of the Swiss cities has on its south side the great mountain mass of the Alps, and on the north, the lower ridges of the **Jura** (jū′rǎ) **Mountains.** Because they are lower than the snow-clad Alps, the slopes of the Jura are all forest covered, hence their name is from the Celtic *joux* == 'forest.' Think back over the names of the many other mountain regions we have already considered; is it not surprising how very few of them have escaped being called forested, or black on account of dark forests, or white on account of snow, or just plain "ridge" or "mountain," in some language other than English? It would seem that when one called a mountain, a mountain; or white, on account of snow; or black, on account of forest; or forested; or high, the ancients had exhausted the names by which a mountain could be called.

It is true that they had little imagination, those barbaric tribes, but with hills and streams all about them, how did they escape needing to give names that would at least distinguish one hill from another? Perhaps it was because

ōld; ôrb; ŏdd; ūse; ûrn; ŭp; fōŏd; fŏŏt; out; oil

each tribe only knew about a few hills, and hence could say to one another "the hill over there." Perhaps it was because only the general names have been preserved, that is, like *joux,* 'forested,' for all the Jura, whereas the names of the smaller features have changed with succeeding kinds and generations of men.

That particular things were more specially named is evident in the names of the peaks of the Alps. Thus the **Matterhorn** (măt'tēr-hôrn) is the *horn* = 'peak' above the *matt,* or 'meadow,' and **Zermatt** (zûr'măt), the town at its base, is 'at the meadow.' The **Jungfrau** (yŭng'-frou), another peak, translates to 'the maiden,' because it is clothed with white snow and remotely resembles a maiden in form. Note, however, how difficult it was for the name-givers to think of anything more complicated than these simple ideas. In the case of the **Rigi** (rē'gē) they had another very elementary comparison in mind; it was to them *der rik* = the 'back' or the 'ridge,' that is, like the backbone of an animal.

**Mt. Cenis** (sē-nē'), in Italy, is a little different; its name seems to be the record of an historic event. When the Carthaginian general, Hannibal, and his armies marched across the Alps to attack the Romans in 218 B. C. they burned down the forest here; because of this the place was called *Mons Cinereus,* that is, 'mountain of ashes.' Notice, however, that *cinereus* was a Latin term, hence a name given by a people that had learned to live broader lives and to have more ideas than do barbaric tribes. It has been said that "the happiest man is he who can think the most exciting thoughts." As one learns exciting things about these old names, they do become much more

āle; câre; ăm; ärm; ēve; ĕnd; makēr; īce; ĭll

interesting. In the case of **Mt. Pilatus** (pǐ-lä'tǔs) the name is a key to a tale that is especially wild and weird. Everyone is acquainted with the history of Pontius Pilate and what he did, or rather, did not do. It is said that Pilate in after years committed suicide by drowning himself in a gloomy lake near the top of Mt. Pilatus. The people who live thereabouts now assert that Pilate's ghost appears on the mountain slopes, and they have a poem which, translated without rhymes, is as follows:

> When the thunder claps ring out,
> When the storm chorus howls,
> Then rises up from the flood
> The ghost of the coward.

Where there are high mountains, people are much interested in ways to cross them. Crossing the Alps is especially difficult; hence one low place is named **St. Bernard** (bêr-närd') **Pass** in grateful remembrance of the labor of a monk, St. Bernard of Menthon, who, about 960, established a hospice on the route and trained dogs to go in search of people who lost their way in the snowstorms which rage there. In recent years crossings have been cut through the mountains under the passes. One of these is the **St. Gothard** (gǒ-thär') **Tunnel,** named for *St. Godelhardus,* the monk who first built shelters in the pass of the same name. Through this, and the **Simplon** (sǐm'plǒn) and Mt. Cenis tunnels, trains are now able to pass. The Simplon was named after a village *Simplon,* but it is not known what the village name meant.

Many streams flow down the slopes of the Alps, and many lakes rest in their valleys. The name of the **Aar**

ōld; ôrb; ŏdd; ūse; ûrn; ŭp; fōod; fŏŏt; out; oil

(är) **River,** like so many of those we have been considering, is again one that means simply 'river.'  In slightly
different forms this also occurs as the **Aire** (är) of England, and the **Ohr** (ôr) and **Ahr** (är) of Germany.  It is
really wonderful how those old names have been kept in
so many slightly different forms.

Most of the Swiss lakes, however, seem to have received
more distinctive names.  **Lake Constance** (kŏn'stăns)
has a Roman personal name; it recalls Constantinus
Chlorus, father of the Emperor Constantine the Great,
who ruled over Gaul before he became Emperor in 305
A. D.  The others were evidently named by the Celtic
tribes before the advent of the Romans.  Thus **Geneva**
(jĕ-nē'vă), the lake and the city, get their title from the
word *genava,* meaning a 'mouth.'  This is similar to the
Welsh word *gen* = 'jaw.'  At Geneva an island divides
the outflowing current from the lake and gives a jaw-like
form to the mouth, the island being like a stuck-out
tongue.  **Genoa** (jĕn'ō-ă), in Italy, with a harbor shaped
like a jaw, gets its name from the same word; indeed, the
Italians call the city *Genova.*  **Limmat** (lĭm'măt) **River**
was formerly called *Lindinmagus,* and this word was
made up of the Celtic words *lejnn* = 'water' and *mac* =
'clean.'  It must be understood that there were many different bands of these Celts, and that, like the North
American Indians, the language of the different tribes
varied much.

Besides Geneva, two other important cities of Switzer-
land have Celtic names.  **Zurich** (zūr'ĭk) was anciently
*Duregum,* and this meant 'water town,' because of another
Celtic word for water, that is, *dur.*  **Bern** (bûrn) was

āle; câre; ăm; ärm; ēve; ĕnd; mākẽr; īce; ĭll

probably the Celtic *bryn* = a 'hill.' **Basel** (bäz'ĕl),
anciently *Basilia,* on the other hand, seems to be a name
of Greek origin and to mean 'Emperor's residence.' **Lu-
cerne** (loo-zûrn') may have been the Latin *lucerna* = a
'watch tower,' used for a lighthouse, erected there at an
early date to aid in navigating the lake of the same name.
**Vevey** (vē-vā'), in like fashion, may be a relic of the
Latin term *bivium* = 'a parting of the roads.' **Neuchatel**
(nū-shä-tĕl') is the French translation of an earlier form
*Neuenburg* = 'new castle.'

Having touched so many high spots in Switzerland, we
need to offset the climb by a visit to the Low Countries,
that is, the Netherlands. Here the rivers flow sluggishly,
swamps and muddy spots are common, and the names
show these conditions. Thus the **Meuse** (mûz) was in
earlier days the *Maas,* and this name goes back to *mos* =
'a swamp.' The **Moselle** (mọ̄-zĕl'), in France, is swampy
only in its upper course, but its name is the Latin way of
saying 'little Meuse.' The **Scheldt** (shĕlt) gets its name
from the Celtic *sgal* = 'to divide,' because it enters the
North Sea by two mouths. The city of **Antwerp** (ănt'-
wûrp), an important seaport in Belgium near the
mouth of the Scheldt, is *æn't werpen,* that is, 'at the
wharf.'

Part of Belgium is known as **Flanders** (flăn'dērz).
Being very low-lying, this region is pounded by the wind
and the waves, and hence may have its name from an old
word *flænderen* = 'to blow mightily.' **Brussels** (brŭs'-
ĕls), the capital city of Belgium, was once the *brouch* =
'marsh' and *seli* = 'house'; that is, the 'house in the
marsh,' according to one explanation of its name. **Liège**

ọ̄ld; ôrb; ŏdd; ūse; ûrn; ŭp; fo͞od; fo͝ot; out; oil

(lē-ĕzh′), once *Luticha,* calls attention to the fact that the residents, *liud,* are 'the people.'

In low, level places, like Belgium, it is a noteworthy matter when even a small object projects above the surface. This explains, then, the names **Ghent** (gĕnt), from *gant* = 'rock'; **Mons** (mōnz), 'a hill'; **Tournai** (tōōr-nā′), from the Latin *turris* = 'tower'; and **Ypres** (ēp′r), 'an elm tree,' locally, *ypereaux.* **Charleroi** (shärl′rwä) recalls that Charles II of Spain, *roi* = 'the king,' built a castle there in the sixteenth century, when the Low Countries belonged to Spain; and **Ostend** (ŏs-tĕnd′), in Belgium, is the 'east end' of a sand bank.

In Holland the names of the two most important cities mean just what they say. **Rotterdam** (rŏt′ēr-dăm) is so called because a dam was built there to shut out the floods from the little River Rotte, and **Amsterdam** (ăm′stēr-dăm) is named for a similar dam on the Amster River. **Haarlem** (här′lĕm) is a name made up of two old Saxon words *hara* = 'estuary' and *lemo* = 'clay' or 'mud.' **The Hague** (hāg) was the *haag,* that is, the 'enclosure,' because its site was once a great enclosed hunting park for the counts of Holland.

āle; câre; ăm; ärm; ēve; ĕnd; makēr; īce; ĭll

# CHAPTER XX

THIS is going to be a short chapter. Denmark, Norway, and Sweden constitute the Scandinavian countries. The first is a very small country with much of its area covered with sand dunes; the other two countries are larger but extend far into the cold north, and are mountainous, rocky, and forest-covered over much of their extent. Not much chance, then, is given for a great number of cities, or for many important names of natural features in these countries. Natural features only have significance when many people live about them, see them, mention them, and need to deal with them.

Of the sandy northern part of Denmark called **Jutland** (jŭt′lănd) we can only say that it was the land of the Jutes, one of the barbaric tribes that lived in Europe as the Indians did in North America; the Jutes took part in the Anglo-Saxon conquest of Britain, where they founded the kingdom of Kent. **Iceland**, the island far to the north of Great Britain, owes allegiance to the king of Denmark, but is otherwise an independent state. Its natural conditions are true to its name. On Iceland there is a great volcano, **Hekla** (hĕk′lă), with a rather unusual name. The word is Norse and means 'a hooded, woolen coat of varying colors.' The idea is that the lower part

ōld; ôrb; ŏdd; ūse; ûrn; ŭp; fōōd; fŏŏt; out; oil

of the volcano is covered with a cloak of white snow, and that this cloak has a hood of darker smoke and bare rock at its summit. The one large city of Denmark is **Copenhagen** (kō′pĕn-hā′gĕn), and that, too, is quite well named, for in Danish it is *Khobenhavn,* which is 'merchant's harbor,' and truly the Danes do a nice business there.

At the end of the Baltic Sea is the smaller **Gulf of Bothnia** (bŏth′nĭ-ă). In Sweden *botten* means the 'end of anything,' especially the head of a bay, so the name Bothnia is quite fitting. Our English word *bottom* has the same origin as *botten.* The great mountain mass of Norway is sometimes called the **Kjolen** (kē-ō′lĕn), that is, the 'keel,' because its summit ridge looks like the bottom of a boat furnished with a narrow keel. As the Scandinavian peoples have been seafarers from time immemorial, they quite naturally thought of such a comparison. One often hears of **North Cape,** at the far north of Norway, because tourists have there the opportunity to see the midnight sun.

Although the capital of Norway, **Christiania** (krĭs-tē-ă′nē-ă), has a name with a familiar enough sound, and, as one could guess, was founded by a king, Christian IV, in 1624, other city names in Norway are more unusual. **Hammerfest** (häm′ĕr-fĕst), for example, is a name made up of the words *hamarr* = 'a steep crag' and *fest* = 'a haven'; in other words, Hammerfest is a rocky harbor where ships can be made fast. **Trondhjem** (trŏn′yĕm) refers to the *hjem,* or 'home,' of the *Throndr,* 'the people there living.' **Bergen** (bĕr′gĕn) tells us a bit more about itself. Its full name was once *Bergenhuis,* that is, the

āle; câre; ăm; ärm; ēve; ĕnd; makĕr; īce; ĭll

'mountain castle,' because it is surrounded by seven peaks.

**Stockholm** (stŏk'hōl'm) is the capital of Sweden. In its original form the name was *Stakholm,* made up of *stak* = 'sound' and *holm* = 'island.' As Stockholm is built on a lot of little islands in a shallow lake, its name is much more appropriate than one would suspect from its rather commonplace sound. In Sweden we must also note **Göteborg** (yû'tĕ-bŏr'y'), or **Gothenburg** (gŏt'ĕn-bûrg). This was the town of the Gotar. But they got their name from a very old language root, or syllable, *aud* = 'brave.' Adding a *g* at the end and *ere* at the other makes this (like the Latin *audere* = 'to dare') *gauder,* that is, 'courageous folk.'

ōld; ôrb; ŏdd; ūse; ûrn; ŭp; fōōd; fŏŏt; out; oil

# CHAPTER XXI

## RUSSIA AND POLAND

RUSSIA is a land of rivers, long snaky streams that wind out from the center of the country in all directions. They are big rivers, too, and in this are unlike many famous European streams, for, as we in North America think of rivers, the Seine and the Thames are small. But of these large Russian rivers, one is greatest, the **Volga** (vŏl′gă), and the Russians have recognized its first place in the name, for *wolkoi,* the old Slavonic form of the word, means 'great.' The Russians also affectionately call this river, "Mother Volga."

Four other rivers in Russia have names beginning with *d,* and these names are based on a single, original root word, *don* or *dan,* meaning simply, 'river.' The **Don** (dŏn) has its root form without change or addition. The **Dvina** (vē′nă) shows it in a form which is supposed to indicate a 'double-sourced' river. In the **Dnieper** (nē′pēr) we have a change from an original form *Danapris,* of which the *apris* ending meant 'northern,' or 'upper' *dan* or 'river'; whereas the **Dniester** (nēs′tēr) was the *Danaster,* the 'southern' or 'lower' river. The **Duna** (dū′nă) might be suspected of belonging in this group, but its name is really a Russian corruption of *dünen,* the German word for 'dunes,' because German sailors found sand dunes at its mouth. One other river, the **Pechora** (pĕ-kôr′ă), has a truly Russian name; it means 'caves,' and there are many caves along the banks of the stream.

**Petrograd** (pĕt′rō-grăd), before the World War the most important Russian city, was formerly called *St. Petersburg,* that is, 'St Peter's fort,' because it was founded by the Emperor Peter the Great of Russia in 1703 in honor of St. Peter. The new form is simply the Russian *Petro* = 'Peter' and *grad* = 'fortress.' However one takes its name, **Moscow** (mŏs′kou), the old capital of Russia and the present seat of the Soviet government, is a "wet" place. First, it is named after a river, the *Moskva.* Second, the word *mokschow,* which is nearest the present form of the city's name, means 'wet.' Third, the Finnic root verb from which these terms may have been derived is *musk,* and means 'to wash clothes.' **Smolensk** (smŏ-lĕnsk′), near Moscow, has its name from *smola* = 'tar' and *ensk* = 'to burn.'

**Nizhni Novgorod** (nyēzh′nyē nôv′gō-rōt) is one of those geographic names that everyone hesitates to pronounce. But somehow that task is much easier after one has learned that *nizhni* means 'under' and *novgorod,* the 'new town'; that is, Nizhni Novgorod is simply the 'new city below (down stream from) the old city.' **Archangel** (ärk-ān′jĕl) is not so puzzling; a monastery was founded there in 1584 in honor of Michael the Archangel.

The city name **Odessa** (ō-dĕs′ă) has a curious history. The Empress Catherine II of Russia, who founded it in 1794, had the task of naming the place and asked for suggestions. Forty-seven different words were put before her, but she did not like any of them. Finally someone

ōld; ôrb; ŏdd; ūse; ûrn; ŭp; fōōd; fŏŏt; out; oil

told her to call it *Odissos,* perhaps in memory of Homer's Greek epic, the *Odyssey.* This pleased the Empress, but she insisted on the feminine form, Odessa. Odessa is on the Black Sea, and, while we are there, we may note the extension of this sea inland as the **Sea of Azof** (ä′zŏf) with a name which is a Mongolian word meaning 'moist place.' Between the Black and the Azof seas is the peninsula called **Crimea** (krī-mē′ă), from the Russian term *kremnoi* = 'crags' or 'rocky cliffs.' **Sebastopol** (sĕ-băs′-tō-pŏl) is a seaport at the far end of the Crimea; its name is made up of *sebaste* = 'august' or 'imperial,' and *opol,* like *polis,* the Greek for 'city,' and the town was given this high title when Catherine II established a naval arsenal there in 1780. **Taganrog** (tă-găn-rôk′), on the inner shore of Azof, ends in *rog,* which means 'cape.' Between the Sea of Azof and the Caspian Sea is found a great depression, and in it a river; both are known as the **Manich** (mă-nĕch′). This is a Tartar tribal word *manatsch* = 'bitter,' and no doubt the waters of the stream are very salt.

On the land-bound Caspian Sea there is an important city at the mouth of the Volga, **Astrakhan** (ăs′trä-kăn). This may be simply 'the city of the star,' or may be named after *Hadschi Terchan. Hadschi* (that is, 'holy') Terchan was a chief who had made a pilgrimage to Mecca, and this was his city. **Yekaterinburg** or **Ekaterinburg** (yĕ-kăt-ĕr-ĭn-bûrg′), though you might not suspect it, is simply 'Catherine's city'; it was founded in 1722 and named in honor of Catherine I, the Empress of Peter the Great.

The greater part of the reëstablished state of Poland was carved out of Russia. Hence it is not out of place here to mention two important Polish cities. **Warsaw** (wôr'sô) started in life as *Varsovia,* a word composed of *var* = 'castle' and *mazovia,* a 'government reservation.' A well known dance, the *mazurka,* originated in Warsaw. **Krakow** or **Cracow** (krā'kō), the other city, was named after a chief whose name was *Krak.*

ōld; ôrb; ŏdd; ūse; ûrn; ŭp; fōōd; fŏŏt; out; oil

# CHAPTER XXII

SPAIN still holds a few islands out in the Atlantic, the last remnant of her once vast overseas possessions. Curiously enough, these **Canary** (kǎ-nā'rǐ) **Islands** in name, and historically also, are connected with the discovery of the New World. *Canaria* means 'dog' island, from the Latin *canis* = 'a dog.' Here the Spaniards found a race of giant wild dogs, and on his second voyage Columbus took a number of these "canines" with him to help fight the Cuban and Haitian natives. Cuban bloodhounds are probably descendants of these beasts.

Other island groups lying off the Iberian Peninsula in the Atlantic belong to Portugal. Of these, the **Madeira** (mǎ-dē'rǎ) **Islands** have the most interesting name. The full Portuguese title is *Ilha da Madeira* = 'island of timber.' The Portuguese word *madeira* was derived from the Latin *materia*. We get our words *matter* and *materials* from this word, too, but originally *materia* meant only lumber for buildings. The **Rio de Madeira**, a tributary to the Amazon in Brazil, is so called because of the unbroken tropical forest through which it flows. In the Madeira Islands, **Funchal** (fŭn-chôl') is the chief city, so named because the "fennel" weed, Portuguese *funchol* = 'a bed of fennel,' grows there so abundantly as to be a nuisance.

Portugal also retains the **Cape Verde** (vĕrd) **Islands** which lie off **Cape Verde,** that is, the 'green cape,' of Africa. When the Portuguese sailed down the African coast opposite the Sahara, they, of course, found confirmation of the old idea that the south of the world was uninhabitable because it must be burnt up by the tropical sun. Aristotle, the Greek philosopher, taught that. But when they had gone far enough south to reach the equatorial latitudes, they found Cape Verde, green with palms, and then they knew that they could go on. Still another Portuguese island group is that of the **Azores** (ă-zôrz'), in Portuguese *Ilhas dos Acores,* or 'Hawk Islands.' Many hawks frequent these islands.

In the Mediterranean, Spain retains the **Balearic** (băl-ē-ăr'ĭk) **Islands,** named for the *Baleares,* that is, the 'sling-shot people.' Modern boys use sling shots and sometimes break windows because they are not skilful enough in handling them. But the Romans found it worth while in ancient times to hire the *Baleares* to "work" in their armies, so good were they in the use of this weapon. We note, also, that the **Cantabrian** (kăn-tā'brĭ-ăn) **Mountains,** on the mainland at the northwest of the peninsula, are named for an ancient tribe, the *Cantabri,* but we do not know why the *Cantabri* were so called.

In view of the way in which the Spanish sprinkled saints' names all over the New World, it seems rather strange that none of their home places are identified by religious names. Not only that, but Spanish and Portuguese names are, most of them, "honest-to-goodness" names, the kind of names one can find pleasure in explaining and knowing about. They are the kind

ōld; ôrb; ŏdd; ūse; ûrn; ŭp; fōod; fŏŏt; out; oil

of names that, either because of their odd form, or the quaint story they contain, make one imagine things. They are the kind of names that lift one out of the ruts which we have grooved in this book by the phrases "named after" and the like.

Take the names of the rivers in Spain and Portugal. Their explanations, it is true, are much the same as those of other river names in Europe. Thus the **Tagus** (tā'-gŭs), in Portugal, is probably Phœnician for 'fish river,' and the **Douro** (dō'rŏŏ) smacks of the Celtic *dur* or *don* = 'stream,' 'flowing water.' These are quite commonplace meanings, but the form is different enough to please. Still better are the **Guadalquivir** (gwä-däl-kē-vēr') and the **Guadiana** (gwä-dē-ä'nä) of Spain. Just roll those names over your tongue to get the correct pronunciation. They are Arabic. They don't mean much; originally, they were *Wad-al-Kebir* and *Wad-al-Anas*. *Wad* is 'river,' *al* is 'of' or 'the,' *kebir* is 'great,' and *Anas* is translated by one writer as 'joy,' hence the Guadiana is the 'river of joy.'

But **Madrid** (mă-drĭd'), the capital of Spain, provides us with a city name having a good ring to it and a good story besides. In fact Madrid is explained in several ways. The *Madrileños,* so the people of Madrid call themselves, particularly relish this first one. They say a boy, who lived in those parts before the city was built, was chased into a cherry tree by a bear. His mother came to help the boy down, unknowing of the bear, and so the boy, to warn her, shrieked *"Madre, id!"* = "Mother, go!" Of course, if one doesn't believe that story, it may be of interest to know that there is an

ăle; câre; ăm; ärm; ēve; ĕnd; makēr; īce; ĭll

Arabic word, *madsherit,* which means 'fresh, invigorating breeze,' and it is quite likely that the founders had in mind that there would be fine breezes at the site of Madrid.

The Arabian terms already mentioned were brought into Spain by the Moors. During the seven centuries the Moors held the country (711-1492) they had their capital at **Granada** (grǎ-nä'dǎ), and the name then was *Garnatha,* that is, 'the pomegranate.' Now if you do not know what a pomegranate is, you will need to look up a picture of one, for the city was so called because it was built on four hills divided somewhat like the parts of a pomegranate. **Barcelona** (bär-sě-lō'nǎ) was probably founded by Hamilcar Barca, the father of the great Carthaginian general, Hannibal; his name goes back from *Barca* to the Hebrew word *barak* = 'the lightning,' and he was well named for he conquered most of Spain in 236 B. C. Here is another unusual significance in a city name. **Valencia** (vǎ-lěn'shǐ-ǎ) was in Roman times *Valentia Edetanorum,* that is, the 'strong place of the Edetani,' from the Latin *valere* = 'to be strong.'

**Cartagena** (kär-tǎ-gē'nǎ) was once *Carthagena,* and earlier still *Carthago nova,* 'New Carthage,' under which name Hasdrubal, the son-in-law of Hamilcar Barca, founded it about 230 B. C. This name meant 'new new town,' because the ancient Carthage was itself a 'new town' when the Phœnicians from Asia Minor established it near the site of the present city of Tunis more than eight centuries before Christ. **Malaga** (mǎl'ǎ-gǎ), like Cartagena, is Phœnician. It started as *malah* = 'salt,' because the Phœnicians used to come there to salt down their fish for export. The present chief export of Malaga is quite different. **Cadiz** (kā'dĭz) was the Phœnician *Gaddir,* that is, the 'walled place.' It has been a great city longer than any other town in Europe, for it was probably founded before the foundation of Rome. **Seville** (sĕ'vĭl) was *Sephela,* that is, the 'plain' or 'lowland,' and it is situated on river lowlands.

**Lisbon** (lĭz'bŏn), the capital of Portugal, in earlier days had the much more intriguing name of *Olisipo.* Sorted apart, Olisipo probably was made up of *alis* = 'pleasant' and *ubbo* = 'sea basin,' two Phœnician words again and in a rather happy combination. Why keep calling a harbor a harbor or a port or a haven all the time; "sea basin" is a refreshing change. **Vigo** (vē'gō) finds itself in the Latin *vicus* = 'village.' **Bilbao** (bĭl-bä'ō), however, is more elusive. Maybe it started as *Balvao* = 'pretty ford'; maybe as *pilla* = 'mountain' and *ba* = 'under,' hence, at the foot of the mountain.

Inland we find our old friend **Cordoba** (kôr-dō'bă), that is, *carta-tuba* = the 'great city,' which we mention because we remember that there is another **Cordoba** in Argentina. **Almaden** (ăl-mă-dēn') is the Arabic *El-Ma'aden,* which is a rather complicated way of saying 'the mine.' There are still great quicksilver mines there. And finally, **Valladolid** (văl-yă-dō-lēth') comes from *Valle de Olid,* probably the 'valley of the olive.'

# CHAPTER XXIII

## ABOUT ALL THESE NAMES

In how many different ways are places in European countries named? We have now considered all of two continents and a large part of a third. We should, therefore, by a review of the names already encountered, be able to get a notion of how place names come about.

Thought of in this way, varieties of names are surprisingly few and simple—so much so as to be almost disappointing. Indeed, only the satisfaction we have in being able to catalogue them easily, because of their fewness and simplicity, makes up for the interest a greater variety would arouse.

The simplest of all are those names which go no further than to say that a place is a river or a mountain. The barbaric peoples said "the river" or "the mountain" in their language; later, when their language had been forgotten, "river" or "mountain" in another language was added to the first, and so we have many "river rivers" and "mountain mountains." It will be found interesting to compile a list of such names.

Then there is the large class of names that preserve the simple descriptive adjectives which the primitive peoples gave to a place: the "black," or the "forested," or the "white" mountains; the "tranquil," the "swift," and the "swampy" river; the "fortified" hill, the "shining"

ōld; ôrb; ŏdd; ūse; ûrn; ŭp; fōod; fŏot; out; oil

swamp, and the "gleaming" summit. Those few terms and "great" river, mountain, lake, include about all that were often used.

Occasionally the memory of an event is preserved in a place name. It may have happened only once, or been a repeated occurrence. Fords across streams seem especially to have been noted in this way, thus *Frankfort* and *Oxford*.

In Europe there are comparatively few names of religious significance. The ancient gods were occasionally remembered, but they were simple fellows only, and the names thus given were almost always after the sun god or the god of war. In the New World the Spanish, Portuguese, and French were, as we remember, most liberal in their bestowal of religious names. But that happened only because they came on so many new places in so short a time, and at a time when all their world was possessed of a special religious fervor. They were all "worked up" over religion in those days.

A very vast group of names remember some individual. He may have been a person of little or no consequence, commonly the man who first settled in the place. Not less frequently, however, the mightiest of the mighty were the ones who imposed their names or had their titles fixed on places—the emperors, the kings, the queens, lords, or chieftains. Their castles, their forts, their cities are so marked. Like these personal names are those given for the kinds, that is, tribes, of people who lived in particular regions.

It is strange, too, how often city names mean only "old city" or "new city." When people moved to a new spot,

 āle; câre; ăm; ärm; ēve; ĕnd; makẽr; īce; ĭll

it was a new city, and those who remained behind thought of their home as the old city. Beyond that, it seemed, human minds in a certain stage of civilization could not go in naming cities. Soon, however, they did say "great city" and "upper city" and a few other easy ideas such as these.

Another large group of names is that wherein the title denotes something found at the place. It is seldom anything unusual, almost always something very abundant, and, by preference, the name denotes something useful. Of these, the "fish place" perhaps most frequently occurs. The Canary Islands, which we have just noted, is another example.

Of course, we do all this sort of naming ourselves, to-day. We refer to "the berry patch," "the swimming hole," the "big woods," and, in cities, to "the square," "the park," "Connie's hotel," "Wilson's yard," and so on. If, however, we were to return to this earth some hundreds of years hence and were then to find that people using a strange language were talking about a *Berrpagh* (berry-patch) city, we certainly should be astonished. And yet that is exactly what we seem to be doing, not only in a few instances, but with almost all our place names. The simple, distinguishing words that the first comers at a place used for their nearby surroundings we have made nationally, even internationally, known. A tribe that never traveled over more than a few miles of country could, of course, make out very well by saying only "the river" or the "big river" or the "chief mountain."

A step up in devising place names was achieved when the name of a place was fixed by naming it so as to denote

ōld; ôrb; ŏdd; ūse; ûrn; ŭp; fo͞od; fo͝ot; out; oil

its position in relation to some other place or object. *Portsmouth,* the *Matterhorn,* and *Aix la Chapelle* are names of that kind. To give them, it was necessary to think of two things at once. We think we are doing this very smartly when we invent such names as Texarkana, but, really, it is a very old idea.

Something bigger and broader, and perhaps the best we can hope for, in manner and method of place names was introduced when comparisons were first used. Under that inspiration a place is named because it looks like something else, or because it suggests something to one—gives one an idea. The last is not exactly a comparison, but it is the end of the series which starts with the most simple comparison. The names that have thus originated are among the most interesting and pleasing that we have, not only in meaning, but also in form and sound. Consider *Parana, Halifax, Valparaiso, Cuzco, Titicaca, Ben Nevis, Uruguay.*

Most interesting, though they are hard to classify, are those names which have a complete story attached to them. Part of these could be put in a "blunder class." *Nome, Yucatan,* and *Texas* are examples. *Potosi, Montevideo,* and *Madrid,* however, are each interesting for a more serious reason.

We purposely avoid here sorting out all the different kinds of names that have been encountered, and we avoid also writing out everything that could be said about how the different kinds came to be, and why some of them are pleasing and others not. We avoid those things because the reader who is sufficiently interested will no doubt enjoy seeking out the facts for himself. Thus, for example, he

āle; câre; ăm; ärm; ēve; ĕnd; makēr; īce; ĭll

may hunt out a group that will show names, first, of the most simple kind in its class, and then include, successively, more and more difficult ones.    Such a list should be accompanied by a statement telling why each succeeding name is more difficult, or better than, the preceding one.

Again, how many different names that have real stories can be found?    Where this book is available in schools, members of a class may try writing out those stories with more of the little things that must have been part of them when they happened, as, for example, what the sailors thought in Patagonia, or why the boy was in the cherry tree at Madrid.

Finally, as we go on, the reader will find it worth while to keep these notions about the different classes of place names in mind, and to reflect on how the rest of the place names in the world would fit into them.    More and new classes may be needed.    He may consider, too, whether the names in Asia are better, in his opinion, than those of other continents.

ōld; ôrb; ŏdd; ūse; ûrn; ŭp; fōōd; fŏŏt; out; oil

# CHAPTER XXIV

## ITALY

How do the place names of Italy fit into the classes we have set forth in the preceding chapter? They afford examples of nearly all of them—most, perhaps, of that class which indicates that the place is *like* something. Hence, it would appear that the Italian group is rather better than the average lot of place names.

Around about Italy are a number of islands, of which **Sicily** (sĭs'ĭ-lĭ) is the largest. It was named for a tribe called the *Siculi,* and this term was probably derived from a word meaning 'sickle.' The idea was to show that these people lived in level, agricultural lands on the west coast of Italy, and were accustomed to cutting, that is, 'sickling' grain, hence 'the reapers.' For another reason the original name of **Messina** (mĕ-sē'nă), one of the chief cities of Sicily, was connected with the same idea. The Greek colonists called it *Zancle* = 'sickle' because of the sickle-like shape of the harbor. Later a Greek tyrant renamed it *Messana* in honor of his native Messenia in Greece, whence comes the modern name.

Sicily is very closely connected with Italy, in fact, only the narrow **Strait of Messina** separates the two. On the peninsular side of the strait is found the town of **Reggio** (rĕj'ĭ-ō), in Latin *Rhegium,* which was derived from a Greek word meaning 'torn apart,' 'split,' 'rent.' Put in

 āle; câre; ăm; ärm; ēve; ĕnd; makēr; īce; ĭll

another way, this is 'the place at the fissure,' and quite probably that is a true name, for tremendous earthquakes occur in these parts, and it is not at all unlikely that the strait is a great rent, or fissure, by which the island was separated from the mainland sometime in the ancient past. **Palermo** (pă-lär′mō), another large city of Sicily, however, simply announces by its name, changed from the Greek *Panormos,* that it is a 'good harbor,' a 'place always fit for landing.'

Another island, **Sardinia** (sär-dĭn′ĭ-ă), was named for the aboriginal inhabitants, the *Sardi.* But we think their name was a Phœnician term *sarado* = 'footprint,' because the shape of the island as a whole looks like a great footprint. **Elba** (ĕl′bă) is a little island near the coast which, like Sardinia, belongs to Italy. Its name once was *Ilva* and perhaps was derived from *alb* = 'mountain,' for Elba is quite mountainous. **Corsica** (kôr′sĭ-kă) belongs to France, but, like Sardinia, has a Phœnician name, which probably meant 'wooded' island. Why should you say that Elba and Corsica have more commonplace names than Sardinia? The chief town of Corsica, however, **Ajaccio** (ă-yät′chō), claims a proud origin, for it is said to have been founded by the Greek hero Ajax.

Southern Italy is a region of active volcanoes, the ones first known to history. The largest of these volcanoes, **Etna** (ĕt′nă), is on the island of Sicily. Its name is either from the Greek *aith* = 'to burn' or 'to smoke,' or the Phœnician *attuna* = 'the furnace.' Both terms have the same sound and an appropriate meaning. **Vesuvius** (vē-sū′vĭ-ŭs), the big volcano on the mainland, was once called *Ocre fisov, ocre* = 'mountain' and *fisov* = 'smoke.'

ōld; ôrb; ŏdd; ūse; ûrn; ŭp; fōōd; fŏŏt; out; oil

The root word for *fisov* is *fesf* = 'to steam' or 'to smoke.'
This is an old tribal word. If the reader will say *fesf* out
loud, he will appreciate that geography has done very well
in keeping this sound in Vesuvius, also that *fesf* sounds
like escaping steam. **Stromboli** (strŏm-bō′lĭ), another
island volcano, nearby Vesuvius, had a Greek descriptive
name to start with, *Strongyle* = the 'round island,' on
account of its shape.

The **Apennines** (ăp′ĕ-nīnz), the mountain ranges
that form the backbone of Italy, may have their name
from the Celtic word *pen* = 'summit,' but the Romans
thought of them as the *Pœnine,* or *Punic,* mountains,
because Hannibal, the Carthaginian general, crossed these
mountains when he invaded Italy. The **Tiber** (tī′bĕr),
like the Thames, a small stream but almost equally
famous, has its name probably from the Celtic *dubr* =
'water.' The **Po** (pō) **River** in Roman times was the
*Padus,* and the Romans thought the word came from
the Celtic *padi* = 'pine tree,' because pine trees grew on
its banks.

The largest of the Italian lakes has simply the Italian
name **Lago Maggiore** (lä′gō mä-jĭ-ō′rĕ) ; *maggiore* =
'larger' and *lago* = 'lake.'

**Lombardy** (lŏm′bärd-ĭ), a district of northern Italy
often mentioned, was once *Langobardia,* because it was
settled by the Lombards, *Langobards* or 'long beards.'
Those who are not satisfied with that explanation suggest
that the name is from *longis bardis,* that is, 'long halberts,' or 'those with long halberts.'

Now we come to the names of the Italian cities. One
of the more interesting is the capital **Rome** (rōm). If

āle; câre; ăm; ärm; ēve; ĕnd; makēr; īce; ĭll

its origin is in a Greek word of the same form, the name means 'force' or 'strength.' The Romans were not lacking in those characteristics. Perhaps, however, Rome is only a corruption of *groma,* a place where roads crossed each other in the center of a camp and made a square or open space. But best is the story that the city is named after Romulus, of the brothers Romulus and Remus, who were nursed by a she-wolf and, when they grew up, founded the city. As Livy tells the story, it appears that Remus was rather unappreciative of the importance of the work in hand. Accordingly Romulus very effectively put him out of the business. And so the city was named for Romulus only.

**Naples** (nā'p'lz) is in Greek *Neapolis,* one of those stale 'new cities.' Vesuvius is near Naples, and in the year 79 A.D. an eruption of Vesuvius destroyed **Pompeii** (pŏm-pā'yē), and **Herculaneum** (hĕr-kyū-lā'nē-ŭm), the latter named for the giant Greek hero, Hercules. Tradition credited Hercules with the founding of Pompeii also, and the name arose from the *pompeion* = 'pomp' with which he was said to have celebrated it. **Venice** (vĕn'ĭs) was named for the *Veneti* tribe, and their name seems to have meant 'marsh dwellers.' **Turin** (tū'rĭn), likewise, was so called for a tribe, the *Taurini,* but we know that this name was from the word *tors* = 'hills,' hence 'people of the hills.' The Italians even now call the city *Torino.* We have clipped off most of the ancient Roman name of **Milan** (mĭ-lăn'); it was *Mediolanium,* that is, 'middle of the plain.'

**Florence** (flŏr'ĕns) is the way the French want the Italian word *Firenze* spelled, and we have followed the

ōld; ôrb; ŏdd; ūse; ûrn; ŭp; fo͞od; fo͝ot; out; oil

French style. Anyway the old Latin form was *Florentia,* and this may have meant either that the city was 'flourishing,' 'blooming,' or that it was actually full of flowers, as, indeed, it is even now. Some, however, point out that *Fluentia* is probably the correct old form, that is, a 'confluence' of two rivers. For **Leghorn** (lĕg'hôrn) the Italians say *Livorno*; English sailors are responsible for our name, as they said they bought hats at Leghorn, meaning Livorno.

**Trieste** (trē-ĕst'), anciently *Tergeste,* was Austrian, is now Italian, and has its name from *terst* = 'a reed' or 'rushes.' **Carrara** (kär-rä'rä) has its name from the Celtic *kaer* = 'stone' or 'rocky cliff,' and, if anywhere in the world stone is fitting as a city name, perhaps the famous Carrara marble makes this the best place.

**Brindisi** (brēn-dē'sē), anciently *Brundusium,* has a harbor with many branching arms; hence the comparison with a *brention* = 'stag's head' is quite in keeping. **Bellagio** (bĕl-lä j'ĭ-ō) should probably be translated directly from the words *bel* = 'pretty' and *lago* = 'lake.'

# CHAPTER XXV

## THE SOUTHEAST OF EUROPE

WE shall have one more try at European place names, and then we shall be ready to invade a new continent, Asia.

In the southeast of Europe we are at the gateway from Asia into Europe. It would seem that groups, large and small, from different peoples who passed through that gate in the various ages, lingered and settled down around the portals. For we find there a jumble of nationalities, with Slavs, Greeks, Turks, and Magyars the most prominent strains.

Just now the **Slavs** (slävs) are dominant over most of the region. The Slavs derive their name from a term in their own language, *slovo* = 'a word.' On the basis of this, they, the Slavs, are 'the speakers,' 'the people of the word.' The Germans to the north of them they refer to as *Niemez* = 'dumb,' 'unintelligible.' One may infer that the Slavs are not at all disdainful of themselves.

Well surrounded by the Slavs are the **Magyars** (măg′yärs), who control Hungary, and formerly ruled much of the country now possessed by independent Slav nations. The Magyars also have a good opinion of themselves, as is shown by the fact that they call themselves *gyer* = 'man' and *ma* = 'land,' hence 'men of the land,' the original owners, if you please.

ōld; ôrb; ŏdd; ūse; ûrn; ŭp; fōōd; fŏŏt; out; oil

Before the forming of the larger state of Jugoslavia, part of the Slavs had attained independence in **Serbia** (sĕr′bĭ-ă). That name, too, is pointed, for it comes from the root *srb* in the Serbian language which means 'the people,' 'the nation.' Another little, formerly independent Slav country, **Montenegro** (mŏn-tā-nā′grō), was more modest, however, for it only proclaimed by its name that its hills were dark. The Italians translated Montenegro from the native tongue, in which it has the same meaning. One should remember that *Turk* means 'robber,' that the *Bulgarians* are 'rebels,' and that the group of Slavs who occupied the district formerly called **Bohemia** (bō-hē′mĭ-ă) got their name from *Boii* ═ 'terrible ones.' Then one will understand what a nice, modest, and peaceful lot of neighbors there are in this part of the world.

Before the arrangement of territory which now prevails was made, for the most part as a consequence of the World War, a number of other districts, no longer recognized as politically separate areas, had a considerable importance, and these are often mentioned. Hence we note their names here. **Croatia** (krō-ā′shă) was from the Slavic word *chrawat* and meant 'men of the hills.' We get our word *cravat* from this. See if you can find out why. Another group of Slavs, those in **Herzegovina** (hĕr-tsĕ-gō-vē′nă), borrowed the German title for 'duke,' that is, *herzog,* for their ruler, called him *Herzega,* and hence his land became Herzegovina. The people of **Bosnia** (bŏz′nĭ-ă) took their name from that of the River *Bosna,* meaning probably 'cold,' 'clear.' **Dalmatia** (dăl-mā′shĭ-ă) was earlier *Dalminium,* a capital city

āle; câre; ăm; ärm; ēve; ĕnd; makẽr; īce; ĭll

name, and this meant, most likely, 'sheep pasture.' The
**Dinaric** (dĭ-năr'ĭk) **Mountains** have a name which is
a modification of *Dalminium*. The district of **Tyrol**
(tĭ'rŏl) took its name from the counts of *Tirol* who took
possession of it in the thirteenth century. One more district, that of the **Transylvanian** (trăn-sĭl-vā'nĭ-ăn) **Alps,**
has a name of Latin origin meaning 'the Alps or mountains beyond the woodland.'

. One river in this section has a name with ᴧn unusual
meaning, the **Tisza** (tē'sŏ) **River** in Hungary. This
name is made up of *tis* = 'yew' and *za* = 'behind.' Hence
it is 'the river behind, or beyond, the yew trees.' The
remaining rivers have names that are odd sounding, but
of commonplace derivation. Thus the **Morava** (mō-
rä'vä) comes from the Slavic *morje* = 'water'; the **Save**
(sä'vē), from the Magyar *sab* = 'a stream'; and the
**Drave** (drä'vē), from a Dalmatian word *dru* = 'hurrying river.'

The city names also are, on the whole, disappointing.
**Karlsbad** (kärls'băd), in Czecho-Slovakia, is simply
'Charles bath,' because at a hot spring here in the four-
teenth century the Emperor Charles IV recovered from
wounds received in battle; he was the first to avail himself of the healing power of its waters, which are still
visited by invalids from all over the world. In the same
country we find also **Marienbad** (mă-rē'ĕn-băd), the
'bath of Mary,' another health resort famous for medici-
nal springs. **Prague** (präg) is a little better. It is
derived from *praha* = 'the threshold,' because the Mol-
dau River runs over a reef at this point.

**Vienna** (vĭ-ĕn'ä) is the chief citv of Austria, and

ōld; ôrb; ŏdd; ūse; ûrn; ŭp; fōōd; fŏŏt; out; oil

has a name that in Celtic was evidently *Vindobna,* of which the first two syllables mean 'white,' and the last 'castle.' This name has suffered many changes since it was first used. **Innsbruck** (ĭns'brōŏk) has a German name meaning 'bridge over the Inn River'; whereas **Inn,** itself, may be a variation of *aar* = 'something flowing.' **Eisenerz** (ī'sĕn-ĕrts) also is German; it translates simply as 'iron ore.'

**Budapest** (bŭ'dă-pĕst), in Hungary, is made up of two Slavic words *buda* = 'huts' and *pesth* = 'oven' or 'grotto.' The idea is that huts were built at a place where hot sulphur springs (ovens) occur, and also caves (grottos). There is probably no other city in the world that admits in its name that it started as a collection of huts.

In Jugoslavia we have **Belgrade** (bĕl'grăd), originally *Beograd,* meaning 'white fortress.' The white walls and towers of the city rear up boldly above the Danube River. **Nish** (nĭsh) was the Greek word *naisos* = 'birthplace,' that is, of the Emperor Constantine the Great.

There are two Scutaris, one spelled **Scutari** (skōō'tär-ē), in Albania, and another, **Skutari,** in Turkey in Asia, just across the Bosporus Strait. The Albanian Scutari is possibly derived from the Latin *scodra,* and means 'hill town.' The Asiatic Skutari, however, was the Persian word *uskudar* = 'a messenger.' The place is directly opposite Constantinople, and from it messengers started on the Asiatic side for places in the east. That is quite a romantic situation. **Durazzo** (dū-räd'zō), in Albania, also has the merit of being enough different to make us interested in its site. It is a name corrupted from the Greek *Dyrrhachion* = 'evil surf,' or perhaps bet-

āle; câre; ăm; ärm; ēve; ĕnd; makĕr; īce; ĭll

ter, 'dangerous breaker place,' hence difficult landing place.

**Bucharest** (bū-kă-rĕst'), in Rumania, is locally termed *Bucuresci*. *Bucurie* means 'pleasure' and *boukoure,* 'beautiful.' **Galatz** (gä'läts), also in Rumania, is a modification of *Kladsko,* a Slavic word meaning 'a place palisaded with trees.' In Bulgaria, **Sofia** (sō-fē'yă), formerly *Sophia,* which in Greek means 'wisdom,' was founded in the sixth century by the Roman Emperor Justinian, who also built the famous mosque of St. Sophia in Constantinople.

We conclude our study of European place names with those of Greece, which was the first country of that continent to develop civilization as we know it. The most famous city of Greece is **Athens** (ăth'ĕnz), presumably named for the goddess of wisdom, *Athene*. Athene's name is guessed by some authorities to have been developed from the root word *ath* = 'a long-handled spear.'

For all the fact that the ancient Greeks rose to greater imaginative heights than have been attained by any people since, their important place names are quite ordinary in the main. **Corinth** (kŏr'ĭnth) is a term descriptive of a 'helm-shaped rock.' **Salonica** (să-lŏn-ī'kă) is a contraction of Thessalonica; it was named for *Thessalonica,* who was a half-sister of Alexander the Great. **Piræus** (pī-rē'ŭs), the harbor town of Athens, was on an island to which one went on a ferry, hence the Greek *pera* = 'opposite' or 'pass over.' Finally, there is **Adrianople** (ăd-rĭ-ăn-ōp'l), returned to Turkey in 1923, which was *Hadrianopolis* = the 'city of Hadrian,' the Roman Emperor who refounded it in the second century A.D.

ōld; ôrb; ŏdd; ūse; ûrn; ŭp; fōod; fŏŏt; out; oil

# CHAPTER XXVI

## A SURVEY OF WESTERN ASIA

THIS, which we are to make next, is going to be a long trip all around Asia. And Asia is a big continent. It will be well to have a map close at hand on which each place may be located as we come to it. If the reader can remember the situations of the big places first to be considered, he will later be able to use them as sign posts to the smaller places mentioned further on.

Asia (ā′shǎ) is the 'land of sunrise,' for its name is the Semitic word *azu* = 'sunrise.' It is the East, the Orient, as Europe is the West, the land of sunset. As soon as we step from Europe into Asia, across the Bosporus, we encounter **Anatolia** (ǎn-ǎ-tō′lǐ-ǎ), which repeats the name of Asia in Greek, for *anatolea* is 'morning,' 'land of the rising sun.'

**Brusa** (brōō′sǎ), sometimes spelled Brussa, is the largest city of the Turkish possessions in Asia; it was named for *Prusias,* the king of Bithynia with whom Hannibal sought refuge after his defeat in the war with Rome. A little to the south and west we note another city, **Smyrna** (smûr′nǎ), which has the distinction of having kept the same name unaltered, and not changed in any way, throughout its long existence of nearly three thousand years. Smyrna was named for a certain one of the legendary female warriors, the Amazons, of whom we have already heard. Now crossing over to the east and north, we pass along the base of the Caucasus Mountains, and note **Mt. Elbruz** (ĕl-brōōz′), the highest of their peaks, with a Persian name meaning 'shining mountain.' The name of the **Elburz** (ĕl-bōōrz′) **Mountains** in Persia is derived from the same word.

This region, at the southern base of the Caucasus, was formerly known as **Transcaucasia** (trăns-kô-kā′sĭ-ă) and had Russian government. It is now divided up into two new states which desire independence. One ᵕf these, **Georgia** (jôr′jă), has a name which is a corruption of *Gurdschistan,* which means 'land of the Gurdschi people.' Its big city has the Georgian name **Tiflis** (tyē-flēs′), from *tbili* = 'warm,' given because of the hot springs found there. Another Georgian city is **Batum** (bă-tōōm′), a name greatly shortened from the Greek *Bathys Limen* = 'deep harbor.' The other state is **Azerbaijan** (ä-zĕr-bī-jän′), a name which may mean 'country of the Tartars.' Its big city, **Baku** (bă-kōō′), has a Persian name *baadku* = 'the mountain wind.' To the east of Azerbaijan lies **Armenia** (är-mē′nĭ-ă), a country with a much more familiar name. This was originally *Har-minni,* that is, 'mountains of the Minni.' The *har* comes from an old Persian word *ara* = 'mountain,' and here accordingly we find **Mt. Ararat** (är′ă-răt). For what is this mountain famous? Two cities in Armenia are **Erzerum** (ĕrz-rōōm′) and Erivan. The inhabitants of the country fled from the early Turkish invaders to a fortress called *Arzek-el-Rum,* that is, 'Arzek (*arz* = 'land') of the Romans'; later this was shortened to *arzi-Rum,* and now

ōld; ôrb; ŏdd; ūse; ûrn; ŭp; fōōd; fŏŏt; out; oil

Erzerum. That is about as complete a change from an original as could be imagined. **Erivan** (ĕr-ĭ-văn′) remembers the Persian chieftain Revan, its founder. **Trebizond** (trĕb′ĭ-zŏnd), a third Armenian city, has an alluring name which, however, is only a corruption of the Greek word *trapeza* = 'table,' so called on account of the shape of nearby mountains.

We turn southwest now and come into **Syria** (sĭr′ĭ-ă). That name is a remnant of the name of the ancient realm of *Assyria*, which at one time included Syria. Assyria was named after *Assur*, name of its chief city, the name meaning 'the water bank,' and, perhaps in its original form, 'the plain.' The god of the Assyrians was also called Assur, and here we have the idea that he was just and righteous, as we say in slang, "on the level."

**Palestine** (păl′ĕs-tīn) is from the Greek *Palaestina* = 'Philistine land,' and *Philistine* means 'stranger.' Palestine lies south of Syria. From thence we enter the great peninsula of **Arabia** (ă-rā′bĭ-ă). Its name is from the Semitic *ereb*, meaning 'dark,' as we have already learned from "Europe," but is also to be translated as 'waste,' 'barren wilderness.' In these latter senses *ereb* fits well to Arabia, for most of the peninsula is desert. Along the borders of Arabia are found, however, areas of more favorable conditions, and these border tracts are divided into a number of governments. At the north is **Hejaz** (hĕj-äz′), a name meaning 'the passage.' Between the low coastlands on the one side and the highlands on the other is the route, through Hejaz, followed by caravans. The Arabs are Mohammedans, and their metropolis, **Medina** (mĕ-dī′nă), is in full *Medinat-al-Nabi* = 'city

āle; câre; ăm; ärm; ēve; ĕnd; makēr; īce; ĭll

of the Prophet,' but this is only one of ninety-two names the city bears, all referring to the holy character of Mohammed. **Mecca** (mĕk'ă), the capital of Hejaz, famous as the birthplace of Mohammed, has a name of unknown meaning, but the Mohammedans call it only *El Blad,* a term which means simply 'the city.' Then we come to **Yemen** (yĕm'ĕn), which has a name with a real story. Yemen is translated as 'fortunate Arabia.' The Arabic term *Yemin* means 'an oath,' and also 'the right hand,' because people "swore an oath" by raising the right hand while facing east. But facing east puts the right hand to the south. Hence the south of Arabia came to be known as *El Yemen* = 'the right hand.' Further, the right hand is considered more lucky than the left, accordingly the south, that is, the right hand of Arabia, became "lucky," or "fortunate" Arabia, that is, *Yemen.* That, to say the least, is complicated. But about the names of **Sanaa** (sä-nä') and **Mocha** (mō'kă), cities in Yemen, we do not seem to have information, although the latter is one of the famous coffee markets of the world.

At the southwest tip of Arabia the British have a possession called **Aden** (ä'dĕn), anciently *Adane,* meaning 'place of delight,' or Eden. It is, too, in comparison with most of the country. About the names of **Oman** (ō-män') and its city **Maskat** (mŭs-kăt') on the southeast corner of Arabia, no one seems to know much. **Hasa** (hä'să), the district north of Oman, may have its name derived from *El Hasi* = 'the little springs,' a term used in Algeria.

But now we come to a famous region, that of **Meso-**

**potamia** (měs-ō-pō-tā′mĭ-ă), whose Greek name means 'between the rivers.' The rivers meant are the Tigris and Euphrates, the sources of which are within five miles of each other and which unite after flowing the length of Mesopotamia. Mesopotamia is, therefore, very truly "between the rivers." The **Tigris** (tī′grĭs) has an ancient Persian name, *tigris* = 'an arrow,' and this refers to the swift flow of the Tigris. Tigers, the 'swift beasts,' have their name through the same origin. **Euphrates** (ū-frā′tēz), on the other hand, comes from *Hufrat,* meaning 'very broad.' *Phrat* in Persian means 'sweet water,' and the upper course of the Euphrates is still called the *Frat.* The earliest form seems to have been *Pura-nunu* = 'the great water.' By juggling all of these forms the word Euphrates eventually emerged.

We must not linger now to consider the ancient and modern cities of Mesopotamia. We have made only a beginning of traveling "by name" over all Asia, and must hurry along if we are to avoid being tired out at the end of the trip. Accordingly, we go east and cross directly into **Persia** (pûr′shă), once called *Parsa,* a Semitic term meaning 'horsemen.' Persian and Arabian steeds are famous, as you know. Passing through Persia we encounter the "stan" states. These are, from the south to north, **Baluchistan** (bă-lōō′chē-stän), **Afghanistan** (ăf-găn′ĭ-stän), and **Turkestan** (tûr′kē-stän), partly under Russian, partly under Chinese control. The Persian word *sitan* means 'one who takes possession'; *sistan* means 'the possession' or 'the country.' Hence, 'the country of the Turks,' 'of the Baluchi,' and so on. Afghana was a nephew of King Saul and had forty sons. The descendants of these sons were deported in captivity with the rest of the Jews and, the Afghans say, were settled in Afghanistan.

Tucked in between the "stans" we note the province of **Bokhara** (bō-kä′rä), with a capital of the same name, which means 'treasury of science.' It is a "college town" to the Mohammedans. Here we find a railway line, and on it we travel west to the city of **Merv** (mērf), which has a name derived from *meregho* = 'bird water,' a pleasing fancy, on account of the swift flow of the waters there. Going east on the same line we arrive at **Tashkend** (tăsh′-kĕnd), which has a Persian name, *tasch* = 'stone' and *kend* = a 'village.'

West from Tashkend the country is desert until we arrive at **Khiva** (kē′vä), the region of an oasis and city. Its name is from the Turkish word *khavak* = 'dry,' as its surroundings certainly are. Khiva, however, touches on the **Aral** (ăr′ăl) **Sea**, that is, in the native tongue, the 'island' sea. There are many islands along the east coast of Aral, but some authorities insist the name was given because the water itself is 'an island in a sea of land.' North of the Aral Sea are the wide **Kirghiz** (kĭr′gēz) **Steppes** (stĕps), *kir*, meaning 'steppe' or 'semi-arid land' and *giz* = 'passing through.' So we will, until we come to **Askabad** (ăs-kä-bäd′), in Transcaspia, where we should rest awhile. For Askabad is Arabic for 'abode of love,' and we may expect therefore to spend some days there in peace and comfort.

# CHAPTER XXVII

## A CIRCUIT OF ASIA

THE parts of Asia over which we have already traveled are, many of them, quite out-of-the-way places. But we have much farther to go on the remainder of our trip, and to even more desolate places. As we have just enjoyed a rest, we may as well do the hardest part first. So we ride back on the railway to the eastern border of Bokhara.

We first climb to the top of the **Pamir** (pä-mēr') **Plateau.** Its name, as given, may mean 'the wilderness,' but locally a better name is used, *Bam-i-Dunya,* meaning 'the roof of the world.' And truly it does seem to be that as we look down on the **Tarim** (tä-rēm') **River** basin. *Ta* in Chinese means 'great' and *ri* is Tibetan for mountain. At the head of the Tarim basin we find two cities located in oases, one, **Kashgar** (käsh-gär'), from *gar* = 'a permanent camp' and *kash* = 'bank.' The other is **Yarkand** (yär-känd'), with a name made up of the Persian *yar* = 'a friend' and *kand* = 'place,' and we are glad to come to a 'friendly place' at nightfall. But *yar* in another dialect means only 'cliff.' After our night's rest, we find the vast ranges of the **Tian Shan** (tĭ-ăn' shän') or, in Chinese, 'celestial mountains,' towering above us on the north. We journey along their base to the east for a glimpse of the **Gobi** (gō'bē) **Desert** with a name which should be *Gobi* only, for *gobi* means 'desert.' We also wish to see the **Altai** (äl'tī) **Mountains.** The Mongolian words from which the name Altai is had are *Altain ula* = 'mountain of gold.' In the seventh century people said the Altai were rich in gold and silver, but no one seems to be keen about working them now, for they are so difficult to reach.

We, too, have no desire to try for Altai's treasures, so we turn next south and across the **Kuenlun** (kwĕn-lōōn'), or 'onion mountains.' Onions grow wild, abundantly, on the Kuenlun slopes. Descending on the south side we have spread below us the vast plateau of **Tibet** (tĭ-bĕt'). The name Tibet was originally an Arabic term *Thupho,* meaning 'strong' or 'capable.' As the Tibetans use the words, both *thub* and *phod* mean 'strong,' so Tibet would be 'strong—strong.' In Mongolian, *bot* = 'country.' The idea, then, evidently is that Tibet is a 'high, strong country,' one difficult to invade. There can be no doubt about that. Because of this strength, probably, the sacred city **Lassa** (läs'ä) is situated south of its center. To the Tibetans, Lassa, or *Lhasa,* is 'God's land,' from *lha* = 'God' and *sa* = 'land.'

Again we have before us a mountain range to cross, the tremendous **Himalaya** (hĭ-mä'lă-yă) **Mountains.** Their name is Sanskrit, *hima* = 'snow' and *alaya* = 'abode,' hence 'abode of snow.' The Himalaya are very well named, too, much better than is **Mt. Everest** (ĕv'ēr-ĕst), their highest peak, and the highest mountain in the world. Everest is a personal name, recalling a surveyor-general of the India Survey, but the English people themselves

ōld; ôrb; ŏdd; ūse; ûrn; ŭp; fōōd; fŏŏt; out; oil

protest against it, and the natives can't pronounce it. The natives call the peak *Gaurisankar, gauri* meaning 'white' and *sankar,* 'the beneficent.' The beneficent part is added, no doubt, because Everest's snows, melted, furnish volume to the rivers. We get through the mountain barrier by way of the **Karakoram** (kä-rä-kō′răm) **Pass,** a native name, of which *kara* is 'black' and *koram* = 'stony ground.' This is really the name of a small cluster of mountains to the west, the **Karakoram Mountains,** which are darker than the Himalaya because they do not have such great snowfields.

Still farther to the west are found the **Hindu-Kush** (hĭn-dōō kōōsh′). From their slopes we look down into **India** (ĭn′dĭ-ă) and the valley of the **Indus** (ĭn′dŭs) **River.** All three of these names contain the Sanskrit word *Sindhu,* meaning a 'river' or, more exactly, 'the irrigator.' Indeed, almost every drop of the water of the Indus is used for irrigation of crops. The people who settled in the Indus valley are known as Hindus, and *kush* means 'killer.' Hindu slaves, carried to market across these mountains, often died of cold because the mountains are so high, hence *Hindu-Kush* = 'Hindu killer.'

India is the home of Sanskrit, and one may therefore expect that many of the place names of that country will be from the Sanskrit language. The great plateau of the **Deccan** or **Dekkan** (dĕk′kăn) is an example. Its name is like Yemen in that it means 'south country,' from the Sanskrit *dakshina* = 'the right hand.' **Ceylon** (sē-lŏn′), the island, is *Sinhala dwipa* = 'the lion island.' A conquering tribe called themselves "the Lions," hence the name. **Bengal** (bĕn-gôl′), the bay and district in

India, is a name corrupted from *Bangalaya* = 'abode of the Bangas.' Coming north we note **Nepal** (nē-pôl'), a name made up of *nipa* = 'the foot' and *alaya,* again as in Himalaya, hence Nepal is 'abode at the foot' like the name Piedmont. **Khatmandu** (kät-män-dōō') is its capital city, the name meaning 'wooden building' and given because an inn of wood was erected there to house religious pilgrims.

Another small state of northern India is **Bhutan** (bū-tän'), originally called *Bhotant,* from *Bhot* = 'Tibet' and *anta* = 'end.' It is at the 'end of Tibet.'

**Burma** (bûr'mä) is another corruption, but a wise one, for the original word was *Mranma,* meaning 'those who are strong.' An English-speaking person would need to be strong and clever of tongue to pronounce the name if the original of Burma were still in use.

Now we are out of India and are proceeding south. **Siam** (sī-ăm') is the name of the people, the *Siyam,* or 'the free.' Beyond Siam we come to a number of states that include **Malay** (mă-lā') in their names. Malay is a variation of the Greek *melas* = 'dark' or 'black,' and applies to the skin color of the natives. The **Straits Settlements,** at the end of the peninsula, refer to the **Strait of Malacca** (mă-lăk'ă). This is named, in Javanese, from *malaka,* a species of palm tree growing abundantly on the shores of the strait.

Turning north now we cross **French Indo-China,** and thus finally we arrive in **China** (chī'nă). China is the East, Asia, expressed in the utmost degree. China's name has two plausible explanations. One makes it from the Greek *Sinae,* that is, from *Seres* = 'silk people.' The

ōld; ôrb; ŏdd; ūse; ûrn; ŭp; fōōd; fŏŏt; out; oil

other explanation says that the Arabs heard of the *Thsin* conquerors of China through the Indians, who called these conquerors *Tschina,* hence China. The north of China, we find, is called **Mongolia** (mŏn-gō′lĭ-ă), that is, the 'land of the Mongols,' and *Monggol* means 'brave and proud.' Beyond Mongolia is **Manchuria** (măn-chū′rĭ-ă), named for the *Manchus,* or 'pure people.' Rather insistent they all are, in this part of the world, about proclaiming their good personal qualities.

As Great Britain lies off the coast of Europe, so Japan lies off the coast of Asia. The name **Japan** (jă-păn′) in several forms repeats the meaning of Asia. Marco Polo first brought word back to Europe of Japan, and he was told the Chinese word for the island empire, *Zipangu* = 'sun-origin kingdom.' This word we have since altered to Japan. The Japanese themselves call their land **Nippon** (nĭp′pŏn), from the Japanese *ni* = 'fire' or 'sun' and *pon* = 'land,' hence again 'land of sunrise.' The Japanese own the **Nansei** (năn′sā) **Islands,** that is, the 'south' islands, *nan* = 'south,' the largest of which is **Formosa** (fôr-mō′să). Formosa is the Portuguese name of the island and means 'full of beauty.' But the Portuguese name is now most used for the **Formosa Strait** between the island and the mainland. The island itself is known by its Chinese name **Taiwan** (tī-wän′), that is, 'terrace site.' In successive steps, the sandy foreground of the island is followed by green foothills, and then by craggy mountains.

We could now float along northward on the **Japan Current** or **Kuro Shivo** (kōō′rō shē′vō), that is, 'black stream,' which follows the Asiatic coast as the Gulf

āle; câre; ăm; ärm; ēve; ĕnd; makêr; īce; ĭll

Stream does the North American continent. But the **Kuro Siwo** (so spelled, also) would carry us too far to the northeast to note the **Kuril** (kōō′rĭl) **Islands** north of Japan, named after the inhabitants, who call themselves *Kurili,* that is, 'men' or 'the people.' The Kuril Islands end at the **Kamchatka** (kăm-chăt′kă) **Peninsula,** a name which the Russians made up from *Kontschalo,* as the people inland called the people on the peninsula. *Kontschalo* meant 'people at the outermost end of the earth.' Look at your world map and pick out all the places that could be so named.

To go back to the mainland we need to sail across the **Sea of Okhotsk** (ō-kŏtsk′), which also has a native name *okat* = 'river,' changed by the Russians to the present form. We land in **Siberia** (sī-bē′rĭ-ă), perhaps the largest unbroken stretch of land in the world known by a single name, and that name one of a little brook, *Ssibirka.* Fur trading with Siberia started at this little brook—no one now knows what this name means—and as the trading gradually extended eastward, the first name given the country kept pace with the traders and conquerors. Yet it is not an inappropriate name, for the biggest things in Siberia are streams.

As we plan now to travel back westward, overland, we shall take note of the names of these Siberian streams. At the south border of the country flowing into the Sea of Okhotsk is the **Amur** (ä-mōōr′). As might be expected from its position, the Amur has a Mongolian name, really *Tamur,* that is, 'great river.' We do not need to cross the Amur, but we shall have to pass over the other Siberian rivers, for these flow northward directly across

ōld; ôrb; ŏdd; ūse; ûrn; ŭp; fōōd; fŏŏt; out; oil

the great plain. The first to be met is the **Lena** (lē′nă), which seems to have a simple name but it is again one of native origin whose meaning is not known. But no fault is to be found with the name of the **Yenisei** (yăn-ē-sĕ′ē), which was originally *neser-nak-yi* = 'I flow down ice.' And so it does, great blocks and cakes of it, each spring with the melting floods, for during the winter the Yenisei is frozen many feet thick. One of the sources of the Yenisei is **Lake Baikal** (bī-käl′), named from the Yakut words *bai-kul,* that is, 'abundant lake' or 'rich sea,' because it contains so many salmon fish.

The **Ob**, or the **Ob-Irtysh** (ŏb ĭr-tĭsh′), **River,** as it is sometimes known, also goes back to fish for its name. The Irtysch part is from the word *erthis* = 'stream.' *Ob* is the native word for 'grandmother' or 'aunt,' used in the loving way, as when we say "granny" or "aunty." This pet name is used because the Ob furnishes the people with so many fish as well as a route for travel, and also because it holds a certain power over their lives, for many drown in it.

South of the Ob is **Lake Balkash** (bôl-käsh′), with a Mongolian name which means 'great lake.' At its shores we discontinue our overland travels and, for a final stage in our Asiatic journey of names, make an airplane flight to three other lakes and seas of Asia. We land first on the far side of Arabia, on the coast of the **Red Sea**, so called from ancient times on account of red marine organisms which live in its surface water and streak it with red color. A short jump takes us north to Palestine and to the **Dead Sea**, its name being due to the fact that its waters are so salt that no fish can live in it. Last of

āle; câre; ăm; ärm; ēve; ĕnd; makēr; īce; ĭll

all we rest at the **Sea of Galilee** (găl′ĭ-lē), that is, the 'circuit,' as it was called by the Hebrews because the Gentiles lived all around it.    Galilee is the Greek form of the Semitic word *g′lil* = 'the circle.'    And since our circle, also, is now complete, we could not well have chosen a better name with which to end this chapter.

# CHAPTER XXVIII

SOME of the countries we visited, on our "name-by-name" trip around the continent of Asia, were regions so sparsely populated, or so little known, that we could note all the features of interest they contained in that rapid survey. Others, however, were regions that, both in ancient times and now, are the homes of many people; hence they have many big cities. Also, some of these well-populated places have natural features that, though not so imposing as the Himalaya Mountains, for example, are, nevertheless, well known. That is because the inhabitants of those parts set much store by their natural monuments and have made them familiar to us. So we need to complete our study of Asiatic names by taking account of all such items.

We have often mentioned the Phœnician language as the source of place names in Europe, and even in North America. The first home of the Phœnicians, and the place from which the Phœnician traders first set out on the travels which spread their language and culture so widely, was in the area which is now Syria. Here were located **Tyre** (tīr) and **Sidon** (sī'dŏn), the early, great commercial cities of the Phœnicians. Tyre was in Phœnician *zor*, that is, 'the rock' on which the city was built.

āle; câre; ăm; ärm; ēve; ĕnd; makĕr; īce; ĭll

Sidon was *zidon,* meaning 'the catch of fish.' Fishing was a very important industry with the Phœnicians. Through it they were led to the dyeing of cloth a "Tyrian purple," that is, crimson red, by means of a juice they obtained from a species of mollusk. As the supply of this shell-fish gave out nearby their homes, the Phœnician fishermen went farther and farther in search of more of this material. Then they took their dyed cloths and other goods along and traded with the peoples they found on other shores. Thus the Phœnicians became the first merchant people of the world, and traveled far, all because they once made a "catch of fish" at *Zidon.*

The Phœnicians not only dyed cloth but also in time manufactured many other kinds of goods, for example, glassware. All of these goods they sold and exchanged. So the region became a manufacturing center at an early date. And even in much later times the city of **Damascus** (dă-măs'kŭs) was the 'place of industry,' as that is what its Arabian name *Dammesq* means. At Damascus very fine sword blades were made. **Aleppo** (ă-lĕp'ō), came from the Arabic *Haleb,* and this in turn grew out of *Khilibu,* the name of an ancient king. The Arabs have a tradition, however, that Abraham stopped there on his way to Canaan and distributed milk to the poor, repeating the words *Ibrahim aleb* = 'Abraham has milked.' **Beirut** (bā-rōot') is had from the Semitic *B'eroth* = 'springs,' of which there are some fine ones at Beirut. Both Aleppo and Beirut are Syrian cities of modern importance.

We turn now to Palestine to learn the meanings of some of the Bible names. **Judea** (jōo-dē'ă) was the Hebraic

ōld; ôrb; ŏdd; ūse; ûrn; ŭp; fōod; fŏŏt; out; oil

*j'hudah* = 'praise,' as Jacob's fourth son was called.
The **Jordan** (jôr'dăn) **River** was the *radan,* that is, the
'rusher' or 'descender,' for it drops 600 feet in its short
course between the Sea of Galilee and the Dead Sea.  **Mt.
Lebanon** (lĕb'ă-nŏn) has its name from *laban* = 'to be
white,' because its cliffs are made up of white chalk and
limestone.

**Jerusalem** (jĕ-rōō'să-lĕm), the most famous city of
Palestine, has a Babylonian name *Urusalim,* of which *uru*
was 'city' and *Salim,* the 'god of peace.'  **Nazareth**
(năz'ă-rĕth) is derived from *nazar* = 'to watch,' and in
the form of the place name meant a 'watch tower.'
**Hebron** (hē'brŏn) was originally *chabron,* meaning 'a
confederacy,' that is, of the Hittites and the Amorites.
**Jaffa** (jăf'ă) was *Jophe,* or 'the white shining place,' on
account of a bold cliff of white chalk there seen.  Finally,
we must mention **Gaza** (gā'ză), in Palestine, not because
it is so big nor to tell the meaning of its name, which is
'the strong place,' but because it was here that "gauze,"
the finest and filmiest cotton cloth, was first made.

Only less well known than Palestine and Egypt from
Bible accounts is Mesopotamia.  Here was situated **Babylon** (băb'ĭ-lŏn), a name which started as *Bab-ilu,* that is,
'gate of God.'  By this was meant that Babylon was the
court of the sun god Bel, the Baal of the Bible version.
Another famous ancient city hereabout was **Nineveh**
(nĭ'nē-vĕ), that is, *Ninua* = 'the habitation' or the 'dwelling place.'  In later times **Bagdad** (băg'dăd), founded
in 763 A. D., has become famous as the home scene of the
"Arabian Nights" stories.  In Persian, Bagdad, or Bagh-
dad, means the 'garden of Dad,' from *bagh* = 'garden'

āle; câre; ăm; ärm; ēve; ĕnd; makēr; īce; ĭll

and *Dad,* a monk who had his home there. The city had great tropical riches in gardens of date palms, in groves of orange and lemon trees, and in wide fields of rice. An older translation of Bagdad as the 'gift of God' is, therefore, quite fitting.

**Basra** (bäz'rä), in Mesopotamia, is simply 'the fortress,' but **Mosul** (mō-sōol') deserves the rest of a paragraph. From Mosul, muslin was first had. In the days of the Venetian traveler Marco Polo, muslins so fine that a whole breadth could be passed through a lady's finger ring were brought by caravan from Mosul to Aleppo and thence to Europe. Perhaps you have seen pictures of the fine ladies of Europe of those times wearing long, flowing white veils. Those veils were made of Mosul muslins. In Arabic, Mosul is *Al-Mausil* = 'the place of connections,' that is, of the caravan routes, for the Tigris was crossed at Mosul by a bridge and a ford.

**Tabriz** (tä-brēz'), in Persia, like Tiflis, is a 'hotwater city,' for *tab* means 'warm' and *riz* = 'to flow.' As you will suspect, Tabriz is famous for its hot springs. **Urumia** (ū-rōo-mē'ä) is a Turkish word *Urum.* By that term the Turks knew the Greeks of these parts. The Persians, however, call Urumia *Daria-i-Shahi,* a much prettier name, for it means 'the royal sea.' There is a beautiful lake of the same name at Urumia. **Teheran** (tĕ-hĕ-rän') is sometimes explained as the 'pure city' or the 'clean city,' and if it has that merit in those parts of Asia, it certainly deserves to call attention to its virtue in its name. **Ispahan** (ĭz-pä-hän' or ĭz-pän') is a corruption of the word *Acpadhane* = 'the horse enclosure.' But the natives of Ispahan scorn that explanation. They

ōld; ôrb; ŏdd; ūse; ûrn; ŭp; fōod; fŏot; out; oil

insist on *Nisf-Jahan* as the original word, because it means 'half the world.' One might judge that the Ispahans are good at what we call "boosting the home town." **Herat** (hĕ-rät') gets its name from the Old Persian *Haraiwa*, meaning 'the water-rich.' That is also a form of boasting in a region like Persia.

**Kabul** (kä′bōōl), the capital of Afghanistan, has a Persian name meaning 'the warehouse.' It is what is known as an "entrepot" city for caravan trade. Many routes come into the city, goods arriving in wholesale lots are stored there, and later these are sent out in smaller lots of many kinds over other routes to the people who use them.

From Afghanistan we progress to India. As you will remember from our "name by name" trip around Asia, India is named for a river, the Indus. But even if it has given its name to the country, the Indus is not the only important stream in that peninsula, perhaps not even the most important. Thus the **Ganges** (gǎn′jēz) has a name which, in the Indian language, as *Ganga*, means 'the river,' in the emphatic sense. The **Brahmaputra** (brä-mä-pōō′trä) is second only to the Ganges in importance, as suggested by its name, for the Hindu word *putra* means 'son' or 'offspring' of the god Brahma, the supreme being of the Hindu religion. Hence it is a very holy river, and the Indians are very religious. At the sources of the Indus and the Ganges we note the district of **Kashmir** (kǎsh-mēr′), also spelled **Cashmere**. The central part of Kashmir is a great valley, and the original name was *Kasyapa-mar*, that is, 'the dwelling place' (*mar*) of the god *Kasyapa*. Kasyapa is said to have opened up

āle; câre; ăm; ärm; ēve; ĕnd; makēr; īce; ĭll

a great gorge across the mountains, through which a river flows out of the valley. You will find it worth while to locate a picture of the Vale of Kashmir and of this gorge. Cashmere has given its name to another textile fabric, the fine cloth which was originally made there from the wool of Tibetan goats.

Strung along the course of the Ganges are a number of important Indian cities. **Delhi** (dĕl′hī) gets its name from the Hindu word *dil* = 'a hill'—how like the *dun* with which we have become so familiar! **Lucknow** (lŭk′nou) is all that is left of the Sanskrit *Lakschmanauti*, which meant 'those who are fortunate and happy.' Students of geography are perhaps fortunate and happy that so much of their original name has been forgotten. **Benares** (bĕn-ä′rĕz) was *Veranasi* = 'those having the best water.' Benares is the holy city of the Brahmans and holy water is bottled up here and sent all over India. **Calcutta** (kăl-kŭt′tă), the great city at the mouth of the Ganges, in the Indian language is *Kali-Kata* = 'the gate to the sacred dwelling of Kali,' wife of the Hindu god Siva.

**Hyderabad** (hī-dĕr-ä-bäd′) lies inland from the east coast of India. It is the 'Haidar's city,' and *haidar* means 'lion' in the Arabic-Persian tongue. Probably Haidar was a chief of considerable repute in his day. **Madras** (mă-dräs′), the city on the coast to the south of Hyderabad, was originally *Mandra-raj*, that is, 'realm of the god Mandra.' **Colombo** (kō-lōm′bō), the capital of the island of Ceylon, is simply *Kolumbu* = 'the harbor.' **Kandy** (kän′dĭ), another city in Ceylon, has a sweet name, but it is only a corruption of the native word for 'hill.'

, ōld; ôrb; ŏdd; ūse; ûrn; ŭp; fōōd; fŏŏt; out; oil

Passing around to the west coast, we find **Calicut** (kăl′ĭ-kŭt) near the south tip of India.  No, this is not like Calcutta.  Calicut was originally *Kolikotta,* that is, 'rooster fort.'  But the place is famous for other reasons. It is where "calico" was first printed by a process kept secret.  Invaders several times tried to capture the city and thus to find out the secret, but they failed.  Also Calicut was the first city in India to be visited by European ships, for Vasco da Gama made his first landing there in 1498.  Calicut, though not very large, is, after all, of some importance.

**Bombay** (bŏm-bā′), the large city of the west coast of India, was first called *Mahi-ma* = 'great mother,' referring to a goddess.  By and by the goddess was probably forgotten, and then the place was called *Mumbai;* later somebody said *Bumbai,* and now it is Bombay.  There is another port on the west coast, **Karachi** (kă-rä′chē), at the mouth of the Indus.  It has a Turkish name which possibly means 'black city,' from the word *kara* = 'black' which we know from the mountains, Karakoram.  But as there is another spelling, Kurrachee, this may be wrong. The place was only a collection of mud huts until artificially developed, in modern times, to be a harbor for the commerce of the Indus valley.

Over in Burma, to the east, we find **Mandalay** (măn′-dă-lā), made famous by Kipling's poem; its name possibly is from *mandala* = 'a flat plain.'  If so, this plain is the valley basin of a branch of the **Irrawaddy** (ĭr-ä-wŏd′ĭ) **River,** which here flows south, and is the *Airawati,* or 'the water possessor,' to the natives.  At the mouth of the Irrawaddy is **Rangoon** (răn-goōn′), a city with a little different kind of name from any we have so far met. Rangoon is the 'city of victory,' but the fact is not so stated. Rather, *ran-kun,* the original form, means 'end of the war' or, quite exactly, 'enmity exhausted.' When a conquering chief had taken the city in 1753 he said the enmity of the defenders was exhausted, *"ran-kun."* This is a very neat way of putting the matter. You attack some one, thoroughly beat him, he lies helpless at your feet; then you say, "his enmity is exhausted!"

**Singapore** (sĭn-gă-pôr'), the great city at the Strait of Malacca, is the Sanskrit *Singhapur,* that is, *singh =* 'lion' and *pura =* 'city.' The lion, however, was not a great beast, but a powerful chief. In Siam, the **Menam** (mā-näm') **River** is properly spelled the *Mei-nam, mei =* 'mother' and *nam =* 'waters,' hence 'mother of waters.' **Bangkok** (băng-kŏk'), at its mouth, is probably the 'city of the wild oil palms' or, perhaps, 'place of the jungle.' The **Mekong** (mā-kŏng'), farther to the east, is from *me =* 'river' and *kong =* 'river' also, hence 'river river.' **Saigon** (sī-gōn') is in **Cochin** (cō'chĭn), or 'little,' **China.** Saigon is from *Sagaing,* which means 'the golden sieve.' This is because the gravels of the rivers hereabout are supposed to have sorted, or sifted out, the gold carried down in their currents. Similarly, we try to sift the gold out of the Asiatic names.

# CHAPTER XXIX

## CHINA, JAPAN, AND SIBERIA

PEOPLE say, "It's like a Chinese puzzle," when they mean that something is altogether beyond their understanding. Spelled out in Chinese characters, the place names of China are in the class of Chinese puzzles. Put in English, the Chinese names are quite short and not difficult to pronounce. Yet the syllables of which these names are made up are quite unfamiliar combinations of letters, and that alone makes the names seem mysterious. However, when we have the key to these syllables, we find that the explanation of the Chinese names is as easy as their spelling and pronunciation. In fact, Chinese names are really on the average more compact and simple than are the European names.

Take the rivers of China for a beginning. In the south of China, the **Si** (sē) **River** is the important stream, and *si* is simply 'west,' hence 'West River.' The greatest Chinese stream is the **Yangtze-kiang** (yäng′tsē-kyäng′), or **Yangtze, River.** Kiang in Chinese is a 'large river,' and *yang* means 'blue.' The Yangtze-kiang flows through the middle of China. North of it is the basin of the **Hwang** (hwäng) **River,** or the **Hoangho** (hwäng-hō′), *hwang,* or *hoang,* meaning 'yellow' and *ho* being the Chinese word for any river, hence the 'Yellow River.'

āle; câre; ăm; ärm; ēve; ĕnd; makẽr; īce; ĭll

We have already noted several provinces of China—Tibet, Manchuria, and Mongolia. Besides China proper, one other province, **Sinkiang** (sĭn-kyäng'), north of Tibet, is 'the land of the new boundary.' *Kiang,* as was just pointed out, means 'large river,' but in this combination it evidently was originally *kiai,* which means 'boundary.' A large peninsula, **Korea** (kō-rē'ă) or **Chosen** (chō'sĕn), which projects from the Chinese mainland in the north, has been taken possession of by the Japanese. Korea is a European version of the Japanese word *Koorai,* apparently the personal name of a warrior chief. Chosen, originally *Choson,* means 'land of the morning calm.'

Across from Chosen we note the smaller **Peninsula of Shantung** (shän-tŭng'), with a name which means 'east of the mountains,' *shan* = 'mountains,' *tung* = 'east.' This is the place the Germans were developing before the World War, and here the Germans built the immense fortress **Kiaochow** (kyou-chō'). In Chinese, *chou* is 'district' and *kiao* means 'bridge,' hence 'bridge district.'

The **Gulf of Pechili** (pā'chē-lē) lies north of Shantung. The name of this gulf is made up of *pe* = 'north' and *chili* = 'court province.' This, then, is the 'Gulf of the North Province,' because close by it is situated **Peking** (pē-kĭng'), the 'North Capital' of China, from *pe* = 'north' and *king* = 'capital.'

**Hongkong** (hŏng'kŏng'), an island off the south coast of China held by the British, has a name which is an English corruption of the Chinese version *Heang Kiang,* meaning 'sweet or fragrant waterway.' *Kiang* is here, once more, 'large river' or 'waterway,' and *heang* =

'sweet.' The reference is to the "sweet," that is, "fresh," water brought by the Si River into the strait between the island and the mainland. **Canton** (kăn-tŏn'), the city on the mainland opposite Hongkong, also has a name modified from the Chinese, which is *kwang-tung; kwang* means 'broad' and *tung* ='east.' The idea is that Canton indicates the broad province toward the east. The Chinese also use a corresponding term *Kwang Si* which is the equivalent of our term, the Great, or Wide, West.

**Foochow** (fōō-chō'), the city farther north along the coast than Canton, is the *fu*, or 'head,' city of the *chou*, 'district' or 'island.' North of Foochow we find **Hangchow** (hăng-chō') with a similar name. The *hang* part means 'dry'; Hangchow, then, is the 'dry district.' But **Hankow** (hăn-kō'), upstream from Hangchow, has a name of which *han* possibly means 'sea' and *kow,* or better *kau,* is 'mouth,' hence 'seaport.' Perhaps this one is indeed a "Chinese puzzle" in city names. Nearby Hangchow, not Hankow, is the smaller city of **Ningpo** (nĭng-pō'). Its name is made up of *ning* = 'rest' and *po* = 'waves,' hence 'repose of the waves' or 'place where the waves come to rest.' We must give the Chinese credit for that as a distinctly worth-while name. At Toronto, Canada, though, it will be remembered that the North American Indians hit on nearly the same idea.

**Chungking** (chŭng-kĭng') has an easy name to explain, for *chung* means 'middle' and *king,* 'capital city.' Chungking, therefore, is the 'capital city of the middle province.' Coming back to the coast once more, we note, near Hangchow, the great city of **Shanghai** (shăng-hī'). *Shang* means 'above' and *hai* means 'the sea.' Notice how many

 āle; câre; ăm; ärm; ēve; ĕnd; makĕr; īce; ĭll

large cities there are in this southeastern part of China. Their number and size suggest the great density of population there and the fertility of the land.

Going north now we see **Tientsin** (tĭ-ĕn-tsēn'), the *tien* = 'celestial,' and *tsin* = 'place,' hence 'celestial city,' near Peking, the capital. With that we leave China proper and go into Chosen and Manchuria where we encounter the great Trans-Siberian Railway. **Mukden** (mōok-dĕn') is a corruption of *Fungtien, fung* = 'wind,' *tien* = 'celestial,' hence 'city of the heavenly winds.' For a final Chinese name, note **Urga** (ûr'gä), in far away Mongolia, north of the Desert of Gobi. The word Urga is from *urgo* = 'palace' or 'residence,' and this is the place where the high priest of the Buddhist religion in Mongolia, the *Khuttukhtu,* or 'resplendently divine one' lives. It would be almost worth while to form a secret society called Urga in order to be its great and exalted *Khuttukhtu.* Any boy will appreciate the fun it would be to have the other fellows call him that.

Of course, we have considered only a few of the many hundreds of Chinese names, but from them you can see how Chinese names are usually put together. Besides the syllables already given, like *kiang* = 'large river,' *pe* = 'north,' *nan* = 'south,' *tong* or *tung* = 'east,' *si* = 'west,' *tien* = 'celestial' (look up the rest), we list here some others that are commonly used. Thus, *ling* = 'a mountain pass,' *yi* = 'a village,' *pai* = 'white,' *hei* = 'black,' *yang* = 'blue,' *tao* = 'an island.'

Suppose, now, one takes the trouble to trace the map of China from a geography text and to letter, on this traced, outline map, the translated English names of all

ōld; ôrb; ŏdd; ūse; ûrn; ŭp; fōod; fŏot; out; oil

the cities, provinces, and natural features shown, using as a key the list of syllables given above and those explained on other pages. That would be solving a Chinese geography puzzle.

The one great natural feature of Japan is the volcano **Fujiyama** (foō'jē-yä'mä). Perhaps this ought to be spelled *Fusijama,* and in that form the name means 'great mountain.' In Japanese poetry the name is often spelled *Fujisan, san* being the same as our English word 'lady'; hence, the 'Lady Fuji.' Look at a picture of Fujiyama and see how nicely this idea fits the splendid form of the mountain. Still other explanations are that *Fuji* means 'riches,' and that the word is from *Huchi,* the God of Fire.

The capital city of Japan is **Tokyo** (tō'kē-ō). It has its name from *to* = 'east' and *kio* = 'capital.' There is also **Saikio** (sī'kē-ō), or 'western capital,' but this is a much smaller place and is found on few maps. **Yoko-hama** (yō-kō-hä'mä), the harbor city for Tokyo, has a name which is thought to mean the 'opposite shore.'

Only one city in Siberia has real quality, but it is the biggest of these places, has the most important position, and its name is the hardest of Siberian terms to pronounce. That is **Vladivostok** (vlä-dǐ-vǒs-tōk'), located at the east end of the Trans-Siberian Railway. *Vladi* is a Russian word meaning 'dominating ruler,' and *vastok* means 'the East.' Three other important Siberian towns are also located on the great railway line. Their names all end in *sk,* which, in Russian, means 'belonging to,' or 'at.' The first part of each name is the name of a river. Thus, going from east to west, we find **Irkutsk** (ǐr-koōtsk'), 'at the river Irkut'; **Tomsk** (tômsk), 'at the

āle; câre; ăm; ärm; ēve; ĕnd; makēr; īce; ĭll

river Tom'; and **Omsk** (ômsk), 'at the river Om.' We do not seem to have any information as to what these river names mean, but in the case of **Tobolsk** (tō-bŏlsk'), a city near the eastern boundary of Russia, we know that *tobol* means 'willows.' Tobolsk, then, is 'the city on the river of willows.'

# CHAPTER XXX

## THE EAST INDIES AND AUSTRALASIA

IT is quite remarkable how much the **East Indies** (ĭn'dēz) resemble the West Indies in position, in arrangement, and in relation to the neighboring mainlands. The Malay Peninsula corresponds to Florida, Australia to South America. Between these two mainlands the East Indies extend from west to east, large islands and small islands, as do the West Indies in the Atlantic Ocean. True, the East Indies lie farther to the south than do the West Indies, and Australia is pushed up too close to the East Indies to make its correspondence with South America exact. Still, Columbus, who did not know all of this, may well be pardoned for his mistake, and, indeed, he might have been even more completely deceived if Australia had been known in 1492 and South America had been discovered on his first voyage. So to derive the names of both these groups of islands from India, is not, geographically, altogether inappropriate.

Beginning at their western end, we note, first of the East Indies, the large island of **Sumatra** (sōō-mä'trä), which has a Sanskrit name, originally *Samudra Dvipa*. *Dvipa* is the word for 'island,' *samudra* is 'ocean'; hence Sumatra is the 'island of the sea.' Close by Sumatra are the small islands **Banka** (bän'kä) and **Billiton** (bĭl-lĭ-tŏn′), which have important deposits of tin. Banka is in Malay *Bangka musuh* = 'hill of the enemy,' but the origin of Billiton is uncertain. In the original name of **Java** (jä′vă), which was *Javadvipa*, we find the 'island' word once more, this time coupled with *java*, which means 'grain,' hence the 'grain island.' The grain referred to was probably rice or millet, and Java does feed a very dense population largely through its production of these crops. The Dutch hold Java, and they have given a Dutch, lower Rhine name to the chief city of the island, **Batavia** (bă-tā′vĭ-ă). The word is made up of the Teutonic terms *bat* = 'good' and *au* = 'land.' Hence Batavia is 'good land,' though it lies far from Europe whence it got the name.

**Borneo** (bôr′nē-ō) and **Celebes** (sĕl′ē-bēz) have names that belong there, for these terms are of native origin. What the name *Borneo* meant does not seem to be known, though Borneo only gradually turned to its present form. At first it was *Brune,* later *Burni,* and then Borneo. Celebes may be derived from *seli besi,* a type of Malay dagger or iron kris. If so, explorers who asked the name of the island were told the name of the dagger—the same sort of mistake made several times in the New World. The **Molucca** (mō-lŭk′ă), or **Spice Islands,** as they are sometimes called, have, however, a name that is unusual in form and of which the whole history, and this an interesting one, is known. The Moluccas were originally called, in Arabic-Malay, *Jazirat-al-Muluk,* that is, ' slands of the Kings,' because each of the five islands in the group had its own particular sovereign.

ōld; ôrb; ŏdd; ūse; ûrn; ŭp; fōōd; fŏŏt; out; oil

**New Guinea** (gĭn'ē) is a name given to one of the East Indies by the Portuguese, because they thought the inhabitants of that island resembled very closely the negroes of the Guinea Coast of Africa, and particularly because the New Guineans had frizzled black hair. Curiously enough, the island is also known as **Papua** (pă'poo-ă), following the Malay word *papuwah* = 'frizzled.' Far to the north of New Guinea are found the **Marianne** (mä-rē-än') **Islands,** which also have two names, the other being **Ladrone** (lă-drōn') **Islands.** Magellan discovered these islands in 1521 and wanted to call them *Islas de las Velas Latinas,* that is, 'Islands of the Lateen Sails,' because the native boats were so equipped. But his sailors would not have this; they insisted that these were the *Islas de los Ladrones,* that is, the 'Islands of the Thieves,' because the natives stole everything in sight when they came aboard ship. But eventually the islands had fixed on them the tame name of Marianne, in honor of Maria Anne, wife of Philip IV of Spain.

When the Spanish discovered the **Solomon** (sŏl'ō-mŏn) **Islands** in 1567, they got some gold from the natives by barter; hence they thought, or said they thought, that they had found the gold mines of King Solomon. A more practical reason for giving the name, however, was their idea that Spanish colonists would be attracted by the possibility of actually finding the mines and getting more gold. An expedition did set sail for the Solomons in 1595 with the purpose of settlement, but could not find the islands. The Solomons remained unknown, therefore, for 200 years after their discovery,

āle; câre; ăm; ärm; ēve; ĕnd; makĕr; īce; ĭll

until rediscovered in 1767 by the English navigator Philip Carteret.

The **Hebrides** (hĕb′rĭ-dēz) are a rugged, mountainous, island group west of Scotland. The **New Hebrides** are situated east of the coast of Australia, and were given the name of the Scottish islands because New Hebrides coasts are also precipitous, rocky, and high. The word *Hebrides* itself is an error; it should be *Hebudæ*, for that was the name used by the Greek geographer Ptolemy, which was copied incorrectly. *Hebudæ* was from the Greek *Ebudæ*, and its derivation has been for many years the despair of scholars.

Near the New Hebrides is **New Caledonia** (kă-lĕ-dō′nĭ-ă), also a Scotch name, for the Roman name *Caledonia* = 'forest country' and referred to the great central forest that once covered Scotland. Like this word is the Gallic word *called* = 'thistles.' The thistle is the national emblem of Scotland. *Cal-led* = Caledonia!

But we are considering the place names of the South Pacific, not those of northern Europe. So your attention is called next to the **Fiji** (fē′jē) **Islands.** Neighbors of the Fijis, the Tonga Islanders, pronounced *Viti,* the true name of the Fijis, *Fiji,* and European missionaries in the Tongas heard this mispronunciation and perpetuated it. What *Viti* means is not apparent. The **Tonga** (tōn′gă) **Islands** were originally *Tonga tabu,* that is, 'sacred island,' for in the native tongue *tonga* means 'island' and *tabu* is 'sacred.' The Tongas are also called the **Friendly Islands,** which accounts for the presence of the missionaries at an early date.

**Australia** (ôs-trāl′yă) enjoys the distinction of having

ōld; ôrb; ŏdd; ūse; ûrn; ŭp; fōōd; fŏŏt; out; oil

been named long before it was found by the Spaniard
Luis Vaez de Torres in 1605. It is the one instance in
which the guesses of the ancient geographers proved to
be correct. These old fellows pointed out that there
should be a great continent in the south to balance the
land masses of the Northern Hemisphere, and they named
this unknown continent *Terra Australis Incognita,* that
is, *incognita* = 'undiscovered,' *terra* = 'land,' *Australis*
= 'of the South.'

In a way, Australia is still an unknown continent, for
much of it is desert land. Because of this there are not
many Australian names to consider. Of the comparatively
few that need to be noted, quite a number are English
personal names, for Australia is exclusively a British possession—the only continent entirely owned by a single
nation. **Cape York,** in the north, was so named by Captain Cook in honor of the Duke of York. The **Murray-
Darling River** recalls a British Secretary of State for the
Colonies, Sir George Murray, and Sir Ralph Darling, the
Governor of **New South Wales,** one of the provinces
of Australia, at the time when the river was discovered.
**Brisbane** (brĭz'bān), the chief city of the province of
**Queensland,** was named for another Governor of New
South Wales, Sir Thomas Brisbane; **Adelaide** remem-
bers Queen Adelaide, wife of King William IV; and
**Palmerston** (päm'ēr-stŭn), in the north of Australia,
also called **Port Darwin,** recalls in its names Viscount
Palmerston, British Prime Minister, 1855-1865, and
Charles Darwin, the famous scientist. **Sydney** (sĭd'nĭ),
the capital of New South Wales, was named for Viscount
Sydney who was Colonial Secretary at the time of its

āle; câre; ăm; ärm; ēve; ĕnd; makēr; īce; ĭll

settlement in 1788. **Melbourne** (mĕl'bŭrn), the capital
of the province of **Victoria** and the present seat of the
Commonwealth government, was founded in 1837, the
year of Queen Victoria's accession, and named for Viscount Melbourne, her first Prime Minister.

**Bendigo** (bĕn'dĭ-gō), although it is a personal name
also, has a much more sprightly history than the other
stodgy British names of Australia. William Thompson
was a celebrated English prizefighter in the days when
Australia was largely populated by miners and gold
seekers, with whom prizefighters were very popular.
Thompson was one of three boys, triplets, who, early in
life, were nicknamed by their friends Shadrach, Meshach,
and Abednego. William was Abednego, and he went by
that name during his fighting career. Accordingly, the
miners, who admired him, named their settlement in the
rich gold diggings Bendigo, Abednego being a bit "too
difficult" for them.

**Ballarat** (băl-ă-răt'), another rich gold field, has the
common prefix *bal* derived from the Celtic *baile* = 'place'
or 'enclosed place.' **Canberra** (kăn-bĕ'ră), the place
where Australia expects to have a capital which will be
modeled after, and rival, our Washington, D. C., has its
name from a ranch which occupied that site.

**Tasmania** (tăz-mā'nĭ-ă), the island just south of Australia, is named after the Dutch navigator, Jansz Tasman,
who discovered it in 1642. Tasman called it Van Diemen's Land in honor of the then governor of the Dutch
East Indies who had aided Tasman's expedition. More
than a century later the English acquired the island by virtue of its rediscovery by Captain Cook in 1769. They had

ōld; ôrb; ŏdd; ūse; ûrn; ŭp; fōōd; fŏŏt; out; oil

the bright idea of making all this island a huge penal settlement for British criminals. The result was that Van Diemen's Land became a pandemonium, and it had a very "bad name" with respectable people. When the practice of sending criminals to it was stopped in 1853 and respectable colonists settled there, the name was changed to Tasmania in accordance with the wishes of the honest newcomers. However, **Hobart** (hō'bärt), the capital city, still retains the name of Lord Hobart, who sent out the first warship filled with robbers and ruffians in 1803, and the site of Hobart is the one first picked out for the landing of the criminals with their guard of soldiers. **Zeehan** (zē'ăn), also in Tasmania, is named for one of Tasman's ships.

**New Zealand** (zē'lănd) repeats the Dutch name *Zeeland,* that is, 'sealand.' These islands were inhabited by **Maori** (mä'ō-rĭ) when discovered, the word meaning 'natives.' Hence, to say, or write, Maoris, as the word is spelled in most texts, is as incorrect as saying 'mens.' **Auckland** (ôk'lănd), in New Zealand, is named for the English Lord Auckland who was Governor-General of India when the town was founded in 1840; his name originally meant 'field' or 'farmland,' from *auch* = 'field.' **Wellington** (wĕl'ĭng-tŏn), likewise, was named for an English nobleman, the famous Sir Arthur Wellesley, Duke of Wellington, the victor of Waterloo. In the Anglo-Saxon, Wellington was *Weolingtun,* that is, the *tun,* or 'enclosure,' of the *Weolings.*

If Australia is the continent that one nation owns completely, Antarctica has the distinction of being a continent owned by no nation. We already know about its name,

 āle; câre; ăm; ärm; ēve; ĕnd; makĕr; īce; ĭll

but we may close our discussion of Southern Pacific place names by noting **Mt. Erebus** (ĕr′ē-bŭs) and **Mt. Terror,** two great volcanoes on Antarctica, discovered by the English explorer, Sir James Ross, and named by him after his two ships, the *Erebus* and the *Terror,* with which he spent eight years (1834-1843) in the Antarctic. In Greek mythology *Erebus* was the place of darkness between heaven and earth and as it is dark in Antarctica for six months, this fits very well.

ōld; ôrb; ŏdd; ūse; ûrn; ŭp; fōōd; fŏŏt; out; oil

# CHAPTER XXXI

### AFRICA, THE DARK CONTINENT

THIS final one of the list of continents has been, throughout all history, the Dark Continent. Vast and mysterious, place of one of the earliest civilizations, yet in part unexplored until very recent times, Africa is now only incompletely known. Hence, it is the shadowy, the dark, continent. More than that, it is peopled by blacks, and further, its place names suggest and indicate those dusky bodies and countenances, and so complete the picture of a realm of obscurity.

For to the ancients this continent was **Ethiopia** (ē-thē-ō'pǐ-ă), the land of the *Æthiopes,* a Greek word meaning 'the burnt faces.' *Helios,* the sun, said the ancients, "burns the faces and curls the hair" of human beings who live in the interior of Africa, "so parching are the rays of Helios there." **Africa** (ăf'rǐ-kă), the name we use for the continent, is a term which carries the same idea, if it is derived from the Latin *aprica* = 'sunny' or 'heated by the sun.' However, it may be a Phœnician word *Afryquah,* meaning only 'a colony'; and in that sense it was first used in reference to Carthage, but later was applied to all the continent.

Of all Africa, the ancients really knew well only the country of the **Nile** (nīl) **River.** This the Phœnicians

 āle; câre; ăm; ärm; ēve; ĕnd; makĕr; īce; ĭll

called *Nahal,* that is, 'the valley.' The Greeks modified *Nahal* to *Nilus,* and we now call it Nile. The Nile was the one important stream of Africa until recent times, but in the future the **Kongo** (kŏn'gō) **River,** in the middle of the continent, may become equally significant. Its name is a native word *kong,* meaning 'mountains,' and refers, not to the river, but rather to the mountains where the stream has its source, or, perhaps, only to the chief who ruled over this mountainous district. In any event, a third river of Africa, the **Niger** (nī'jẽr), is more directly named. Its title is, in full, the Berber term *N-eghir-reu,* of which *ghir* = 'river.' Thus Niger has no connection with the term "nigger," which is had from the Latin word *niger* = 'black.' One other African stream, the **Zambezi** (zăm-bē'zē), derives its name from the native *Luambeji,* that is, 'the great river.' Trace out on the map the course of each of these Dark Continent streams.

The lakes of Africa are, all of them, situated in the very nearly equatorial latitudes. Why is this location for lakes to be expected in Africa? **Lake Chad** or **Tchad** (chäd) is about as far north of the equator as **Lake Nyasa** (nyä'să) lies south of it. The names of both mean simply 'lake,' the first in one native dialect, the other in another. Like the second in origin and meaning, though slightly different in form, is **Victoria Nyanza** (nyän'ză), which is situated right on the equator. This supplies us with an instance where a native class term has been rightly coupled with a distinctive European name, for Victoria Nyanza means 'Victoria Lake.' It was so named by its discoverer in 1858 in honor of Queen Victoria. The smaller **Albert Edward Nyanza,**

ōld; ôrb; ŏdd; ūse; ûrn; ŭp; fōōd; fŏŏt; out; oil

discovered by Henry M. Stanley in 1889, recalls the given names of Queen Victoria's eldest son, the late King Edward VII. **Lake Tanganyika** (tän-gän-yē′kǎ) has an interesting name which may be related to the *nyasa* and *nyanza* forms, and again may not. The native word *tanganya* means 'collect.' Accordingly, if *nyika* is a form of *nyasa,* this lake is the 'collecting' or 'gathering place of waters.' However, *nyika* is held by some to mean 'water chestnut,' for great masses of these edible nuts collect on the surface of the lake.

One reason why Africa remained for so long the Dark Continent is that its interior is very completely an area of plateau and highland. These highlands end abruptly near the ocean in steep cliffs, which are difficult to ascend and cause the rivers to be interrupted by great waterfalls, and hence to be unnavigable. Here and there true mountains and volcanoes rear themselves to still higher levels. In the north are the **Atlas Mountains** which gave their name to the Atlantic Ocean. At the equator the **Ruwenzori** (rōō-wĕn-zôr′ĭ) **Mountains** have a native name which means 'cloud king.' **Kilimanjaro** (kĭl-ē-män-jä′-rō), a great volcanic peak, also has a native name, composed of *kilima* = 'mountain' and *Ndjaro* = 'Demon of Cold'; hence this is the 'mountain of the demon of cold,' and no doubt the upper, snow-clad slopes of the volcano appeal to the equatorial savage as being a very cold place. **Mt. Kenia** (kā′nē-ă), also spelled **Kenya,** has a native name which means 'mist'; fogs frequently do hide its summit. South of these volcanic peaks lies the great **Katanga** (kä-tän′gä) **Highland,** its name a native word which means 'the wall.'

 āle; câre; ăm; ärm; ēve; ĕnd; makēr; īce; ĭll

The **Drakensberg** (drä′kĕnz-bûrg) **Mountains,** in
South Africa, are the 'Dragon Mountains.' Not far from
this range is the **Great Karroo** (kä-rōō′), a steppe-like,
plateau country which introduces us to the desert regions
of Africa. *Karoo* is a Hottentot word meaning 'hard.'
The Karroo has a clay soil which is soft during the rainy
season but dries out to a "flint-like" hardness in the
months of drought. North of the Karroo there is encountered the **Kalahari** (kä-lä-hä′rĭ) **Desert.** Its name
is more correctly spelled, according to the native version,
*Karri-karri* and means 'those who are tormented by
thirst' or 'the parching ones.' The name, no doubt, refers to those who dwell within the confines of the Kalahari, or need to travel across it, and is very vividly suited
to the place.

Equally far to the north of the equator as the Kalahari lies to the south of the earth's central girdle is the
heart of the **Sahara** (să-hä′ră) **Desert.** The Sahara,
however, is much vaster in dimensions than the Kalahari.
It is evident that the Sahara is better entitled to its name
than the Kalahari would be when one learns that Sahara
is the Arabian word for 'desert.' The singular form of
the word is *sahra,* which means 'a wide flat destitute of
vegetation,' and related forms suggest 'white appearing,'
'burnt by the sun' and so on. All these fit the glaring,
hot expanses of the Sahara. Not that the Sahara is
altogether lacking in habitable spots. It has, for example,
the city of **Timbuktu** (tĭm-bŭk′tōō), in the native
tongue *Timbutu,* which means a 'hollow.' Timbuktu is
built in a hollow among the sandhills, near the course of
a former creek, the bottom of which is still marshy and

ōld; ôrb; ŏdd; ūse; ûrn; ŭp; fōōd; fŏŏt; out; oil

furnishes the needed water supply.  People, the **Bedouins**
(bĕd'ŏō-ĭnz), also occupy the desert spaces, as in fact
their name indicates, for Bedouin is the French form of
the Arabic word *bedew* = 'one inhabiting a desert.'  One
can not escape the pun that no doubt they are grateful
when they are "bedewed."

The northeast corner of the Sahara is known by a special name, the **Libyan** (lĭb'ĭ-ăn) **Desert,** so called after
a native woman with the Semitic name *Lubim,* although
the Greeks, who applied the name *Libya* to the whole of
Africa, attributed the name to one of the minor figures
of their mythology.  **Libia** (lĭb'ĭ-ă), the Italian colony
comprising much of the area of the Libyan Desert, of
course derives its name from the same source.  The chief
city of Libia is **Tripoli** (trĭp'ō-lĭ), a Greek word, *Tripo-
lis,* meaning 'three cities.'  This name was given because
Tripoli in ancient times was the meeting place for a
council of three cities.

The coast line of Africa is notably straight and unbroken; bays, inlets, headlands, islands, and harbors are
not numerous.  Hence it will not be too tedious to consider the names of practically all of those which do occur.

The largest single indentation of the coast line is the
**Gulf of Guinea** (gĭn'ē), which occupies what may be
termed the "armpit" of Africa.  Look at the map and
see how this idea fits.  But the name Guinea does not
mean "armpit."  It is, rather, a corruption of a negro
term *ginnie* = 'town.'  The English used to have "guinea"
coins, gold pieces originally made from gold found in
these parts, coins often mentioned in pirate stories; and
we have guinea fowls, which also came originally from

āle; câre; ăm; ärm; ēve; ĕnd; makēr; īce; ĭll

this region. **Walfish** (wôl′fĭsh) or **Walvis** (vôl′vĭs) **Bay** is a tiny place in comparison with the Gulf of Guinea; its name is the German *Walfisch* which means 'whale' and was given because American whaling ships stopped there in numbers at one time. Note how greatly this name has been changed from the original form in a very few years.

Many African names have interesting histories, but none other of these is so important, in the course of world events, as that of the **Cape of Good Hope** at the south tip of the continent. Until ships went around this cape, all traffic between Europe and India was over the long and difficult caravan route overland across Asia. In 1487 the Portuguese navigator Bartholomew Diaz first sailed around the south end of Africa, and though he did not proceed farther, the cape was then named *Boa Esperanza* = 'good hope,' in the good hope that India could be reached by a sea route. A few years later this good hope was realized when Vasco da Gama did succeed in sailing all the way to India over this course. Columbus' discovery of America, Vasco da Gama's voyage to India, and Magellan's trip around the globe were the three achievements that make us now the inhabitants of a world, instead of being only separate peoples of various continents and islands.

An opening on the east coast of Africa, opposite to and not much larger than Walfish Bay, is known as **Delagoa** (dĕl-ă-gō′ă) **Bay**. This term is a jumbled form of the Portuguese name *Bahia de Lagoa* = 'bay of the lagoon,' which was given it by Vasco da Gama, who discovered it in 1498. Off to the northeast of Delagoa Bay is situated the large island of **Madagascar** (măd-ă-găs'kăr). Its name was fixed by Marco Polo, though he applied it to the wrong place. Madagascar is derived from the word *malagasi* in the language of one of the negro tribes. The first part, *mala,* may mean 'Malay'; the second part is a form of *ni-gozi* = 'men'; hence Madagascar means 'Malay men.' **Tananarive** (tä-nä-nä-rēv'), the capital of Madagascar, has a good place name, one with an appeal to the imagination. In full it is composed of *an* = 'at,' *tana* = 'place,' and *arivo* = 'a thousand.' Hence Tananarive is 'at the place of a thousand,' that is, of a thousand houses.

In the **Indian Ocean** beyond Madagascar are two small islands: one French, **Reunion,** so called because of the reunion of the French in a republic after the revolution of 1848; the other British, **Mauritius** (mô-rĭsh'-ŭs), named after the Dutch Prince, Maurice, by the Dutch explorers who took possession of it in 1598. Passing by several smaller island groups, we note next **Zanzibar** (zän'zĭ-bär), lying quite near the African coast. Zanzibar has an Arabic name made up of *zanje* = 'negro' and *bar* = 'coast.' Last of coast features, if it may be called that, is the **Suez** (soō-ĕz') **Canal.** It has an Arabic name, *Bir Suweis,* which meant 'well of Suweis,' but we do not seem to know who, or what, Suweis was.

Now we are ready for a "round-up" of the countries and colonies of Africa. To accomplish this successfully, and with most profit to the reader, it will be necessary that it be made a "name-by-name" trip, like the one we made over Asia. Then we follow a definite route on the map which may be traced as we go along. In this way one may easily become acquainted with all the little subdivi-

āle; câre; ăm; ärm; ēve; ĕnd; makẽr; īce; ĭll

sions of Africa, and where each is located. And there are many of them. No other continent has been so cut up by foreign powers as has Africa. Moreover, many new arrangements have been made since the World War, so the reader will do well to be sure that his map is up to date. In slave-holding days Europeans took Africans away from Africa; now they have taken Africa away from the Africans.

As we left off at Suez, we will begin at that point on this trip of the countries and cities. Starting there is proper in any event, for it was in **Egypt** (ē'jĭpt) that the civilization of Africa, and perhaps of the world, began. Egypt is variously explained. Perhaps it is a Greek term made up of *aia* = 'land' and *guptos* = 'vulture,' hence 'land of the vulture.' Possibly this *guptos* is a Greek misconception of the name of an ancient Egyptian city, *Koptos,* from which goods were first sent to the Red Sea by caravan. Again, Egypt may be all that has survived of the phrase *Het-ka-Ptah* = 'house of the genius of Ptah,' Ptah being the oldest of the Egyptian deities, "father of the gods," the principal place of whose worship was at the ancient city of Memphis. The ancient Egyptians themselves called their land *Kem* = 'the black,' on account of the color of its soil.

Egypt with its dense population has numerous cities. Nearest Suez is **Port Said** (sä'ēd), named for Said Pasha, the khedive or ruler of Egypt when the digging of the Suez Canal was begun in 1859, whose Arabic personal name *Said* means 'the fortunate.' **Alexandria** was the first and greatest of the twelve cities founded by Alexander the Great, to all of which he gave his own

ōld; ôrb; ŏdd; ūse; ûrn; ŭp; fōōd; fŏŏt; out; oil

name. **Cairo** (kī'rō), beloved of tourists, is the Arabic *El Kahira* = 'the victorious,' so called because Mars, the planet of war and victory, was visible on the right when the city was founded by an Arabian conqueror in 970 A.D. **Assuan** (äs'wän), better **Aswan**, up the river from Cairo, has its name from the Arabic *Aswan,* meaning 'the opening,' so called because of the gap here, at a cataract of the Nile, between Egypt and the regions south.

These regions south of Egypt are now known as the **Anglo-Egyptian Sudan** (sōō-dăn'). Sudan is another Arabic term, in full *Beled e' Sudan,* that is, 'the land of the blacks.' Here we find a city, **Khartum** (kär-tōōm'), built on a spit of land shaped like an elephant's trunk; hence the name *Ras el Khartum, ras* = 'cape,' *khartum* = 'elephant's trunk,' thus 'Cape of the Elephant's Trunk.'

The Italians have a colony on the Red Sea which they call **Eritrea** (ā-rē-trĕ'ä), after *Erythraeum Mare,* the Greek for 'red sea.' Inland from Eritrea is **Abyssinia** (ăb-ĭ-sĭn'ĭ-ă), one of the two independent countries in all the continent of Africa. Abyssinia is 'the land inhabited by a mixture,' for that is the meaning of the Arabic word *Habasha,* which was the original form of Abyssinia. It was so called because a "mixture" of Arabic tribes first settled the country. **Adis Abeba** or **Addis Ababa** (ä'dĭs ä-bä'bä) is the capital city of Abyssinia, and has its name from *addis* = 'new' and *ababa* = 'flower,' because it is a comparatively new city founded in 1892 by Menelek II, who died in 1913, the great modern ruler of Abyssinia who claimed descent from Menelek, son of King Solomon and the Queen of Sheba.

South and east of Eritrea, the French, British, and Italians, all three, have **Somaliland** (sō-mä'lē-lănd) colonies. *Somali* is the native word for 'blacks' or 'negroes.' Turn back now and set down in a list all the African place names already encountered that, like Somaliland, indicate that Africa is a Dark Continent. South of Italian Somaliland we note the British **Kenya Colony, Tanganyika Territory,** and **Uganda** (ū-gän'dă) **Protectorate.** With the names of the first two we are already familiar; Uganda means *u* = 'the country' of the *Ganda* people. Then follows another French colony, **Mozambique** (mō-zăm-bēk'), with a **Channel** opposite it with the same name. Mozambique is a Portuguese corruption of the native words *ma-sam-buco* = 'the seamed boats.' This odd term applies, actually, to the harbor of the small, coral island on which the capital city, also called Mozambique, is built. **Beira** (bā'rä), another town in the colony Mozambique, has a name which is the Portuguese term for 'a spit of sand.' Inland from Mozambique lies **Rhodesia** (rō-dē'zhǐ-ă), named for Cecil Rhodes, the great English promoter and imperialist, whose work for the extension of British territory and influence in South Africa kept African politics "stirred up" during the last quarter of the nineteenth century.

All the country south of Rhodesia in Africa is now combined in the British dominions known as the **Union of South Africa.** Linked up in this Union are a number of formerly separate states. The **Transvaal** (trăns-väl') is the region *trans* = 'beyond' the *Vaal* = 'yellow' river. As may be judged by the name Vaal, this is the region occupied by the Dutch Boers. Hence, also, the name of its capital city, **Pretoria** (prē-tō′rĭ-ă), after the Boer general, Andries Pretorius, one of the leaders of the great Boer emigration from the Cape Colony in 1838 and chief founder of the Transvaal Republic ten years later. Pretorius had a good name, too, for a general, as Pretorius is probably derived from the Latin word *prætor* = 'an army leader.' **Johannesburg** (yō-hän′nĕs-bûrg) = 'John's castle,' in the south of France which was once the property of the royal house of Holland, was probably so named by the devout Boer settlers in honor of the Apostle John. The **Orange Free State** is named for the principality of Orange, but the name has nothing to do with oranges, for it was originally *Arausia*. In it is **Kimberley** (kĭm′bēr-lĭ), the diamond city, named for the Earl of Kimberley, a British Secretary of State for the Colonies in the 70's of the last century. **Natal** (nā′-tăl), in Portuguese, *dies natalis* = 'the day of the birth,' was reached by Vasco da Gama on Christmas Day, 1497. **Durban** (dûr′băn), capital city of Natal, bears the name of Sir Benjamin D'Urban, who at the time of the founding of the town in 1834 was governor of **Cape Colony,** at the south tip of the continent, of which **Cape Town** is the capital.

Now, like Vasco da Gama returning on his great voyage to India, we have rounded the cape once more and are on the home stretch. The protectorate of **Southwest Africa** is administered by the Union of South Africa. North of it lies **Angola** (ăn-gō′lă), a Portuguese possession. The full name of Angola was originally *Dongo Angola*, which meant 'land of Angola.' The King of Congo presented this *dongo* = 'area' to his faithful

āle; câre; ăm; ärm; ēve; ĕnd; makēr; īce; ĭll

aide, Angola. **Loanda** (lō-än'dä), chief city of Angola, has its name from the native word *luanda* = 'tribute.' Here the natives obtained a certain kind of shell, much prized by the blacks, and paid tribute in these to their king.

The interior country of Africa situated directly under the equator is the **Belgian Kongo.** This Belgian possession extends to the coast at the point where **Boma** (bō'mä), its chief city, is located. According to its name, native *boma* = 'palisade,' this was once a fortified town. **French Equatorial Africa** includes territory formerly known as the **Kamerun** (kä-mä-rōōn'). Kamerun is derived from the Portuguese name *Rio dos Camaraos,* that is, 'river of shrimps.' The River of Shrimps was only a small stream, but the shrimps found there are now celebrated by the name of a wide land. **Libreville** (lē-br'-vēl') is, of course, the French way of saying that this place in French Equatorial Africa is a 'free city.' And we must note that the Spanish have a little tract, **Spanish Guinea,** cut out of the coast lands of French Equatorial Africa.

Right in the center of the "armpit" of the Gulf of Guinea is another British protectorate, **Nigeria** (nī-jē'-rǐ-ă), about the name of which we are already informed. From here on the coast is very much cut up into little states. The first of these has a name, **Dahomey** (dä-hō'-mä), which suggests this cutting up, and is, moreover, one of those unusual place names that make us take especial interest. Dahomey started as *Da home,* became *Da omi,* and is now Dahomey. As *Da home* the name meant 'city on the belly of Da.' And this is the story. Da was a

ōld; ôrb; ŏdd; ūse; ûrn; ŭp; fōōd; fŏŏt; out; oil

great chief back in the 1600 years, but he had a rival
who was more powerful. This rival killed Da, ripped
open his belly, and buried Da so mutilated. Then the
rival founded a new city on the site of the grave, *Da
home.*

Next west of Dahomey, which is French, is the British
**Ashanti** (ă-shăn′tē), named after the Ashanti tribe of
negroes. This is followed by the **Ivory Coast,** so called
because of the ivory tusks there obtained, which is part
of **French West Africa.** Then comes **Liberia** (lī-bē′-
rĭ-ă), 'the land of the free,' the other independent country
of Africa, which was founded in 1820 as a colony for
freed slaves from our Southern States. The capital of
Liberia is **Monrovia** (mŏn-rō′vĭ-ă), so named for James
Monroe, fifth President of the United States, who en-
couraged the American Colonization Society in the Li-
berian enterprise.

**Sierra Leone** (sē-ĕr′ă lā-ōn′ē) is, in Portuguese, *Serra
Leao,* that is, the 'lion range.' When the Portuguese navigators first sailed down this coast in 1462, they heard
the roar of the surf on the beach and thought the noise
was the roaring of lions in the adjacent forest. At **Free-
town,** in Sierra Leone, negroes rescued from slave ships
by English sailors were landed and set free again. Next
is found a little **French Guinea,** then an even smaller
**Portuguese Guinea,** followed by the tiny British colony
**Gambia** (găm′bĭ-ă), which in name is an English-
Portuguese corruption of the name of a native tribe, the
Gambre. **Senegal** (sĕn-ē-gôl′), likewise, is a much modified name. It recalls the *Azanague* tribe who lived there.
Senegal and the territory next north are now parts of

 āle; câre; ăm; ärm; ēve; ĕnd; makẽr; īce; ĭll

French West Africa. Last of these small divisions of
the west coast of the continent is the Spanish colony of
**Rio de Oro** (rē'ō dā ō'rō), that is, 'River of Gold.'

As the final group of all in our study of place names,
we come to the north coast and the **Barbary** (bär'bĕ-rĭ)
**States**. These states are the countries of the Berbers, a
name which is probably made up of the word *ber* = 'men'
repeated. Perhaps our word *barbarian* has a similar
source. At any rate, the Berbers are apt to be rough.
Even the United States had a war with the Barbary
States in the early 1800's.

Farthest to the west of these Barbary States is
**Morocco** (mō-rŏk'ō). The name Morocco is a Spanish
modification of the Arabic *Moraksch,* which meant 'the
adored city.' We know it better as a kind of leather.
The name of this city was later used for all the country.
In Morocco, the country, is the city **Fez** (fĕz), with a
name which is probably an Arabic word meaning 'fertile'
or 'beautiful.' Then we note the little neutral territory
of **Tangier** (tăn-jēr'), south of Gibraltar. Here Europe
and Africa nearly touch, so we need not be surprised that
this was originally *Tigisis* = 'the place of staples,' for
here would be just the place to exchange goods.

**Algeria** (ăl-jē'rĭ-ă) and **Algiers** (ăl-jērz') have names
that are simple in their present form but which started
out as *El-Jezair Beni Mezghanna.* That meant 'islands
of the children of Mazghanna.' It was wise to save only
the *Jezair* part, which meant 'islands.' In another Arabic
form islands are *dschesire*; perhaps that was enough to
start Algiers.

Last of all, since we have already considered Libia and

Egypt, we come to **Tunis** (tōō′nĭs). Tunis was named for the Phœnician goddess *Tanith*. Tunis the city was dedicated to her. *Tanith* was known to the Greeks as Artemis and to the Romans as Diana. She was pictured as very beautiful—so we have a pretty thing with which to close our account of the place names of Africa.

āle; câre; ăm; ärm; ēve; ĕnd; makēr; īce; ĭll

# CHAPTER XXXII

### THE END

Now we are done. We have made the round of all the world—its continents, its islands, its countries, and the seas; and we have considered the names of all their principal places and natural features. What has been gained from the study of these names?

We know the meaning and pronunciation of many geographical words which before seemed mysterious and difficult to remember. Quite to our surprise, we found that many of them were commonplace in origin, easily understood when translated. It was very pleasant, though, to chance occasionally upon a sprightly or a splendid name. There were too few of these. The peoples of the world seem too often to have been dull in giving names to their surroundings.

But in making our review we have become familiar, to a degree not otherwise so easily possible, with these geographical places, with their locations, and with something of their geographical significance, as well as with the meanings of their names. When now the reader sees or hears of any of these places, however remote from his home it may be, whether mentioned in newspapers, magazines, books, or by travelers, he will think at once, "That's the 'sandy spit' or the 'shining mountain' of so and so." Then immediately a picture will come to mind of all the setting and one will be more able to appreciate what further is said about that place.

"Familiarity breeds contempt." A superficial familiarity, which is altogether bad, arises from not paying sufficient attention. But there is a knowledge bred by familiarity which is not contempt at all; rather it is mastery. Let the motto of this volume then be

THE CONSCIOUS MASTERY OF GEOGRAPHIC NAMES

# INDEX OF NAMES AND TERMS

# INDEX OF SUBJECTS

(1)